Klaus Mühlhahn,
Nathalie van Looy (Eds.)

The Globalization of Confucius and Confucianism

Berliner China-Hefte
Chinese History and Society

Edited by
Mechthild Leutner

Editorial Management
Hauke Neddermann

Ostasiatisches Seminar
der Freien Universität Berlin

No. 41

LIT

The Globalization of Confucius and Confucianism

Edited by

Klaus Mühlhahn and Nathalie van Looy

LIT

Bibliographic information published by the Deutsche Nationalbibliothek
The Deutsche Nationalbibliothek lists this publication in the Deutsche Nationalbibliografie; detailed bibliographic data are available in the Internet at http://dnb.d-nb.de.

ISBN 978-3-643-90305-1

A catalogue record for this book is available from the British Library

Klosbachstr. 107
CH-8032 Zürich
Tel. +41 (0) 44-251 75 05
Fax +41 (0) 44-251 75 06
E-Mail: zuerich@lit-verlag.ch
http://www.lit-verlag.ch

LIT VERLAG Dr. W. Hopf
Berlin 2012
Fresnostr. 2
D-48159 Münster
Tel. +49 (0) 2 51-620 320
Fax +49 (0) 2 51-23 19 72
E-Mail: lit@lit-verlag.de
http://www.lit-verlag.de

Distribution:
In Germany: LIT Verlag Fresnostr. 2, D-48159 Münster
Tel. +49 (0) 2 51-620 32 22, Fax +49 (0) 2 51-922 60 99, E-mail: vertrieb@lit-verlag.de

In Austria: Medienlogistik Pichler-ÖBZ, e-mail: mlo@medien-logistik.at
In Switzerland: B + M Buch- und Medienvertrieb, e-mail: order@buch-medien.ch
In the UK: Global Book Marketing, e-mail: mo@centralbooks.com
In North America: International Specialized Book Services, e-mail: orders@isbs.com

Contents

The Globalization of Confucius and Confucianism

Conference Reports

Reviews

Calligraphy: Chen Ning
Orders: Lit-Verlag Münster-Hamburg-London, Grevener Str. 179, 48159 Münster, Germany, lit@lit-verlag.de.
Submission of Manuscripts (Articles, Reports, and Reviews):
Chinese History and Society/Berliner China-Hefte, Freie Universität Berlin, Ostasiatisches Seminar, Ehrenbergstr. 26-28, 14195 Berlin, eChina@zedat.fu-berlin.de.
Manuscripts should conform to the style of Chinese History and Society/Berliner China-Hefte: <http://www.chinesehistoryandsociety.de>

Einleitung

Totgeglaubte leben länger. Dieser Satz mag einem in den Sinn kommen, wenn man die aktuelle Erfolgsgeschichte von Konfuzius und seinen Lehren in China betrachtet. Während er zu Lebzeiten (ca. 551-479 v. Chr.) mit seinen Ideen über eine gerechte Staatspolitik und funktionierende Gesellschaftsordnung kein Gehör bei den Herrschern fand, avancierte die nach seinem Tod in den *Analekten* verschriftlichte Form seiner Gedanken einige Jahrhunderte später in der Han-Zeit zur staatlichen Leitideologie. Auch in den folgenden zwei Jahrtausenden befassten sich Generationen von chinesischen Intellektuellen neben den *Analekten* vor allem mit den von Konfuzius redigierten oder kommentierten fünf klassischen Schriften bestehend aus dem *Buch der Wandlungen* (*Yijing*), dem *Buch der Lieder* (*Shijing*), dem *Buch der Urkunden* (*Shangshu*), den *Frühlings- und Herbstannalen* (*Chunqiu*), und dem *Buch der Riten* (*Liji*) (Makeham 2003). In der Gegenwart genießt der Konfuzianismus erneut Aufmerksamkeit. Universitäten gründen Zentren zum Studium des konfuzianischen Erbes; Seminare über das Leben und Wirken von Konfuzius – eigentlich seit den 1920er Jahren vom Lehrplan gestrichen – erfreuen sich zunehmender Beliebtheit unter Studenten; auch andere Bildungseinrichtungen von der Grund- bis zur Abendschule ergänzen den Lehrplan zunehmend mit entsprechenden Kursen. Es gibt Seminare für Geschäftsleute und Beamte zur konfuzianischen Ethik, Selbststudienkurse in öffentlichen Bibliotheken und Gemeindezentren und Plakate über die konfuzianischen Tugenden in Parkanlagen und Straßen aller großen Städte (siehe den Beitrag von Hans van Ess in diesem Band). 2006 wurde eine Neuinterpretation der *Analekten* mit über einer Million Exemplare in wenigen Monaten zum Bestseller (Tu 2010: XV). Doch nicht nur die innerchinesische Popularität des „Meisters Kong" steigt rapide, auch international verweist China immer häufiger auf seine wohl berühmteste historische Persönlichkeit als Synonym für die chinesische Kultur (siehe z.B. die weltweiten Konfuzius-Institute). Dieses „Konfuzius-Fieber" in der Gegenwart gibt Grund genug, um das Phänomen auch von wissenschaftlicher Seite zu beleuchten und sowohl Hintergründe zur Entstehung als auch unterschiedliche Manifestationen zu analysieren.

Dabei wurde an der Wende vom 19. zum 20. Jahrhundert das konfuzianische Erbe noch einer vernichtenden Kritik unterzogen. Während in China bereits seit Mitte des 19. Jahrhunderts die Unzufriedenheit mit dem politischen und gesellschaftlichen Zustand der konfuzianischen Gesellschaft schwelte, begannen auch immer mehr westliche Stimmen von den negativen Seiten der konfuzianischen Kultur zu sprechen. Der deutsche Soziologe Max Weber hat sich als einer der ersten Wissenschaftler mit dem Verhältnis von Konfuzianismus und Moderne auseinandergesetzt und den Konfuzianismus als die „Weltreligion" benannt, die am wenigsten für den kapitalistischen Fortschritt geeignet sei. Diese Meinung fand Anfang des 20. Jahrhunderts nicht nur im gesamten Europa, sondern im Zuge der Selbststärkungs- und Modernisierungsbestrebungen mit Augenmerk auf den Westen auch zunehmend Verbreitung unter chinesischen Intellektuellen, die nun im Konfuzianismus den Grund für Chinas Unfähigkeit mit den westlichen Imperialisten gleichzuziehen sahen. Aufgrund seiner reaktionären und feudalen Inhalte wurde er als fortschrittsfeindlich gebrandmarkt und – wie so oft zitiert – von den Mitgliedern der 4. Mai-Bewegung und später auch von den Kommunisten entweder ganz zu Grabe oder zumindest ins Museum getragen. Bei der Frage nach dem richtigen Weg zur Moderne standen zwar diverse Modelle von Kapitalismus bis zum Marxismus zur Debatte, die Idee einer

konfuzianisch geprägten Moderne blieb jedoch komplett außen vor, denn „modernity had come to mean overcome Confuciansm“ (Bell/Hahm 2003: 2).
Diese negative Bewertung des Konfuzianismus dominierte im Wesentlichen bis zur zweiten Hälfte des 20. Jahrhunderts. Erst der wirtschaftliche Aufschwung in Staaten wie Japan, Singapur, Korea in den 1960er bis 1980er Jahren ließ Webers Prognose fragwürdig erscheinen und verlangte nach einem neuen Erklärungsmodell. Westliche Beobachter fanden nun den Grund für die rasche Industrialisierung in den so genannten „asiatischen Werten“. Der Rekurs auf diese Wertenormen, die in der Folge unschwer einem konfuzianischen Ursprung zugeordnet werden konnten, erlangte innerhalb Asiens rasch Popularität, insbesondere als sie in den 1980er Jahren von der Politik wiederentdeckt wurden, um als Erklärungsmodell für mangelnde Demokratisierungsbestrebungen autoritärer Regime zu dienen. Doch nicht nur für die politische Legitimation ließ sich der Konfuzianismus gut verwenden, auch bei der Bekämpfung von sozialen und ökonomischen Problemen schienen die konfuzianischen Tugenden zumindest einen guten Ansatz zu bieten. Die Wiederbelebung von ethischen Qualitäten wie Mitgefühl, Gerechtigkeit, Fürsorge, Bescheidenheit und Nächstenliebe gemäß der Ausdehnung der Familienbeziehungen auf alle Gesellschaftsmitglieder sollten als Lösung für diverse gesellschaftliche Probleme dienen. Diese Probleme waren entstanden durch soziale Ungleichheit, innergesellschaftliche Spannungen auf Grund ökonomischen Gefälles, des Auseinanderdriftens von Gesellschaftsgruppen bis hin zum Zerbrechen von Gemeinschaften, des rapiden Verlustes eines verbindlichen moralischen Wertekanons und gültiger Handlungsnormen sowie übertriebener Individualisierung und urbanen Hedonismus. Zugleich bestärkte die Finanzkrise 1997 diesen Trend. Die Instabilität der Märkte eröffnete eine veränderte Sicht auf die negativen Seiten des westlichen Kapitalismus. Dies war die Stunde des Neu-Konfuzianismus. Er markiert symbolisch die Umkehrung der bisher eher postkolonialistisch geprägten Beziehung zum Westen. Statt weiter dem Westen als Ideal und Vorbild nachzueifern, wird die Universalität des westlichen Werte- und Denksystems infrage und ihm das chinesische Modell als positiver Kontrast gegenüber gestellt. Vertreter des konfuzianischen Humanismus wie Tu Wei-ming und Jiang Qing verweisen auf die Missstände der Moderne in den Bereichen soziales Kapital, kulturelle Kompetenz, ethisches Bewusstsein und geistige Werte als Preis für das schnelle ökonomische Wachstum. Eine tragfähige Wertebasis kann nach Tu Wei-ming aber nicht auf Materialismus, Rationalität und Progressivität allein gründen, sondern nur eine gesamtheitliche kulturelle Identität, die durch eine Auseinandersetzung mit den Dichotomien des Eigenen/Fremden, Traditionellen/Modernen herausgearbeitet werden muss, kann in allen Bereichen neue Orientierung geben. Denn sämtliche politischen und gesellschaftlichen Agenden „formulated by the technocratic mentality without reference to culture and ethics are not sustainable“ (Tu 2010: XVI).
Die Rückbesinnung auf „eigene“, traditionelle Werte verkörpert zugleich aber auch ein neues chinesisches Selbstbewusstsein. Begünstigt durch den wirtschaftlichen Erfolg, machen sich in China zunehmend Tendenzen bemerkbar, die vor allem auf eigenständige chinesische Leistungen und Erfolge im Modernisierungsprozess verweisen. Darunter fällt auch der Konfuzianismus als eine wichtige kulturelle Errungenschaft und die Essenz von „Chineseness“. Im Zuge der Suche nach einer authentischen kulturellen Identität zeigt sich ein China „that will not be shaped in the image and likeness of the West, but is on its way to realizing a Confucian culture“ (Fan 2011:1).

Die Beiträge des vorliegenden Bandes sind das Ergebnis eines internationalen Workshops über „Globalization of Confucius and Confucianism" im Juni 2011, der in Kooperation mit dem Institut für Sinologie der Freien Universität und Wissenschaftlern der Peking-Universität anlässlich der 30-jährigen Kooperation zwischen der Freien Universität Berlin und der Peking-Universität 2011 am Konfuzius-Institut an der Freien Universität Berlin stattfand. Die Autoren erörtern die Rolle der konfuzianischen Schriften und philosophischen Ideen in Geschichte und Gegenwart sowie die Frage nach der künftigen Gestalt neuer konfuzianischer Kultur. Die Texte sind zum einem kritische Reflexion eines neuen Trends, zum anderen Versuche einer Zukunftsprognose.

Li Wenchao nimmt eine historische Perspektive ein, wenn er die europäischen Übersetzungen und Rezeptionen von Konfuzius' Schriften im 17. und 18. Jahrhundert und ihrem Einfluss auf die Ideen der Aufklärung untersucht. Beispielhaft greift er hierfür die Philosophen Leibniz, Thomasisus, Wolff und Bilfinger und ihre Interpretation des konfuzianischen chinesischen Staates heraus. Die erste vollständige Übersetzung u.a. der *Analekten* und weiterer philosophischer Texte aus China durch Philippe Couplet im Jahr 1687 erregte Gottfried Leibniz' Aufmerksamkeit und schürte sein Interesse auf China. Ihm genügten die darin gelieferten Informationen jedoch nicht, denn er interessierte sich stärker für den linguistischen und historischen Vergleich und vor allem den praktischen Wissensaustausch zwischen Ost und West als für philosophische und theologische Betrachtungen. Auch Christian Thomasius wertete die chinesische Philosophie zwar als fruchtbare Ergänzung, sah in Konfuzius aber keinen bahnbrechenden Philosophen. Seine Ideen hätten schon Seneca und Epikur gehabt, und sein Ruhm beruhe vor allem auf dem Neuigkeitswert zur damaligen Zeit in Europa. Christian Wolffs *Oratio de Sinarum philosophia practica* im Jahr 1721 wurde von seinen Zeitgenossen als „Signal der deutschen Aufklärung" gewertet. Er sah in Konfuzius eine Art Propheten, der die traditionelle Kultur inkarniert und fortführt. Hierbei liegt für Wolff der Schlüssel für die gesellschaftliche Harmonie im fernen Osten in einer „philosophia practica", welche sich in der konfuzianischen Idee der Selbstkultivierung exemplifiziert und nur damit kann eine inhärente Unterscheidung zwischen gut und böse gelingen und somit beweist sich – ganz im Sinne der aufklärerischen Grundidee – die Bedeutung von Vernunft und Rationalität und der Einsatz des Verstandes zur Begründung einer besseren Welt- und Gesellschaftsordnung. Zeitgleich mit Thomasius lieferte Bernhard Bilfinger eine systematische Analyse der konfuzianischen Schriften nach Couplets Übersetzung und führte darin den Denkweg von Leibniz und Wolff fort. Er kam zu dem Schluss, dass die christliche Theologie und Philosophie der chinesischen ohne Frage überlegen sei und schwenkt damit am Ende in eine ähnliche Denktradition, wie sie bereits bei den jesuitischen Missionaren vorherrschte, indem er weniger auf den Kulturvergleich abzielte als vielmehr die Vorreiterposition des Westens für China hervorheben zu wollen. Li Wenchao nimmt diesen „Denkfehler" Bilfingers als Anlass, um resümierend dieses Überlegenheitsgefühl der westlichen Philosophie, die stets latent die westliche Rezeption von China und seiner Kultur beeinflusste, infrage zu stellen und damit den Bogen bis zur heutigen Auseinandersetzung mit den konfuzianischen Schriften zu spannen. Wenn ihnen heute nun wieder verstärkte Aufmerksamkeit zukomme, so solle dies nach wie vor im Geiste der Aufklärung geschehen, und man solle sich der Herausforderung, fremde Kulturen und Denktraditionen als Bereicherung und Ergänzung zu akzeptieren anstatt sie in vorhandene Muster zu pressen, stets bewusst sein.

Inwiefern dies bei der Auseinandersetzung mit den konfuzianischen Klassikern Ende des 20. und Anfang des 21. Jahrhunderts gelungen ist, beleuchtet *Klaus Mühlhahn* in seinem Beitrag, in dem er die Entstehung und das Grundkonzept des Neu-Konfuzianismus nachzeichnet. Dieser versucht den philosophischen Konfuzianismus durch eine Aneignung, Neuerfindung und kreative Transformation wiederzubeleben, um dadurch neue Impulse für den Selbstbehauptungsdiskurs, die Frage nach einem alternativen Konzept von Moderne und die Eingliederung in den globalen moralphilosophischen Diskurs zu liefern. Angetrieben wird diese neue Ideenschule durch Zweifel an der Vereinbarkeit von Moderne und nicht-westlichen Traditionen sowie dem Revival von konfuzianischen Weisheiten als politische Legitimationsquelle und sozialer Blitzableiter seit der Reformzeit. Neben den Vorarbeiten von Xiong Zhili, Mou Zongsan, Tang Junyi vom Beginn bis Mitte des 20. Jahrhunderts, setzte sich besonders seit den 1980er Jahren Tu Wei-ming für einen konfuzianischen Humanismus ein, da er ein alternatives Modell der Moderne für Ostasien fordert. Sein Konzept sieht u.a. die Einmischung des Staates in die Marktwirtschaft als Vertreter gesellschaftlicher Interessen vor, betont respektvolles Verhalten anstelle von Verboten und Gesetzen, sieht die Familie als Grundprinzip der Gegenseitigkeit und Herausbildung von Menschsein, nach deren Modell auch der Staat agieren sollte, und spricht sich für die Wertschätzung von Bildung und Selbstkultivierung als eine Art „Zivilreligion" aus. Klaus Mühlhahn erkennt darin den Versuch einer Versöhnung einer konfuzianischen und westlichen – China bisher eher aufgezwungenen – Moderne, sowie die Bestrebungen nach einer authentischen Selbsterneuerung, die aufgrund des gemeinsamen konfuzianischen Erbes sowohl China, Taiwan und Hongkong als auch Auslandschinesen wieder näher zusammen bringt. Die Auseinandersetzung mit dem Neu-Konfuzianismus bietet nicht nur Gelegenheit, um sich die Frage nach der Rolle von Traditionen in der Moderne neu zu stellen, sondern mag auch dazu anregen, das Erbe der Aufklärung durch den Einsatz von pluralistischen und hybriden Modellen zu überdenken und zu erneuern.

Um die Aktualität konfuzianischer Ideen zu untermauern, widmet sich *Tan Mingran* in seinem Beitrag einem zentralen Aspekt des Konfuzianismus, dem Mitgefühl (*ren*), um diesen – anstatt wie bisher von rein ontologischer Warte – aus einer evolutionistischen Position heraus zu untersuchen und zu beweisen, dass dieses Grundprinzip auch nach Darwins Theorie eine sinnvolle Berechtigung in der Entwicklung von Gemeinschaften hat und somit auch auf heutige Gesellschaften angewandt werden kann. Er beginnt seine Argumentationskette mit Darwins Evolutionstheorie, nach der sich Organismen an die sich wandelnde Umgebung anpassen, um zu überleben. Auch das Mitgefühl sei somit prinzipiell eine instinktive Macht, die das Überleben der Spezies begünstigen würde, indem es Altruismus und Selbstaufopferung für das Wohl von Nachwuchs und Gruppe fördere. Soziale Instinkte und ein gewisses Intelligenzniveau führen zur Herausbildung eines Bewusstseins und Mitgefühl, das jedoch nicht nur im Dienste der Gemeinschaft steht, sondern auch dem Individuum Vorteile im Überlebenskampf bringt. Mit dieser Ausbalancierung von Eigen- und Gruppeninteressen findet auch eine Unterscheidung zwischen Familienaltruismus und reziproken Altruismus statt, wobei letzterer diese Balance in Form von gerechten sozialen Verträgen absichert. Im Gegensatz zu der sonst häufigen Annahme, das konfuzianische Mitgefühl stelle eine Ausdehnung des familiären Altruismus auf die gesamte Gesellschaft durch eine Universalisierung der familieninternen Beziehungen dar, sieht Tan Mingran jedoch die Liebe zum Nächsten eher im reziproken Altruismus verwurzelt. Er führt dafür insbesondere die Praktiken der kindlichen Pietät und brüderlichen Liebe an, um zu beweisen, dass beides keine instinktiven Handlungen zur Sicherung des Überlebens sind, sondern eine bewusste Gegenleistung für einen vorausgegangenen sozialen Akt. Damit ist der Konfuzianismus mit seinen Handlungsnormen vor allem ein sozialer Vertrag, der darauf ausgelegt ist, die Stabilität der Gemeinschaft zu erhalten, indem alle Verhaltens- und Handlungsimperative auf Reziprozität ausgelegt sind. Zugleich sieht Tan im Konfuzianismus aber auch einen „Mehrwert" zur Natur: Da Praktiken wie die kindliche Pietät evolutionär nicht notwendig sind, stellen sie eine Ergänzung des instinktiven Handlungsschemas dar, um das Zusammenleben in der Gemeinschaft zu verbessern. Nichtsdestotrotz muss auch Tan Mingran erkennen, dass das konfuzianische Mitgefühl in der Lebenspraxis oftmals vor allem zur Pflicht und Bürde wird, indem sich Familienclans zu stark auf dieses Prinzip der sozialen Kontrolle stützen, was letztlich zu einer Schwächung von Staat und Gesellschaft führt.

Der Beitrag von *Gu Zhengkun* liest sich zuallererst als ein Plädoyer und Beispiel für den aktuellen chinesischen Neu-Konfuzianismus. Als überzeugter Neu-Konfuzianer sieht er die Rückkehr zu konfuzianischer Ethik als Lösung für alle sozialen Probleme der modernen Gesellschaft, da sie seines Erachtens zum besten Wertesystem im 21. Jahrhundert gehört. Der Konfuzianismus sei der universellste moralische Ratgeber für die Menschheit, den je eine frühere Generation hinterlassen habe. Insbesondere seine soziale Strukturierung rund um die Familie als Zentrum vom Individuum bis hin zum Staat verleihe dem Konfuzianismus besondere Qualitäten als moralisches Leitsystem in der heutigen kapitalistisch orientierten, egoistischen Welt. Um seine Einschätzung zu stützen, geht Gu Zhengkun zurück zur Entstehungszeit der konfuzianischen Schriften und betont, dass nicht Konfuzius selbst dieses Ideensystem entwickelte, sondern es nur tradierte, generalisierte und in eine komprimierte Form brachte. Damit umfasse der konfuzianische Regelkanon im Grunde das gesammelte, von unzähligen Gelehrten zusammengetragene Wissen der Xia- bis zur Zhou-Zeit und kann daher den Anspruch eines gesamtgesellschaftlichen ethischen Grundpfeilers erheben. Davon weiterführend richtet sich sein Fokus vermehrt auf die Rolle der Familie in Staat und Gesellschaft und auf den Einfluss des frühzeitlichen Clan- und Familiensystems in China auf das konfuzianische Gesellschaftsmodell. Das Grundprinzip des „Familien-Vertrags" anstelle eines sozialen Vertrags setze sich seit der Zhou-Dynastie bis heute fort und bilde das Fundament einer „family-nation". Diese wäre einer reinen Interessengemeinschaft vorzuziehen, denn nur in der Familie seien – ganz im Gegensatz zu Tan Mingrans Einschätzung – selbstlose Bande und uneigennütziges Verhalten möglich. Der Autor untermauert seine These mit weiteren Argumenten des chinesischen Nationalismusdiskurses, wie z.B. dass alle Chinesen im übertragenen Sinne von einem Urahnen abstammen würden und daher die traditionelle Gesellschaft in natürlicher Weise nach dem Modell einer großen Familie funktioniert habe, sowie mit zahlreichen Beispielen für die positiven Auswirkungen der konfuzianischen Tugenden (Mitgefühl, Gerechtigkeit, Riten, Weisheit, Ehrlichkeit, Freundlichkeit, Demut, Loyalität, etc.) in der Gesellschaft. Damit kommt Gu Zhengkun zu dem Schluss, dass „die Welt das konfuzianische Konzept, die Welt wie eine Familie zu strukturieren, über alle anderen Werte setzen sollte".

Auch *Hans van Ess* sieht im Konfuzianismus großes Potential zur Erweiterung des bisher gültigen westlichen Wertesystems in Zeiten der globalen Krise; er betrachtet die Lage jedoch weit skeptischer als Gu Zhengkun. Indem er die kontroversen Debatten um den Konfuzianismus in China während des gesamten 20. Jahrhunderts resümiert, stellt er fest, dass es schon immer sowohl Verfechter als auch Verurteiler des Konfuzianismus gab. Während sich Kang Youwei für eine konfuzianische „Staatskirche" aussprach, kritisierte Chen Duxiu zeitgleich den Konfuzianismus als Hemmschuh des Individualismus und der ökonomischen Unabhängigkeit, da er feudalistische Moralvorstellungen, Hierarchiedenken und eine patriarchische Gesellschaftsordnung propagiere. Diese Einschätzung des Konfuzianismus als fortschrittsfeindlich herrschte im weiteren Verlauf des 20. Jahrhunderts auch in der westlichen Auseinandersetzung mit China – wie u.a. bei Hegel, Weber und Franke – vor. Erst die Bewegung des Neu-Konfuzianismus stärkte die Reihen der Befürworter – die schon in u.a. Richard Wilhelm und Feng Youlan Vorläufer hatten – und der Konfuzianismus fand zum ersten Mal seit Jahrzehnten der Verdammung nicht nur eine positive Bewertung, sondern auch ein neues Selbstbewusstsein, das sich vor allem auf dem Überlegenheitsgefühl des neuen chinesischen Humanismus gegenüber westlichen Philosophien gründet. Auch wenn es heute noch genügend Anti-Traditionalisten in China gibt, prognostiziert van Ess durch zahlreiche Beispiele aus dem alltäglichen Leben eine tendenzielle Neuorientierung an konfuzianischen Werten. Dies sei vor allem dadurch möglich, weil der Konfuzianismus heute weniger als soziale Organisationsform betrachtet, sondern eher das darin enthaltene positive Menschenbild in den Vordergrund gestellt wird, jedoch ohne sich klar zu machen, was die traditionelle Kultur, die man wiederbelebt, eigentlich bedeutet.

Die Beiträge des Heftes machen somit deutlich, dass und wie der Konfuzianismus seit dem späteren 20. Jahrhundert reinterpretiert wurde. Zunehmend sieht man den Konfuzianismus als lebendiges Denksystem und positive Alternative zu westlichen Einflüssen und Konzepten. Auf Konfuzius wird die Eigenständigkeit einer chinesischen Tradition begründet; von dort aus soll die Auseinandersetzung mit anderen Traditionen in der Gegenwart erfolgen. Ob in der Rückbesinnung auf den Konfuzianismus tatsächlich eine Ressource zur Lösung der Probleme der Gegenwart gefunden werden kann, ist bisher allerdings eher postuliert als nachgewiesen worden.

Klaus Mühlhahn und Anett Dippner

Literatur

Bell, Daniel/Hahm, Chaibong (Hrsg.) (2003) *Confucianism for the Modern World*, Cambridge: Cambridge University Press.

Fan, Ruiping (Hrsg.) (2011) *The Renaissance of Confucianism in Contemporary China*, Heidelberg: Springer.

Makeham, John (2003) *Transmitters and Creators: Chinese Commentators and Commentaries on the Analects*, Harvard: Harvard University Asia Center.

Tamney, Joseph/Chiang, Linda (2002) *Modernization, Globalization, and Confucianism in Chinese Society*, London: Praeger.

Tu, Wei-ming (2010) *The Global Significance of Concrete Humanity*, New Delhi: Munshiram Manoharlal Publisher.

Li Wenchao

Confucius and the Early Enlightenment in Germany from Leibniz to Bilfinger[1]

Europe's greatest cultural discovery during the seventeenth and eighteenth centuries came through its encounter with China, a powerful civilisation which, in conjunction with the concerted efforts of missionaries to convert the country to Christianity, increasingly became the focus of European interests. Detailed firsthand accounts of the Middle Kingdom were in circulation from the beginning of the seventeenth century onwards. These covered every conceivable field and topic, ranging from the age of Chinese civilisation, the conventions of Chinese scholars and the secrets of the Chinese language and characters through to the lustre of Chinese porcelain, the allure of polygamy and the deplorable custom of female infanticide; from Confucian classics, Daoist elixirs of immortality and acupuncture through to the science of the pulse, geomancy and the exact height and width of the Great Wall of China. Together they offered a comprehensive overview of the country, albeit one diametrically opposed to the view of America that emerged upon its discovery: here a civilisation on a par with Europe, or perhaps even superior in some regards; there, for better or worse, the most alien of wildernesses – two motifs that were to occupy the European imagination for centuries (Bitterli 2004).

That this varied cultural discovery of the "foreign" was not without effect on the people "at home" is clearly discernible in the at times controversial response elicited by reports on China among the European intelligentsia, irrespective of their leanings. This had much to do with the European reception of the Chinese scholarly tradition as personified by Confucius. Also highly regarded in China, or perhaps even considered holy, the name of Confucius was unequalled when it came to confronting the missionaries in China and their readership in Europe with the question of heathen morality and, moreover, the potential for heathens to achieve salvation in view of their ignorance of the Gospel (Stolle 1714; De La Mothe Le Vayer 1642). The purportedly prosperous Chinese political system, being largely governed by this scholarly tradition, appeared to radically call into question the Christian notion of faith and virtue (Le Comte 1696: 119; Li 2000: 342ff). This, in turn, called for an explanation which, if it were to be plausible at all, had to rely either on the autonomy of reason or on natural theology with its ambiguity in respect of revelation. Some of the ensuing interpretations, prejudices and misunderstandings were to have an enduring impact right through to the present day. That said, the task of the present essay will be to provide a brief sketch of the process of this reception, limiting what is a vast historical spectrum to the Early Enlightenment in Germany. Here I will focus on two large Latin volumes of writings from the Chinese scholarly tradition attributed to Confucius and their reception in the work of Gottfried Wilhelm Leibniz (1646-1716), Christian Thomasius (1655-1728), Christian Wolff (1679-1754) and Georg Bernhard Bilfinger (1693-1750).

1 This paper is a revised version of a German text published under the title *Konfuzius in der deutschen Frühaufklärung*, in: *Die Kunst der Aufklärung*. Eine Ausstellung der Staatlichen Museen zu Berlin, der Staatlichen Kunstsammlungen Dresden, der Bayerischen Staatsgemäldesammlungen München und des National Museum of China, Beijing 2011, pp. 84-94.

Berliner China-Hefte/Chinese History and Society 41 (2012), pp. 9-21

Two Editions on Confucius and His Teachings

In 1681, Philippe Couplet (1623-1693), a Belgian Jesuit and missionary in China, travelled back to Europe on behalf of the China Mission in order to recruit new missionaries and obtain permission from Rome to conduct services in Chinese. He was accompanied by a Chinese man known as Michael Alphonse (Chinese: Shen Fuzong) (c. 1658-1692), who later assisted the renowned Orientalist Thomas Hyde (1636-1703) with his Chinese studies in London. Couplet is alleged to have had in his luggage over 400 books in Chinese penned by missionaries as presents for the Vatican library as well as a large number of Latin manuscripts for the purpose of publication in Europe. Couplet landed in the Netherlands in October 1682. In Antwerp he had several meetings and discussions with Daniel Papebroch (1628-1714), editor of the *Acta Sanctorum*, with whom Leibniz maintained regular correspondence; in Paris and Berlin further significant encounters took place, with Jean de Fontaney (1643-1710), one of the five French Jesuits in China, who later gained fame as a royal mathematician, Melchisédec Thévenot (c. 1620-1692), royal librarian in Paris and editor of several travel accounts, Andreas Cleyer (1634-1697/98), botanist and physician, Christian Mentzel (1622-1701), personal physician and electoral counsellor in Berlin and Andreas Müller (1630-1694), the well-known Orientalist. Through François d'Aix de la Chaise (1624-1709), Jesuit priest and confessor to Louis XIV (1638-1715), he procured an audience with the French king at Versailles. Apparently the king promised Couplet generous support in the realisation of manifold projects, as the *Nouvelles de la république des lettres*, a journal published in Amsterdam, reported in its April issue of 1686 (428f).

However, Couplet's lasting achievement was the publication of the *Confucius Sinarum Philosophus* in 1687 in Paris, which he dedicated to Louis XIV (Couplet 1687) – all the more so, as it fulfilled a dream the Jesuit had held for decades, his first attempt at publication lying ten years back. Boasting an exceptionally beautiful design, the 550 page-strong folio volume contains three of the so-called Four Books of Confucianism in Latin translation – *Daxue*, *Zhongyong*, *Lunyu* and *Mencius*; no less important and momentous are the *Proemialis Declaratio* (IX-CXIV) prefacing the translations and the *Confucii Vita* (CXVII-CXXIV). Two writings by Couplet on Chinese chronology are included in the appendix: the *Tabula genealogica* describes the Chinese history from the legendary Three Monarchs through to the year 2457 B.C., whereas the *Tabula chronologica*, which had already been published separately one year earlier, presents the history of China from the beginning of the legendary reign of Fuxi through to the year 1683. Reviews in leading periodicals bear witness to the extraordinary enthusiasm with which the *Confucius* edition was received all across Europe immediately after its publication. Examples can be found in the *Philosophical Transactions* in London (1687, no. 189), the *Journal des Sçavans* in Paris (1688: 99-107), the *Acta Eruditorum* in Leipzig (May 1688: 254-265), the *Bibliothèque universelle et historique* in Amsterdam (1687, no. 7: 387-455), the *Nouvelles de la république des lettres* (August 1687: 910), the *Histoire des ouvrages des savants* in Rotterdam (September 1687, 65-79), the *Giornale de' letterati* in Parma (1687: 163-166) and the *Monatsgespräche* by Christian Thomasius (1655-1728), which will be looked into in more detail later in this essay.

Another brilliant Jesuit achievement followed a quarter of a century later. This time, the success belonged to François Noël (1651-1729), likewise a Belgian Jesuit, who had returned to Europe in 1708 having spent a good twenty years in the Middle Kingdom. Published in Prague in 1711, the *Sinensis Imperii libri classici sex* (Noël 1711) was translated and edited solely by Noël himself. Besides the Four Books – *Adultorum Schola* (Daxue), *Immutabile Medium* (Zhongyong), *Liber Sententiarum* (Lunyu), *Memcius* (Mencius) – the volume contains two further books in Latin translation: the *Filialis Observantia* (473-484) and the *Parvulorum Doctrina, seu Schola* (485-608). It was this edition that provided the intellectual and spiritual occasion for Christian Wolff's ceremonial speech *Oratio de Sinarum philosophia practica* on 11 July 1721 at the University of Halle, although the Halle-based mathematician and philosopher would not be able to avoid dealing with Couplet's Parisian publication either. The very plain edition received reviews by Christian Wolff, remaining anonymous, in the Leipzig *Acta Eruditorum* (June 1711: 284ff, March 1712: 123-128; May 1712: 225-229) and in the *Mémoires de Trévoux* (November 1713: 2002-2005).

The significance of these two editions, or rather the furore they created, among European intellectuals up until the middle of the eighteenth century can be gleaned from Johann Heinrich Zedler's (1706-1751) *Universal Lexicon Aller Wissenschafften und Künste* (Universal Dictionary of All Sciences and Arts, 1732-1754), where Zedler succinctly states: "These are the two books wherein all truth is founded and great store is set" (Zedler 1961-1964, vol. 37, column 1627). However, a little over half a century later, when Hegel lectured on the history of philosophy in Berlin, he would announce to his audience regarding those two great editions of Confucius: "that for the fame of Confutse it had been better if they had not undergone translation" (Moldenhauer/Michel 1986: 142f).[2] The venerated "Confucius" became a simple "Confutse".

Gottfried Wilhelm Leibniz and the Couplet Edition

The polymath Gottfried Wilhelm Leibniz heard about Couplet's publication even before the book saw the light of day in Paris. As early as 26 January 1687, the Antwerp Jesuit and Leibniz's main source of information, Daniel Papebroch, told Leibniz of Couplet's intention of publishing a Confucius edition (Leibniz 1923ff: I, 7, no. 541).[3] At the same time, Papebroch notified Leibniz that he had informed Couplet as to Leibniz's questions and interest in the Chinese language and letters (Leibniz 1923ff: A I, 7, no. 510; A I, 7, no. 503). Whether or not Leibniz was acquainted with the Prague edition has never as yet been ascertained.

Now that he was aware of Couplet's plans, Leibniz found it worth his while to send Papebroch the beginning of a Confucius book in his possession. Which publication this was, Leibniz did not disclose, but he went on to write:

> Hopefully now R. P. Coupletius, too, will be at liberty to include the Chinese characters [...] in the Latin version, for perhaps it may be possible at some point in time to divine the etymology or key to some of the characters, of which I have no doubt, although I dare not believe this already accomplished, as a certain braggart [here he means Andreas Müller] has been known to claim. Furthermore, it would be worth the effort to extract the simpler among the Chinese characters and to determine their designation, for it is very likely that such a catalogue would contribute to a better understanding of the composites. (Leibniz A I, 7, no. 517)

2 Georg Wilhelm Friedrich Hegel, "Vorlesungen über die Geschichte der Philosophie", in: Hegel: *Werke in 20 Bänden*, auf der Grundlage der Werke von 1832-1845 re-edited by E. Moldenhauer und K. M. Michel, Frankfurt am Main: Suhrkamp, 1986, vol. 18, 142f.

3 Cited in the order of: series, volume, number.

If the context is anything to go by, the booklet sent by Leibniz must have been Prosper Intorcetta's (1625-1696) *Sinarum Scientia politico-moralis* (1667). Fairly widespread at the time (Lambeck 1672: 418f, Lambeck 1675: 349f), this booklet was reprinted several times, although only the first two editions published in China and India are bilingual, that is, in Latin and Chinese. By contrast, *La science des Chinois ou le livre de Cum-fu-cu* sourced by Thévenot for his *Relations de divers voyages curieux*, Part 4 (1672) offers only a Latin translation, the title being the only exception.

On 1 April 1687, Leibniz received further information from Papebroch: Couplet was planning to have completed his *Confucius* by mid-April and then travel to Rome; upon asking the Chinese man, "Michael Sinensis", who was accompanying Couplet on his journey, what title the edition was to have, the reply was: "Confutianae moralis Philosophiae". Leibniz also learned that, while the bilingual edition he had hoped for would not be possible, the book would nevertheless incorporate a number of select samples (Leibniz 1923ff: A I, 7, no. 525). As it happened, no samples of Chinese characters were included in the publication, although the numbered references to them in the text are still clearly recognisable today. On 22 July 1687, Papebroch reported, amongst other things, that by now the *Confucius Sinarum Philosophus* had been published in Paris with a very useful *Praefatio* (Leibniz 1923ff: A I, 7, no. 542), but that he would have to reject Leibniz's wish for the missionaries to be more attentive to the "artificijs Sinensium".

At the time of its publication, the Couplet edition offered the most comprehensive and indeed the best collection of sources thus far on China, its history and culture, not to mention its philosophy and the various schools of thought and interpreters that comprise it. Yet even so, the Couplet edition did not satisfy Leibniz's curiosity, nor did it whet his appetite for an in-depth examination of Chinese thought per se. Two reasons for this seem plausible: first, no publication, no matter how good or qualified, could possibly have quenched Leibniz's thirst for knowledge; and second, the content of the Couplet book was hardly what Leibniz was most interested in at that time. Of course, this does not mean that the authors had nothing to offer in this regard, but rather that, of all things, the very material that might have captured Leibniz's attention – material that had long existed in the form of manuscripts merely waiting to be printed – was omitted. This decision was made by Couplet, the chief editor, for various reasons. Perhaps the most significant of these has to do with the seventeen-page folio *Digressio de Sinarum Literis*. Both Athanasius Kircher (1602-1680) and Andreas Müller had already profited in their studies from this manuscript, and it was precisely for this reason that the editors did not consider it necessary (any more) to include it in their own publication. Yet even the inclusion of certain key words such as "res" or "significatio" would have been appreciated by Leibniz. As things stand, Leibniz's impression of *Confucius* was scant. Indeed, even five years later, as it stands in his letter of 21 March 1692 to Claudio Filippo Grimaldi (1638-1712), he still found that "Your fellow friar Couplet [...] has begun to give us a certain foretaste of genuine Chinese history; but he encourages one's thirst a good deal more than he quenches it" (Leibniz 1923ff: A I, 7, no. 348).

Leibniz's discontentment by no means diminishes the value of Couplet's work, for ultimately it attests only to the fact that the back contains little that Leibniz desired to know. In other words, both at that point in time and in the years that followed, the focus of Leibniz's work lay elsewhere. Chinese characters, for example, played a role in the context of his *Characteristica universalis* project, while Chinese history provided a useful comparison to the Biblical transmission of knowledge, which he hoped might serve to reconcile the longstanding conflict of opinions over the history of the Biblical Patriarchs. And ultimately, he was interested in the exchange of practical knowledge between China and Europe, for the glory of God and the benefit of everyday life. The possibility of engaging in a critical analysis of Chinese thought in a narrower sense – of its philosophy, knowledge of Deity, or even theology – did not enter Leibniz's mind at this point in time. Even so, Couplet's publication played a significant role for Leibniz and was repeatedly mentioned in his correspondence; it was a kind of handbook on China for casual reference: after Thévenot's death in 1692, Leibniz expressed his hopes (Leibniz 1923ff: A I, 8, no. 202f) for a continuation of the scholar's research into the possibility that Christianity, as found in Arabic writings, may have reached China earlier than long thought to be the case, thereby explicitly referring to Couplet's *Histoire d'une dame chrétienne de la Chine* (1688) and his *Table chronologique* "publiée avec *Confutius*" (1686) (Li 2010); when Joachim Bouvet (1656-1730) wrote from Peking to inform Leibniz in his famous letter of 4 November 1701 of the parallels between the hexagrams in the *Book of Changes* and Leibniz's binary arithmetic, while also including a diagram (Leibniz 1923ff: A I, 20, no. 318), Leibniz, putting his surprise and elation aside, consulted his old Couplet edition and found a different order from the one Bouvet had sent. In his letter 18 May 1703, Leibniz advises his correspondent as follows:

> [I] have looked at the characters by Fuxi in the Parisian Confutius, which were printed on the basis of P. Couplet's notes. I find there only the 4 and 8 gua in their right order; the alignment of 64 is disturbed. Yet meanings such as 'air', 'water' etc. have – falsely, it would seem – been added; one would, or could, think that these line figures actually had such meanings. Could it be that the characters around the printed circle you sent me also have the meanings as given in the Parisian Confucius? I beg you, Reverend Father, to reassess this and let me know [the result]. For I have no doubt that you in Peking are in possession of this book printed in Paris. (quoted in Widmaier 2006: 431ff)

It has meanwhile been historically verified that Couplet's *Confucius* accompanied Leibniz right up until his death. When he wrote his *Discours sur la theologie naturelle des Chinois* between 1715 and 1716 upon the request of Nicolas-François Rémond and intended to again discuss the "Philosophia Fo-hiana", that is, the binary numeral system and the hexagrams – presumably encouraged to do so by Bartholomäus Des Bosses (1688-1732) (Li/Poser 2002: 5ff) –, Leibniz again consulted Couplet. Since there a different order was given, which did not quite match Leibniz's discovery, Couplet could not help him any further. This could also explain why the *Discours* could not be completed in spite of several corrections.

What characterised Leibniz's activity was its vast, all-encompassing focus on the one hand and its longevity on the other. More than most of his contemporaries, the politically-minded polymath realised early on – or at least suspected – that the discovery of China as the high culture of the Far East held more promise for Europe than merely spreading the Good News. He thus consistently endeavoured to unite all fields of knowledge within an intellectual, intercultural, global synthesis, advocating – with incredible foresight – a mutually advantageous exchange of knowledge between Europe and China. In none of these points would he be surpassed by subsequent generations.

Christian Thomasius and "Confucius says"

Owing to the work of Christian Thomasius, Confucius as a person once again become the focus of attention in Europe. In 1689, in the August edition of *Freymüthiger jedoch vernunfft- und gesetzmäßiger Gedancken über allerhand, fürnemlich aber neue Bücher* (Forthright Yet Reasonable and Lawful Thoughts on All Manner of, But Mostly New, Books), which was also called *Monatsgespräche* (Monthly Conversations), Thomasius published a thorough and critical review of Couplet's *Confucius Sinarum Philosophus* (Thomasius 1690: 599-630). As Thomasius himself explained, his interest in the teachings of Confucius had been awakened by the treatise *De la vertu des payens* (1642) by Franciscus de la Mothe le Vayer (1588-1672), who believed he had discovered in China a dominion of philosophers longed for in Europe since Plato, and in Confucius "le Socrate de la Chine" – the Socrates of China (de la Mothe le Vayer 1647: 231). It instilled in him the "desire to obtain more detailed news of this Confucio", and at some point he heard word of Couplet's *Confucius Sinarum Philosophus.* Because he was not able to lay hands on the book immediately, however, his curiosity moved him to consult the numerous reviews published in the scholarly journals mentioned above. Disappointed with what he had read, he felt obliged to concede that the much-fêted *Confucius* was more appropriately subsumed "under the *Scripta paraenetica*" than "the *Scientifica*" and that, as such, it was comparable at best with a biography of Socrates – here, Thomasius was able to draw upon his German translation of François Charpentier's (1620-1702) *Les choses memorables de Socrate* (1650), which had been published several years beforehand under the title of *Ebenbild eines wahren und ohnpedantischen Philosophi, oder Das Leben Socratis* (Image of a True and Unpedantic Philosopher, or The Life of Socrates) (Thomasius 1693). He argues that it was for this reason that he refrained from examining Couplet's *Confucius* more closely when it came "to our book shops", "for the said extracts by those journalists made it sufficiently clear to me" (Thomasius 1690: 600) that there was little new material in the book at hand not already known to Greek and Latin philosophy.

When reprimanded by a friend for acting upon the prejudices of others instead of relying on his own judgement ("praejudicium auctoritatis alienae", Thomasius 1690: 602), where the *Confucius* was in fact a book "by no philosopher ever [...] written" in the "social science" (*Scientia Civili*) and thus one that should be "eagerly explained at higher and lower schools [...] and taught to the studious youth" all over Europe (Thomasius 1690: 601), Thomasius examined the *Confucius Sinarum Philosophus* in depth. Following his close reading, he quite frankly admitted to the necessity of correcting his premature verdict as based on the reviews he had read in journals alone. The comparison of these books translated into Latin with "biographical accounts of Socrates", he conceded, was probably not appropriate. Rather, the Books of Confucius reminded him of the popular *Scaligerana* (Cologne 1669) or, for the reader's better understanding, of "D. Luther's Table Talk":

> Luther and Scaliger both may well remain two famous people / although the aforementioned books contribute least to their fame; Thus Confutius may well remain a sagacious and wise philosopher, although this Scientia Sinica is by no means the most sagacious. Those Scaligeranis contain many learned comments; but there are also a good many things therein that are all too liberal / and which deserve little acclaim; The Table Talk of Luther includes pious and useful things; but there are also other histories therein / of which the papists, as is well-known / will be able to make good use against us / or which come across in a rather ludicrous manner [...] Thus while it cannot be declared untrue / that in those three books of Scientiae Sinensis many most wise and subtle teachings of Confucii are contained / which it would be highly desirous / to see

> observed at higher schools or in daily life, there are also many base things therein / at which one can barely contain one's laughter [...]. (Thomasius 1690: 605f)

Such base things, which, according to Thomasius, one found in the books ascribed to Confucius, cannot, however, be attributed to Confucius himself, but rather to his disciples; they had noted these things and compiled them in the writings, either due to an excessive, blind love of their teacher or due to a lack of judgement. The requisite differentiation between the person on the one hand and the writings ascribed to him by his disciples on the other served to create a much more human image of Confucius, who had been wrongly stylised as a role model and an authority, for a "man may excel in sciences and virtues as much as he will / he still remains a human being / and has much in common with lesser people; is also subject to those human weaknesses" (Thomasius 1690: 606). Yet to transform a human with his virtue and erudition into a role model worthy of emulation, one would need to conceal his imperfections and weaknesses and only tell of things well admirable, much like the clever artist who "designed the portrait of a one-eyed king in such a manner / as to place the figure of the king sideways / so as to conceal the missing eye" (Thomasius 1690: 607).

According to Thomasius, then, the books contained in the *Confucius Sinarum Philosophus* were nothing less than a compiled concoction. And even though many "exceedingly beautiful" ideas proved that Confucius was indeed a wise man with a "righteous manner of teaching", no small number of base and even ludicrous things had crept into the collection, things that better would have been left out (Thomasius 1690: 608). It is interesting and surprising to note that among these "exceedingly beautiful" ideas, none of which is of any major significance, are precisely those programmatic passages of text from the beginning of *The Great Learning* (Adultorum Schola) (Wolff 1711: 10f; Couplet 1687: 1f; Li 2000: 362ff) which were later expounded by Christian Wolff for the purposes of his own philosophy and in which G. Bernhard Bilfinger went on to discover the fundamental principles of Chinese moral philosophy (Bilfinger 1999: 25). Whereas the "most ludicrous things" include certain episodes and anecdotes from the life of Confucius, which are either considered traditional codes of behaviour (and thus good conduct) – hence fulfilling a certain model function – or which might in themselves after all contain a meaning accessible through adept interpretation. Even the notion of charity, with which Confucius "could put many Christians [...] to shame", Thomasius could not accept without further ado: "But where are we to seek this love? Among the authorities? Or among the subjects? Among scholars or the unlearned?" Did not Confucius himself complain that clever "worldly people" scorn virtue and that scholars deviate along dangerous paths!" (Thomasius 1690: 611f)

In other words, Confucius may by all means have been a righteous, wise and sensible man, though, as Thomasius would have it, it would not have taken much effort to excerpt his so-called tenets from Seneca or Epicurus, were either of the two to have possessed the authority of Confucius! Thus, he concludes, Confucius owed his fame not to original thoughts but merely to the prejudice of authority holding "today's world" in its grasp. For instead of paying heed to the tenets and their truth, judgement was passed "according to the distinction made by teachers between the truth or untruth of things". Even distasteful things were taken at face value and elevated "to the heavens" the moment one began their narration with a "Confucius says" (Thomasius 1690: 627).

Christian Wolff's Oratio de Sinarum philosophia practica

Christian Wolff similarly focused on Confucius as a person in what was, with hindsight, his notorious speech of 12 July 1721, held on the occasion of his passing on of the prorectorate to his successor at the Friedrichs-Universität in Halle. Differing from Thomasius in his evaluation of the significance of Confucius, Wolff claimed that Confucius was to the Chinese what "Moses was to the Jews, Mohammed to the Turks, why, even as much as Christ is to us", of course, "in as far as we venerate him [Christ] as a prophet or teacher given to us by God" (Wolff 1988: 18f). In this vein, Wolff interpreted Confucius' confession of not having invented anything new but of merely renovating the old (Wolff 1988: 44f) as an expression of his commitment to a long philosophical tradition, a tradition which, through having Confucius as its role model and teacher, had once again come into its own.

That China was a prodigious realm which, in stark contrast to the highly fragmented reality of Europe, was home to vast numbers of ultimately peaceful inhabitants, was as clear to Wolff as it was to Leibniz and many others before him. Yet Wolff saw in this image of China not an expression of religious motivation or even divine revelation. For him, the magic words were "philosophia practica", a philosophy based on the natural powers of the human mind. Accordingly, he argued, the task of reason was to investigate the essence of things and, by means of this investigation, to deduce a precise concept of good and evil. This, in turn, would lead to a strengthening of the will in such a way that it might learn to love good and hate evil. The criterion for good is its consonance with the nature of the human spirit which will refrain from doing evil, provided it recognises it for what it is. The aim of all actions lies in the perfection of the individual on the one hand, and of the world at large on the other. The pursuit of this perfection is called felicity. Precisely this concept – Wolff's very own –, he argued, formed the basis of the practical philosophy represented by Confucius (Wolff 1988: 22f; 44f). Even in the preface to his *Vernünfftige Gedancken von dem Gesellschaftlichen Leben der Menschen* (Reasonable Thoughts on the Social Life of Man, 1721) Wolff would clearly stress this fundamental correspondence between his philosophy and that of the Chinese: "From the days of old the Chinese have applied much diligence to the art of rulership: that which I have, on occasion, made an effort to examine in their writings, I find in accordance with my teachings."

In order to make his prime example convincing and indeed valid for his own philosophy, Wolff had to safeguard himself as much against theism – the Chinese did indeed know God – as against atheism. For there were dangers lurking on both sides. In classifying Confucianism as theism, the example would lose its significance, while classifying it as atheism would create the impression that the speaker, Wolff, was advocating an ethics governed not by the laws of nature but by atheism. Wolff was able to evade both dangers by skilfully creating a kind of buffer zone between theism and atheism, which could be called theological agnosticism. He then cordoned off the 'zone', as it were, to exclude atheism, thus making room for the autonomy of the law of nature: he who denies God, argued Wolff, is an atheist; yet in order to be able to deny God, one must first have known him. If one has never perceived God, one cannot deny him either. At most, this would make one a poor, pitiable, agnostic, but neither a theist nor an atheist (Wolff 1988: 246f, Adnotatio 182; 152f, Adnotatio 54). Since they did not know God, they could not have denied him, thus what else were they to do but use the *lumen rationis* (light of reason) (Wolff 1988: 155f, Adnotatio 56) in order to achieve felicity! Indeed, the whole quarrel about rites (Mungello 1994) was really much ado about nothing (Wolff 1988: 154f, Adnotatio 54). In this cunning gaining of ground for the autonomy of reason within the thicket of theology and metaphysics lies one of Wolff's main contributions to the German Enlightenment. Here, his interpretation of China played no small part.

There also occurred something one might call divine providence: when Wolff chose China as the topic of his pro-rectorate speech in 1721, he only had Noël's Prague translation at his disposal, having not yet discovered the translation by Couplet (Wolff 1988: 214, Adnotatio 128; 208ff, Adnotatio 113). This circumstance was of great significance insofar as Wolff himself also realised in retrospect that Noël's translation deviated considerably from the texts published in Paris and vice versa (Wolff 1988: 210f, Adnotatio 113). Wolff justified himself by claiming that, at the time, he had had "more confidence" in the translation by Noël (Wolff 1988: 210f, Adnotatio 113), an assertion he neither took any pains to substantiate, nor could have substantiated it had he been put upon to do so.

Of course there are many differences between the two translations. The essential difference, however, which seems to have caused Wolff a good deal of trouble after his speech, lies in the fact that the authors of the Parisian translation were "bent on proving that the Chinese had from the very beginning possessed knowledge and veneration of the true Deity and had probably remained steadfast in this for several centuries" (Wolff 1988: 145ff, Adnotatio 54).

The difference is substantial indeed, and in Wolff's case especially serious. Hence, it is fairly easy to understand why Wolff had "more confidence" in Noël's translation (Wolff 1988: 210f, Adnotatio 113). There was too much at stake for him: adopting the theses of the Parisian translation would have called into question Wolff's entire speech on China and toppled at least part of his philosophy in the process.

Yet "confidence" alone would not suffice. Wolff was obliged to come to grips with the Parisian translation and this he did with diligence and élan. Yet since he had no access to the Chinese original source, he had to operate at a different level, the level of philosophy and concepts: what did knowledge of God actually mean? And how was this cognizance expressed in the teachings of virtue and ethics? As Wolff defines:

> The natural religion consists of veneration of the true God, which is derived from his attributes and deeds, these having been perceived through the light of reason. Therefore, where there is no proof of a cognizance of God; where there is no urge towards love, fear, respect of and deference to the deity in combination with a trust in that deity, there is no natural religion. (Wolff 1988: 150ff, Adnotatio 54)

He continues:

> Yet natural religion requires a clear conception of the deity, for the divine attributes and deeds provide the motivation for actions serving the veneration of the deity. (Wolff 1988: 150ff, Adnotatio 54)
>
> Now that the definition had been stated and fairly high standards set, it was not difficult to evaluate the relevant passages of the Parisian translation and come to a conclusion, namely that the Chinese „had a confused notion of the deity and no clear notion at all. (Wolff 1988; 152ff; cf. 244ff, Adnotatio 182)

Even so, Wolff's speech on China (Wolff 1988: XL V), which was considered the "signal of German Enlightenment" (Wolff 1988: Introduction, XLV) and also cost the speaker his chair in Ducal Prussia, was to pose a challenge to European scholars for a long time to come. Even good old Ludovici (1707-1778) in his *Ausführlicher Entwurf einer vollständigen Historie der Wolffischen Philosophie* (Detailed Outline of a Complete History of the Wolffian Philosophy, 1735-1738) castigated the "great master of world wisdom", "such as Mr Wolff was then already" for his lack of circumspection. He saw too much of a collision between "heathen" philosophy and "Christian" philosophy. Both doctrines drew on the light of reason,

> … only who would want to deny that This had not great advantage over That, since he, in his teachings, benefits splendidly from the Light of Revelation. The Light of Reason and of Revelation can be so wonderfully compared with the light of the Moon and the Sun. For just as the Moon does not possess the light, whereas the Sun does, sharing its light with the former, so is foul reason unable to boast of light, if it is not illuminated by Revelation. Indeed, just as the Moon must receive its Light from the Sun, and is all dark if the rays of the Sun cannot strike it, so does he, who makes Reason his guiding star, wander perpetually in darkness. Hence, it would be a bad philosophy on the part of a wise Christian, were it to boast of nothing more than its perfect resemblance to the tenets of a wise heathen, especially in practical materials, although one never should confound Reason and Revelation. (Ludovici 1977: II §137, 91f)

G. Bernhard Bilfinger's Comparative Studies

In all probability, it was Georg Bernhard Bilfinger who drew Wolff's attention to the Parisian edition by Couplet. Years before Wolff submitted his *Oratio* for printing in 1725/26, complete with 216 *Adnotationes*, each up to several pages in length, Bilfinger had already delivered a substantial and systematic study of China entitled *Specimen doctrinae veterum Sinarum moralis et politicae* (Wolff 1962ff).

Bilfinger is considered the inventor of the term "Philosophia Leibnitio-Wolfiana"; indeed, he contributed more towards the popularisation and defence of the Leibniz-Wolffian philosophy than we might imagine. Ludovici reported several times, that "everyone in the scholarly world admires the clarity, thoroughness and skill of Mr Bilfinger in the presentation and defence of truth" (Ludovici 1977: I, § 161, 149). Published a century later, Wilhelm Traugott Krug's (1770-1842) *Allgemeines Handwörterbuch der philosophischen Wissenschaften* (General Handbook of the Philosophical Sciences, 1827) still states that: [Bilfinger] "was one of the most perceptive and thorough thinkers of the Leibniz-Wolffian school, who skilfully defended and explained its system, and in so doing, observed the ideas of Leibniz even more strictly than his teacher [Wolff]" (Krug 1832: art. Bilfinger). Regarding Bilfinger's examination of the ancient Chinese doctrine of ethics and political science, Jacob Friedrich Reimmann (1668-1743) wrote in his *Historia philosophiae Sinensis* (1727) that Bilfinger had been the first to bring into order the writings of Confucius, to systematically set out the Chinese state philosophy and compare Chinese philosophy with Christian philosophy and theology (Reinmann 1727: 29, 20). Wolff, on the other hand, had, in his "public oration of the harmony between his philosophy and the principles of the Chinese Confucii", shown no qualms in "publicly proposing such things as are entirely objectionable and adverse to Christian Religion" (Reimmann 1727: 8; Brucker 1975: 891-893, 979-981).

In his study, which up until now has been afforded only scant attention in research literature, Bilfinger does indeed deliver a systematic study of the source materials he encountered in reading Couplet – he justifies his decision to work with Couplet with the argument that the Prague edition had become rare: "Nescio, quae caussa illos faciat rarissimos?" (Bilfinger 1724: § 19, 17) – although he had none of the difficulties that Wolff was to have with Couplet: in order to prop up his thesis and partly even his own *philosophia practica*, Wolff had to deal – as shown above – with the key message of the Couplet translation, namely that the Chinese people, at least in ancient times, did know God and had a certain cognizance of deity. Bilfinger does not have such problems; he concentrates on a sample of the ethical and political doctrine of the ancient Chinese in respect of its application to politics, systematically elucidating this doctrine with the aid of numerous excepts from the Couplet edition and other sources: from a training of the mind to recognise good and evil to a refinement of the will, from the control of affects, the rectification of the external actions, rights and duties of rulers, to the administrative structure of the realm. Here, even the terminology indicates the degree of Bilfinger's indebtedness to the fundamental ideas of the Wolffian *philosophia practica.* Once again, it is interesting to observe that by and large Bilfinger, too, refers to the very same passages dismissed by Christian Thomasius as amounting to a wise man's "beautiful ideas" and "righteous manner of teaching".

Nevertheless, Bilfinger went far beyond Wolff's adoption of Chinese practical philosophy. For in his *Oratio*, Wolff only hinted at certain ideas, but could not (or did not want to) expand upon them. These include first and foremost the claim of revelation theology to be the highest possible form of knowing God and the distinction between natural virtue (*virtus naturalis*), philosophical piety (*pietas philosophica*) and theological or Christian virtue (*virtus theologica seu Christiana*). In his *Specimen*, Bilfinger returns to these ideas, which Wolff either ran out of time or consciously decided not to assign with any clarity. However, by placing the motivations themselves in the foreground, and thus deviating from Wolff, who, in spite of highlighting the various forms of motivation, stresses their similarity in the practical "adaptation" of actions to the "natural law", Bilfinger succeeds in formulating a clear classification. This enables him to go beyond a philosophical *Comparatio specialis* (Bilfinger 1724: §§ 231, 233) to arrive at a *comparatio generalis* par excellence between philosophy and theology.

Bilfinger lists eight points in which the *Theologia moralis* was far superior to philosophy. Now that the conceptual-analytical superiority of European philosophy had been established (Bilfinger 1724: §§ 233, 280), philosophy no longer referred to Chinese philosophy alone, but more generally to *Philosophia Societatis Civilis* ("non Sinicae solum, sed universae Philosophiae"), among which not least the Wolffian *philosophia practica* figures. These eight points are: knowledge of human decline is only delivered by Christian religion; theological commandments and prescriptions can be deemed superior, as, for example, in the case of the commandment to love one's enemies; God's instructions are prescribed more clearly – this clarity can never be achieved by philosophy, not even by means of a lengthy *ratiocinatio*; if indeed role models and examples (*exempla*) are of importance for moral improvement, as seemingly is the case in China (and in Wolff's speech on China), then Jesus Christ is more perfect a model than Confucius; fifth, the origin of motivation (*ad motiva pertinet*); sixth, salvation and sanctification (*redemptio et sanctificatio*); seventh, philosophers have no remedy for crimes committed, for only Christianity can transform injury into integrity and confusion into conscience. The last point concerns the word and sacraments of God: they are superior and more effective than, say, the Chinese veneration of ancestors and masters.

It would require in-depth study to determine the extent to which Bilfinger, in his comparison between the tenets of Chinese thought and "our" philosophy and moral theology, still followed Wolff. Yet it would be misguided to presume Bilfinger was somehow trying to reignite old quarrels. To the contrary: he was not concerned whether the Chinese were atheists or not – God was mentioned only rather infrequently in Chinese booklets ("Non est multa Dei mentio in libellis Sinicis", Bilfinger 1724: § 281); neither was he interested in a simple condemnation of Chinese rites and customs. Rather, he takes up the missionary idea and asks what actual benefit the Christian message could bring to China. The answer is provided by a Chinese man, whom he quotes from Couplet: rectify deficiencies of Confucianism, dispel superstition and idolatry [Buddhism] – "supplet illa defectus Philosophiae nostrae [Confucianism]; superstitionem atque idollatriam evertit" (Bilfinger 1724: § 288). Thus, once again Bilfinger arrives at the Christian-divine doctrine of revelation and restores the primacy of theology over philosophy. Having always been latent in the European reception of China, it was a motif to which people would return over and over again.

Hence, today more than ever, it is important to render cultures of different origins translatable and representable to one another and seek a comprehensive understanding, and particularly where we want not to annihilate those cultures on account of their distinctiveness, but to conserve their diversity as the intellectual and spiritual wealth of our world.

References

Bilfinger, Georg Bernhard (1999, first published 1724) *Specimen doctrinae veterum Sinarum moralis et politicae; tanquam exemplum philosophiae gentium ad rempublicam applicatae: excerptum libellis sinicae genti classicis, Confucii sive dicta, sive facta complexis. Accedit de Litteratura Sinensi dissertatio Extemporalis.* Frankfurt am Main: Andreae; reprint: Hildesheim: Olms, 1999 (= Wolff 1962ff).

Bitterli, Urs (2004) *Die „Wilden" und die „Zivilisierten": Grundzüge einer Geistes- und Kulturgeschichte der europäisch-überseeischen Begegnung*, München: Beck.

Brucker, Jacob (1767) *Historia critica philosophiae*, vol. 6, Leipzig: Weidmanns Erben; reprint: Hildesheim: Olms, 1975.

Couplet, Philippe (1687) *Confucius Sinarum Philosophus, sive Scientia Sinensis latine exposita: Studio & Opera Prosperi Intorcetta, Christiani Herdtrich, Francisci Rougemont, Philippi Couplet, Patrum Societatis Jesu ... Adjecta est Tabula Chronologica Sinicae Monarchiae ab hujus Exordio ad haec usque Tempora*, Paris: Hortemels.

de la Mothe le Vayer, Franciscus (1642, 2. ed. 1647) *De la vertu des payens*, Paris: Sommaville.

Hegel, Georg Wilhelm Friedrich (1832) „Vorlesungen über die Geschichte der Philosophie", in: Moldenhauer/Michel 1986.

Krug, Wilhelm Traugott (1832) *Allgemeines Handwörterbuch der philosophischen Wissenschaften nebst ihrer Literatur und Geschichte nach dem heutigen Standpuncte der Wissenschaft*, 2. ed., Leipzig: Brockhaus.

Lambeck, Peter (1672) *Commentarii de Augustissima Bibliotheca Caesarea Vindobonensi* , Teil 5, Wien: Cosmerovius.

Lambeck, Peter (1675) *Commentarii de Augustissima Bibliotheca Caesarea Vindobonensi* , Teil 7, Wien: Cosmerovius.

Le Comte, Louis (1696) *Nouveaux Mémoires sur l'état présent de la Chine*, Paris: Jean Anisson, vol. II.

Leibniz, Gottfried Wilhelm (1923ff.) *Sämtliche Schriften und Briefe*, edited by the Prussian (later German, now Berlin-Brandenburg) Akademie der Wissenschaften, Darmstadt, later Leipzig, now Berlin: Akademie.

Li, Wenchao (2000) *Die christliche China-Mission im 17. Jahrhundert: Verständnis, Unverständnis, Mißverständnis*, Stuttgart: Steiner (= Studia Leibnitiana Supplementa 32).

Li, Wenchao (2010) „Wegen monument[i] Sinici", in: Friedrich Beiderbeck and Stephan Waldhoff (eds) *Pluralität der Perspektiven und Einheit der Wahrheit im Werk von G. W. Leibniz*, Berlin: Akademie, pp. 121-138.

Li, Wenchao and Hans Poser (eds) (2002) *Gottfried Wilhelm Leibniz: Discours sur la Theologie Naturelle des Chinois, mit einem Anhang von Niccolò Longobardis Traité sur quelques points de la religion des Chinois, Antoine de Sainte Maries Traité sur quelques points importants de la Mission de la Chine, Nicolas Malebranches Entretien d'un Philosophe Chrétien et d'un Philosophe Chinois sur l'Existence et la Nature de Dieu, jeweils mit Leibnizens Marginalien, Rezensionen aus dem Journal des Savans und Leibnizens Brief an Des Bosses vom 12. August 1709 (Appendix)*, Frankfurt/Main: Klostermann.

Ludovici, Carl Günther (1977) *Ausführlicher Entwurf einer vollständigen Historie der Wolffischen Philosophie Zum Gebrauche seiner Zuhörer*, 3 vols., Leipzig: Löwe, 1737-1837; reprint: Hildesheim: Olms.

Moldenhauer, Eva and Karl Markus Michel (eds) (1986) *Georg Wilhelm Friedrich Hegel Werke in 20 Bänden, auf der Grundlage der Werke von 1832-1845*, vol.18, Frankfurt/Main: Suhrkamp.

Mungello, David E. (1994) *The Chinese Rites Controversy: Its History and Meaning*, Nettetal: Steyler.

Reimmann, Jacob Friedrich (1727, 2nd ed. 1741) *Historia philosophiae Sinensis nova methodo tradita*, Braunschweig: Schröder.

Stolle, Gottlieb (1714) *Historie der Heydnischen Morale*, Jena: Pohl.

Thomasius, Christian (1690) *Freymüthiger jedoch vernunfft- und gesetzmäßiger Gedancken über allerhand, fürnemlich aber neue Bücher durch alle Zwölff Monat des 1689: Jahr Durchgeführet und allen seinen* Feinden [...] zugeeignet von Chritian Thomas Halle: Salfeld.

Widmaier, Rita (ed.) and Malte-Ludolf Babin (transl.) (2006*) Gottfried Wilhelm Leibniz, Der Briefwechsel mit den Jesuiten in China (1689-1714)*, Hamburg: Meiner.

Wolff, Christian (1711) *Sinensis Imperii libri classici sex, nimirum Adultorum Schola, Immutabile Medium, Liber Sententiarum, Memcius, Filialis Observantia, Parvulorum Schola, e Sinico idiomate in latinum traducti a P. Francisco Noel Societatis Jesu missionario*, Prague: Kamenicky.

Wolff, Christian (1962ff) *Gesammelte Werke*, new edition by Jean Ecole et al., Hildesheim: Olms, sect. 3, vol. 55.

Wolff, Christian and Michael Albrecht (ed, transl.) (1988) *Oratio de Sinarum philosophia practica / Rede über die praktische Philosophie der Chinesen*, Hamburg: Meiner.

Zedler, Johann Heinrich (1961-64) *Großes, vollständiges Universal Lexicon aller Wissenschafften und Künste*, Graz: Akademische Druck- u. Verlagsanstalt, 1961-1964 (reprint), first published in Halle and Leipzig 1732-1754.

Klaus Mühlhahn

Der Beitrag des Neu-Konfuzianismus zum Dialog der Zivilisationen in einer globalisierten Welt[1]

Der folgende Beitrag beschäftigt sich mit dem so genannten „Neu-Konfuzianismus" im späten 20. Jahrhundert – einer Bewegung, die auf die Wiederbelebung des philosophischen Konfuzianismus zielt. Der Schwerpunkt liegt vor allem auf den Arbeiten von Tu Wei-ming, dem gegenwärtig wohl philosophisch innovativsten und einflussreichsten Vertreter dieser Denkströmung. Zwei Aspekte werden diskutiert: Erstens der Versuch der Selbstbehauptung und die Suche nach dem Konzept einer konfuzianischen Moderne sowie zweitens die Bereicherung des globalen moralphilosophischen Denkens durch einen Dialog mit dem Neu-Konfuzianismus.

Die Diskreditierung des Konfuzianismus im 19. Jahrhundert

Rund ein halbes Jahrhundert lang bekundete der Philosoph Leibniz im 17. Jahrhundert in Briefen und Schriften sein starkes und anhaltendes Interesse an China. Konzentrierte sich dieses anfangs auf Fragen zur Sprache, vornehmlich der besonderen Schriftsprache Chinas – wie funktionierte dieses gleichsam für Taubstumme geschaffene System, lag ihm zur Gedächtnisentlastung ein längst vergessenes Kalkül zugrunde, folgte es gar ähnlichen logisch-mathematischen Gesetzen, wie sie Leibniz für seine eigene *ars characteristica universalis* vorsah? – so erweiterte und vertiefte sich dieses Interesse nachhaltig durch die im Jahre 1689 in Rom mit dem Jesuitenpater Grimaldi geführten Gespräche. In ihnen entstand Leibniz' Vision eines bis dahin unbekannten Kultur- und Wissensaustausches mit China: Nicht der Handel mit Gewürzen und Seide gegen Edelmetalle sollte die Beziehung zu Europa prägen, sondern ein Erkenntnisaustausch auf allen Gebieten, in Theorie wie Praxis. Allein China, als älteste und beständigste Kulturnation der Erde, konnte diese Vision erfüllen und Leibniz' „Marotte" für die Wissenschaften stillen und im Verein mit europäischen Theorien den Fortschritt der Wissenschaften um Jahrhunderte beschleunigen. China faszinierte das Jahrhundert und Leibniz, erschien es doch „wie eine andere Welt" und zugleich in seinem besonderen Genius ein Komplement zum Geist Europas. Dieses im Vorwort zu den *Novissima Sinica* gezeichnete Chinabild verdankten Leibniz und Europa den Jesuitenmissionaren in China, die in Briefen, Berichten und Büchern damals am verlässlichsten über das Land berichteten (Widmaier 1990, Li 2000, Li/Poser 2000).

Für die Philosophie im Zeitalter der Globalisierung und des Dialogs der Kulturen liegen Aktualität und Bedeutung dieses ersten Versuchs eines geistigen Austausches zwischen China und Europa in seinem interdisziplinären und komparatistischen Ansatz, nämlich dem Fremden und Eigenen, chinesischem „Universismus" (De Groot) und europäischem Universalismus, auf die Spur zu kommen. Die aktuelle Bedeutung der Leibniz'schen Offenheit liegt auch in dem Bestreben, die mögliche Relevanz konfuzianischer Lehren für globale Probleme der Moderne zu erkunden. Leibniz geht in diesem Zusammenhang sogar so weit, vorzuschlagen, chinesische Missionare nach Europa zu entsenden.

Im Europa der Restauration und Gegenaufklärung kam diese Bereitschaft dann jedoch weitgehend zum Erliegen. Im Verlauf des 19. Jahrhunderts verdüsterte sich das Chinabild, und damit auch die Perspektive auf den Konfuzianismus. Die konfuzianische Tradi-

[1] Mein Dank gilt Susanne Ebermann für ihre Hilfe, den Text in eine druckfähige Form zu bringen.

tion wurde nun weithin als eine konservative und autoritäre Doktrin angesehen, die in ein Museum antiquierter und obsoleter Artefakte verbannt werden sollte, wenn sie nicht sogar in den sprichwörtlichen Mülleimer der Geschichte gehörte. Hegel, Marx und Max Weber teilten die Auffassung, dass der moderne Westen, informiert durch die Aufklärung, sich grundsätzlich vom Rest der Welt unterschied. Das konfuzianische Ostasien, der islamische Mittlere Osten oder das buddhistische Süd- oder Südostasien wurden als die empfangende Seite des historischen Prozesses der Modernisierung angesehen. Modernisierung oder Konvergenz würden kulturelle Vielfalt früher oder später obsolet machen. Es war weitgehend unvorstellbar, dass irgendeine nicht-westliche intellektuelle Tradition einen gestaltenden Einfluss auf den Prozess der Modernisierung nehmen würde. Die Entwicklung von der Tradition zur Moderne galt als total, unumkehrbar und unausweichlich.
Auch in China begannen Intellektuelle und Studenten sich zum Modellcharakter einer westlichen Moderne zu bekennen. Solche Positionen fanden sich am prononciertesten unter den Ikonoklasten der „Bewegung des 4. Mai“ (1919), die auf das Ende des Kaiserreiches mit einer radikalen Abrechnung mit der chinesischen Tradition reagierten. Viele spätere Führer der Kommunistischen Partei Chinas hatten in der Bewegung des 4. Mai eine ihrer Wurzeln. Nach 1949 wurden daher der Anti-Traditionalismus und der Anti-Konfuzianismus gleichsam zur Grundlage der offiziellen Politik. In der Kulturrevolution wurden die Roten Garden aufgefordert, die Existenz der „Vier Alten“ (alte Denkweisen, alte Kulturen, alte Gewohnheiten und alte Sitten) zu bekämpfen. Erst nach 1978 änderte die Partei ihren Standpunkt. Sie ersetzte ihren einstigen Anti-Traditionalismus durch die Berufung auf die „fünftausendjährige chinesische Geschichte“, und je schwieriger die sozialistische Selbstdarstellung angesichts des real existierenden Kapitalismus wurde, desto mehr nutzte sie den Konfuzianismus als neue Legitimationsquelle.
Im globalen Kontext hielt die Mehrzahl der Denker und Theoretiker im Westen und in China somit die Inkompatibilität nicht-westlicher Traditionen mit der Moderne für eine unumstößliche Wahrheit, aber wir wissen heute, dass diese Auffassung sich höchstens in Teilen als zutreffend erwiesen hat. Erstens hat im Rest der Welt, aber wohl auch in Westeuropa und Nordamerika, der behauptete eindeutige Übergang von der Tradition zur Moderne nie stattgefunden. Als Normen existieren Traditionen auch in der Moderne wieter, und die Modernisierung selbst wird ständig von einer Vielzahl von kulturellen Formen in unterschiedlichen Traditionen geprägt. Zweitens scheint aufgrund der voranschreitenden Globalisierung das 18. Jahrhundert mit seiner positiven Anerkennung der Relevanz radikalen Andersseins für das eigene Selbstverständnis heute viel bedeutsamer zu sein als die Annahme eines Kampfs der Kulturen und die Fixierung auf die so genannten Herausforderungen westlicher Werte durch nicht-europäische Kulturen im 19. und 20. Jahrhundert.

Die Entstehung des Neu-Konfuzianismus

Im frühen 20. Jahrhundert begann eine Minderheit von Philosophen und Historikern sich dafür zu interessieren, ob und wie konfuzianische Ideen und Ideale von Zeitalter zu Zeitalter überlebt hatten, und zwar nicht nur aus ideologischer Trägheit und aus Macht von Gewohnheit und Tradition, sondern aufgrund der ihnen eigenen Vitalität, d.h. durch eigene Verdienste und positive Möglichkeiten, die sich dann ergaben, wenn große Denker in der Vergangenheit oder Gegenwart den Konfuzianismus auf zentrale Fragen von sowohl dauerhafter als auch zeitgenössischer Relevanz bezogen.
Daraus entstand eine Bewegung, die als Neu-Konfuzianismus bzw. Neuer Konfuzianismus bezeichnet wird. Der Neue Konfuzianismus ist vom „Neo-Konfuzianismus“, der bei

bestimmten konfuzianischen Denkern der Song-, Yuan- und Ming-Dynastie Anwendung findet, grundsätzlich zu unterscheiden. Der philosophische Neu-Konfuzianismus ist zu Anfang des 20. Jahrhunderts bereits einmal in Erscheinung getreten. Xiong Shili (1885-1968) gilt als sein Begründer (Makeham 2003).[2] Er geht von einer Insensibilität der westlichen Philosophie gegenüber Fragen der Moral aus. Der Westen verstehe die moralische Dimension menschlicher Existenz nicht – so könnte man Xiongs Haltung zugespitzt formulieren, die er allerdings gewonnen hat, ohne sich mit westlicher Philosophie in expliziter Weise auseinanderzusetzen. Die diesbezüglichen Versäumnisse des Westens und die entsprechenden Stärken der chinesischen Tradition herauszuarbeiten, werden dann seit den 1950er und 1960er Jahren zur zentralen Aufgabe Xiongs.

Der vielleicht wichtigste, ganz sicher aber einflussreichste Vertreter des frühen Neu-Konfuzianismus ist Mou Zongsan (1909-1995). Er wird von seinen zahlreichen Schülern heute als der bedeutendste chinesische Denker des 20. Jahrhunderts gefeiert. Auch seine ebenfalls nicht wenigen Kritiker müssen zugestehen, dass ein Verständnis des zeitgenössischen Konfuzianismus nur auf dem Wege einer Auseinandersetzung mit seinem Denken möglich ist. So einflussreich Mous Werk also war und ist, es ist geprägt von einer Vielzahl innerer Spannungen. Dies steht im Widerspruch zu seinem Bestreben, dem Konfuzianismus ein systematisches und kohärentes Gepräge zu geben und ihn damit im Kontext der Auseinandersetzung mit dem Westen philosophisch konkurrenzfähig zu machen. Zu den Besonderheiten von Mous Konfuzianismus gehört, dass er in seinen späten Werken den Versuch unternimmt, den philosophischen Gehalt der konfuzianischen Tradition in einer Begriffssprache zu artikulieren, die vor allem dem Denken Immanuel Kants entnommen ist. Ferner wendet sich Mou Zongsan gegen die als „Szientismus" verschmähte Auffassung, dass alle Probleme menschlicher Existenz – wenn überhaupt – nur einer wissenschaftlichen Behandlung zugänglich sind und die Philosophie, will sie zu dieser Behandlung ihren Beitrag leisten, sich folglich dem Erkenntnis- und Methodenideal der modernen Wissenschaften anzupassen habe.

Die Gegner des Neu-Konfuzianismus sind zunächst die Vertreter einer radikalen Verwestlichung – z.B. Hu Shi – und später sind es die Marxisten und Kommunisten auf dem chinesischen Festland (fast alle Neu-Konfuzianer arbeiteten nach 1949 außerhalb der VR), die den Konfuzianismus als Hemmschuh auf dem Weg der Modernisierung betrachten.

In den 1980er und 1990er Jahren erfuhr der Neu-Konfuzianismus dann eine Weiterführung und Ausweitung. Es setzte sich unter den Wissenschaftlern in Taiwan, Hongkong und China die Auffassung durch, dass der Neue Konfuzianismus eine philosophische intellektuelle Bewegung darstellt, die in Teilen zurückgeführt werden könnte auf die ersten Jahrzehnte des 20. Jahrhunderts, so dass Phasen der inneren Entwicklung, eine Kohorte von repräsentativen Denkern und Werken sowie klar definierte Linien der geistigen Überlieferung postuliert werden konnten. Ob es sich insgesamt um eine kohärente Bewegung mit einer klaren intellektuellen Agenda handelt, ist umstritten. Fest steht, dass es unter den so genannten Neu-Konfuzianern erhebliche Unterschiede gibt und auch heftige Kontroversen.

---

2 Der Neu-Konfuzianismus sollte nicht mit jeder anderen Form konfuzianischen Denkens gleichgesetzt werden; vgl. Makehams Abgrenzung der von Xiong Shili begründeten und von Tang Junyi, Mou Zongsan, Xu Fuguan und anderen fortgeführten neu-konfuzianischen Denkströmung von einer breiteren Bewegung des „Confucian revivalism".

Die Bewegung des Neu-Konfuzianismus ist in vielerlei Hinsicht bemerkenswert: Erstens gelang es ihr, die geographischen und politischen Grenzen zwischen China, Taiwan und Hongkong zu überwinden. Der Neue Konfuzianismus spielte zunehmend durch Bereitstellung eines gemeinsamen intellektuellen Diskurses eine führende Rolle bei der Überbrückung der kulturellen und ideologischen Gräben zwischen dem Festland und den chinesischen Gelehrten in Übersee. Der breitere Einfluss dieses Diskurses ist offensichtlich nicht nur in der Art und Weise zu sehen, in der er philosophische Forschung und Debatten generell prägte, sondern auch in der Bereitstellung breiter kultureller und intellektueller Themen und Idiome. Einige Protagonisten sind so weit gegangen, einen „exklusiven" Zusammenhang zwischen „den konfuzianischen Werten" und dem wirtschaftlichen Wohlstand in Ostasien zu proklamieren. Der Neue Konfuzianismus erwies sich somit als die erfolgreichste Form der philosophischen Aneignung, Neuerfindung und „kreativen Transformation" von „Konfuzianismus" im zeitgenössischen China, in Taiwan und Hongkong.

Zweitens gelang es dem Neu-Konfuzianismus, die bis dahin vor allem in der VR China, aber auch anderswo vorherrschende negative Bewertung des Konfuzianismus umzukehren. Als Ergebnis wurde zum ersten Mal seit Jahrzehnten der Konfuzianismus, der bis dahin vor allem als „schädliches feudales Überbleibsel" charakterisiert worden war, in der Form des Neuen Konfuzianismus einem größeren chinesischen Publikum systematisch vorgestellt und erklärt. In China spielte der Staat dabei eine wichtige Rolle, wurde doch 1986 der Neu-Konfuzianismus als zentrales Forschungsthema im Rahmen des nationalen siebten Fünfjahresplanes für die Sozialwissenschaften identifiziert und auch finanziert (Song 2003).

Drittens, in der gegenwärtigen Situation, in der China durch den wirtschaftlichen Aufschwung an Ansehen und Status gewonnen hat, knüpfen viele Intellektuelle in China an den Neu-Konfuzianismus die Erwartung, eine verlorene kulturelle Identität wieder zu gewinnen. Obwohl Tendenzen zum kulturellen Konservatismus und zum Nationalismus im engeren Sinne als Triebkräfte in den Debatten zu beobachten sind, ist gleichzeitig auch das Bestreben chinesischer Intellektueller festzustellen, ein verschüttetes kulturelles Zentrum zu suchen und zu reklamieren.

Tu Wei-mings neu-konfuzianischer Humanismus

Tu Wei-ming, Professor an der Harvard University und Peking Universität, ist einer der bekanntesten und prominentesten Vertreter des Neu-Konfuzianismus, der exemplarisch die Relevanz des Konfuzianismus für die Gegenwart betont. Er ist Befürworter eines Dialogs der Zivilisationen, besonders zwischen der Kultur der Aufklärung in der Westlichen Welt und den modernen Manifestationen des Konfuzianismus in Ostasien. Er setzt sich ein für die Schaffung eines „Neuen Konfuzianischen Humanismus" als „Quelle der Inspiration" im 21. Jahrhundert, in dem dieser Humanismus dazu beiträgt. eine weltweite Kultur des Friedens zu schaffen, welche Kommunikation, Dialog und Aussöhnung zwischen den Kulturen betont.

Tu Wei-ming schreibt nicht nur auf Chinesisch, sondern vor allem auch in Englisch. Er beabsichtigt, eine nicht-chinesische Leserschaft anzusprechen, und daher findet er sich konfrontiert mit Fragen nach einem angemessenen Vokabular, mit Möglichkeiten zur Überbrückung philosophischer Ansichten sowie mit der laufenden Aktualität des kreativen Denkens. In diesem Zusammenhang ist es bemerkenswert, dass Tus Schriften über den Konfuzianismus nicht auf bestimmte Schulen oder Gesprächspartner beschränkt sind; stattdessen sucht er den Dialog mit einer Vielzahl von unterschiedlichen und manchmal widersprüchlichen Partnern, darunter Theologen und Philosophen gleichermaßen. Die daraus resultierende Spannung, die in einem solchen Stil der Darstellung des Anderen in Tus Texten entsteht, erinnert ständig daran, dass eine neue interkulturelle Sensibilität oder Offenheit im Spiel ist.

Tus Ausgangspunkt ist ein Defizit westlichen Denkens: Unter den von der Aufklärung und der Französischen Revolution befürworteten Werten habe die *fraternité* oder Brüderlichkeit, das funktionale Äquivalent der Gemeinschaft, nur wenig Aufmerksamkeit von den modernen politischen Theoretikern erhalten. Seit Lockes Abhandlung über die Regierung bestand eine klare Fokussierung auf die Beziehung zwischen dem Individuum und dem Staat. Auch wenn diese Charakterisierung selbstverständlich kein vollständiges Bild des modernen politischen Denkens im Westen zeichnet, ist es nicht zu bestreiten, dass der Kommunitarismus, d.h. die Stellung und der Wert der Gemeinschaft, keine prominente Rolle im westlichen politischen Diskurs spielte.

Wenn man von der Möglichkeit einer so genannten ostasiatischen Moderne, vor allem einer Form der Moderne unter dem Einfluss der konfuzianischen Traditionen bzw. einer konfuzianischen Moderne ausgeht, ergibt sich die Option eines alternativen Modells. Konkret entwickelt Tu Wei-Ming folgende Aspekte eines solchen alternativen Modells (Tu 1995; Tu 1996):

1) *Die Rolle des Staates in der Marktwirtschaft:* Sie ist für Tu Wei-ming nicht nur notwendig, sondern wünschenswert. Die Lehre, dass die Regierung ein unnötiges Böses sei und der Markt an sich als unsichtbare Hand für die Ordnung der Gesellschaft sorge, stehe im Widerspruch zur modernen Erfahrung im Osten oder im Westen. Eine Regierung, die als Reaktion auf die Bedürfnisse der Öffentlichkeit, verantwortlich ist für das Wohlergehen des Volkes und rechenschaftspflichtig gegenüber der Gesellschaft insgesamt, gilt im Konfuzianismus als von entscheidender Bedeutung für die Schaffung und Aufrechterhaltung gesellschaftlicher Ordnung.

2) *Die Grenzen des Rechts:* Obwohl Gesetze notwendig sind, da sie die Mindestanforderung für soziale Stabilität darstellen, kann die organische Solidarität nur aus der Umsetzung der Rechte in täglichen Interaktionen entstehen. Wichtig ist für Tu Wei-ming also die Idee des respektvollen Umgangs. Respektvolle Verhaltensweisen können nie einfach durch Zwang erzeugt werden. Tu Wei-ming weist darauf hin, dass es in den Vereinigten Staaten vielleicht eine halbe Million oder mehr Gefangene in den Gefängnissen gibt, mehr als in ganz China trotz einer vierfach größeren Bevölkerung. Exemplarische Unterweisung, als Standard der Inspiration, beruhe auf freiwilliger Teilnahme. Gesetze allein können kein Gefühl der Scham erzeugen, das kultiviertes und respektvolles Verhalten anleitet. Es ist die rituelle Handlung, die Menschen dazu ermutigt, gemäß ihrer eigenen Bestrebungen zu leben.

3) *Die Rolle der Familie:* Die Familie als grundlegende universelle Form der Vergesellschaftung ist der Ort, von dem aus die Grundwerte übertragen werden. Natürlich können Familien ganz unterschiedlich aussehen: Jede Art von Familie, nicht nur die konventionelle, ist zu berücksichtigen. Die Beziehungen innerhalb der Familie werden normalerweise nach Alter, Geschlecht, Autorität, Status oder sogar Hierarchie differenziert. Sie bietet eine reich strukturierte natürliche Umgebung für das Erlernen der richtigen Weise des Menschseins. Das Prinzip der Gegenseitigkeit definiert alle Formen der menschlichen Verbundenheit in der Familie: Alter und Geschlecht, möglicherweise zwei der gravierendsten Lücken in der ursprünglichen Umgebung des menschlichen Lebensraums, werden in einen kontinuierlichen Fluss intimer Gefühle und menschlicher Obhut eingebracht.

4) *Die Rolle der Zivilgesellschaft:* Die Zivilgesellschaft existiert nicht, weil sie eine ökonomische Arena oberhalb der Familie und unterhalb des Staates ist. Die innere Stärke der Zivilgesellschaft liegt in dem dynamischen Wechselspiel zwischen Familie und Staat. Die Natur der Familie als Mikrokosmos des Staates, und die Idee des Staates als eine Erweiterung der Familie, zeigen, dass die Stabilität der Familie von entscheidender Bedeutung ist für das Staatswesen und dementsprechend eine lebenswichtige Funktion des Staates darin besteht, organische Solidarität innerhalb der Familie zu gewährleisten. Die Zivilgesellschaft bietet eine Vielzahl von kulturellen Institutionen, die eine fruchtbare Verbindung zwischen Familie und Staat ermöglichen. Das dynamische Zusammenspiel zwischen dem Privaten und Öffentlichen ermöglicht es der Zivilgesellschaft, vielfältige und bereichernde Ressourcen für die menschliche Bildung anzubieten (Madsen 2007).

5) *Bildung:* Bildung sollte für Tu Wei-ming eine Art „Zivilreligion" der Gesellschaft sein. Das primäre Ziel der Erziehung ist die Charakterbildung. In der Absicht der Kultivierung einer vollständigen Person sollten die Schulen ethische sowie kognitive Intelligenz betonen; Schulen sollten die Kunst lehren, „soziales Kapital" durch Kommunikation zu akkumulieren. Neben dem Erwerb von Wissen und Fähigkeiten muss Schule auch zur Entwicklung einer kulturellen Kompetenz und der Wertschätzung geistiger Werte beitragen.

6) Da *Selbst-Kultivierung* die Wurzel für die Regulierung der Familie ist, hängen auch staatliche Governance, gesellschaftliche Ordnung sowie Frieden unter dem Himmel als zentrale Lebensqualitäten in einer bestimmten Gesellschaft von dem Grad der Selbstkultivierung der Bürger ab. Eine Gesellschaft, für die die Selbst-Kultivierung eine notwendige Bedingung für menschliche Entwicklung darstellt, ist eine Gesellschaft, die individuelle Charakterbildung durch eine wert-zentrierte politische Führung, das gegenseitige Ermahnen an den gemeinschaftlichen Weg der Selbstverwirklichung, den Wert der Familie als ein richtiges Zuhause für das Erlernen von Humanität und den respektvollen Umgang als die normale Form der menschlichen Interaktion und Erziehung fördert.

Tu Wei-ming gesteht ein, dass diese sechs gesellschaftlichen Ideen niemals in einer der ostasiatischen Gesellschaften vollständig oder tatsächlich realisiert wurden. Die ostasiatischen Gesellschaften zeigen oft Verhaltensweisen und Einstellungen, die genau das Gegenteil von den Auffassungen des konfuzianischen Humanismus sind. In der Tat, vom Imperialismus und Kolonialismus seit Jahrzehnten gedemütigt, zeigt der Aufstieg Ostasiens, zumindest oberflächlich betrachtet, eklatant einige der negativen Aspekte der Moderne, wie z.B. Ausbeutung, Merkantilismus, Kommerzialisierung, Materialismus, Gier, Egoismus und natürlich brutalen Wettbewerb.

Dennoch, als erste nicht-westliche Region, die sich erfolgreich modernisiert hat, sind die kulturellen Auswirkungen des Aufstiegs Ostasiens weitreichend. Der moderne Westen, inspiriert durch die Aufklärungs-Mentalität, gab die Initialzündung für einen weltweiten sozialen Wandel. Die historischen Gründe für den Beginn dieses Prozesses in Europa sind nicht unbedingt bestimmte strukturelle Komponenten oder konstitutive Aspekte der westlichen Zivilisation. Werte der Aufklärung wie Freiheit, Rechtsbewusstsein, rechtsstaatliche Verfahren, Rationalität, die Privatsphäre und Individualität sind alles universalisierbare Werte. Aber das konfuzianische Leitbild schlägt einige humanistische Werte wie Mitgefühl, Verteilungsgerechtigkeit, Pflichtbewusstsein, Ritual, Gemeinsinn und Zielgruppenorientierung vor, die ebenfalls universalisierbar sind. China muss sich darum bemühen, die Menschenrechte zu realisieren, Freiheiten anzuerkennen usw. Aber auch Europa und Amerika, d.h. die westliche Welt, kann und muss mehr tun für Verteilungsgerechtigkeit, Solidarität, Pflichtbewusstsein, Ritual und Gemeinsinn. Eine dringende

Aufgabe ist es auch, über ökologische Fragen und über den Zerfall der Gemeinschaft auf allen Ebenen innerhalb eines globalen interzivilisatorischen Dialogs zu reflektieren. Für Tu Wei-ming geht es darum, das spirituelle Projekt der Überdenkung und Erneuerung des Aufklärungs-Erbes voranzubringen.

Die Möglichkeit, eine radikal andere Ethik oder ein neues Wertesystem getrennt und unabhängig von der Aufklärung zu entwickeln, ist für Tu Wei-ming aber weder realistisch noch verbindlich. Stattdessen fordert er dazu auf, die geistigen Ressourcen zu entfalten, die in der Lage sind, den Umfang des Aufklärungs-Projekts zu erweitern, zu vertiefen, die moralischen Dimensionen zu erforschen und, wenn nötig, kreativ die wirtschaftlichen oder historischen Zwänge zu überwinden, um das volle Potenzial der Aufklärung als einer Weltanschauung für die menschliche Gemeinschaft als Ganzes zu eruieren (Tu 1998). Und natürlich ist der Schlüssel zum Erfolg dieses spirituellen Joint Venture die Erkenntnis der auffälligen Abwesenheit der Idee der Gemeinschaft oder des Kommunitarismus, geschweige denn der Weltgemeinschaft, in dem Aufklärungs-Projekt.

Für Tu steht das industrielle Ostasien unter dem Einfluss der konfuzianischen Kultur, für eine andere Art der modernen Zivilisation, die weniger auf Gegeneinander beruht und weniger individualistisch und weniger eigennützig ist. Es bestehe ein Nebeneinander von Marktwirtschaft und Regierung, demokratischer Parität und Meritokratie und einzelnen Initiativen mit Zielgruppenorientierung. All dies habe die Region wirtschaftlich und politisch zu einer der dynamischsten gemacht, sowohl im negativen wie im positiven Sinne, einschließlich der aktuellen Situation der Finanzkrise. Die Bedeutung des Beitrags der konfuzianischen Ethik für den Aufstieg des industriellen Ost-Asiens, für die mögliche Entstehung von hinduistischen, buddhistischen und islamischen Formen der Moderne, ist weitreichend. Mit anderen Worten, Tu Wei-ming redet nicht bloß über den Übergang von dem westlichen Modell zu einem ostasiatischen Modell; er spricht eher von dem Übergang eines singulären Modells zu einem pluralistischen Modell, wobei das pluralistische Modell einige grundlegende Wertorientierungen über kulturelle Grenzen hinweg mit anderen Kulturen teilt. Die Verwestlichung des konfuzianischen Asiens – Japan, die beiden Koreas, China, Hongkong, Taiwan, Singapur und Vietnam inbegriffen – hat für immer die geistige Landschaft dieses Erdteils verändert. Aber die einheimischen Ressourcen, einschließlich Mahayana-Buddhismus, Taoismus, Shintoismus, Schamanismus und anderer Traditionen besitzen die Widerstandsfähigkeit, immer wieder aufzutauchen und ihre Präsenz in neuen Synthesen zu behaupten.

Das Ziel Tu Wei-mings ist es somit, eine Art geistige Ressource aus dem Kern des Aufklärungs-Projekts selbst zu entwickeln. Durch diszipliniertes Nachdenken und ein gemeinsames Agieren soll eine Art von kreativer Zone gebildet werden, in der religiöse Führer, ethische Lehrer, Philosophen und die Öffentlichkeit einen globalen Dialog führen. Die Traditionen sollten dabei nicht statisch aufgefasst werden: Die feministische Kritik an der Tradition, das Bewusstsein für die Erhaltung der Umwelt, der Diskurs über kommunitaristische Ethik und die Überzeugungskraft des religiösen Pluralismus sind offensichtliche Beispiele einer kritischen Selbstreflexion. Die Notwendigkeit, über die Aufklärung hinauszugehen ohne sie entweder zu dekonstruieren oder das Engagement für Rationalität, Freiheit, Gleichheit, Menschenrechte, Verteilungsgerechtigkeit völlig aufzugeben, erfordert eine gründliche Überprüfung der Moderne als dem Signifikanten und der Modernisierung als einem Prozess.

Hinter dieser Überprüfung steht die faszinierende Frage nach der Rolle von Traditionen in der Moderne. Das dichotome Denken von Tradition und Moderne als zwei unvereinbaren

Formen des Lebens muss von einer viel differenzierteren Auseinandersetzung mit dem kontinuierlichen Wechselspiel zwischen Modernisierung und Tradition ersetzt werden. In diesem speziellen Zusammenspiel entstehen neue Formen der kulturellen Selbstvergewisserung. Die Traditionen in der Moderne sind nicht nur historische Ablagerungen, passiv abgekapselt in dem modernen Bewusstsein. Auch sind sie in funktioneller Hinsicht nicht einfach hemmende Faktoren, die die Flugbahn der unilinearen Entwicklung der Modernisierung untergraben. Im Gegenteil, Traditionen wirken sowohl mäßigend als auch befördernd und sind damit Kräfte, die die Gestaltung der jeweiligen Kontur der Moderne in einer gegebenen Gesellschaft beeinflussen. Es ist daher konzeptionell naiv und methodisch trügerisch, Traditionen zu einer Restkategorie in unserer Diskussion über den Vorgang der Moderne zu verweisen. In der Tat ist eine Untersuchung der Traditionen in der Moderne wesentlich für unser Verständnis von Modernisierung als ein sehr differenziertes kulturelles Phänomen, im Gegensatz zu der simplifizierenden Vorstellung der Moderne als integraler Prozess der Verwestlichung.

Fazit

Tu Wei-ming betrachtet die konfuzianische Lehre als eine Art von umfassendem Humanismus, der in Anlehnung an sein kulturelles Ideal der Einheit zwischen Himmel und Erde das Säkulare als heilig betrachtet und durch Selbstkultivierung und gute Regierungsweise versucht, die Welt von innen heraus zu verändern. Den Intellektuellen in Europa und in Amerika bietet er den konfuzianischen Humanismus als Beitrag zur Kultivierung einer globalen Ethik an. Die konfuzianische Ethik der Verantwortung, in die konkreten Umstände Ostasiens eingebettet, soll auf die globale Gemeinschaft ausgedehnt werden. Nur dann kann die konfuzianische Denkweise zu einem aktiven Partner der Aufklärung werden.

Zwei Aspekte sind hervorzuheben:

Erstens der Versuch der kulturellen Selbstbehauptung und die Suche nach den eigenständigen Grundlagen einer konfuzianischen Moderne. Die Philosophie des Neu-Konfuzianismus stellt den Versuch einer zunächst kleinen Gruppe von chinesischen Intellektuellen dar, angesichts der Herausforderung durch westliche Zivilisation, Wissenschaft und Philosophie zu einem erneuerten Verständnis der eigenen Tradition zu kommen und dieser Tradition zu einem neuen, philosophisch präziseren Ausdruck zu verhelfen. Der Konfuzianismus im 20. Jahrhundert ist ein Diskurs *kultureller Selbstbehauptung* (Lackner 2003), er wird aber im Verlauf seiner Entwicklung auch ein Bemühen um so etwas wie *authentische Selbsterneuerung* und wird folglich zu einer beständigen Gratwanderung zwischen Bewahrung und Veränderung auf der Suche nach einer genuin konfuzianischen und dennoch modernen Philosophie.

Zweitens geht es um das Beharren auf der notwendigen Bereicherung des globalen moralphilosophischen Denkens durch einen Dialog mit dem Neu-Konfuzianismus. Man könnte auch sagen, es geht um eine Versöhnung des Konfuzianismus mit westlicher (China zunächst von außen aufgezwungener) Moderne, wobei der Konfuzianismus in die globale Debatte eingebracht werden soll.

Doch gibt es selbstverständlich auch kritische Punkte:

Zum einen erscheinen die Ausführungen als zu idealistisch. Da weder in früheren Zeiten noch in der Gegenwart diese Vorstellungen eine praktische Umsetzung erreicht haben, könnte man schlussfolgern, dass sie einfach nicht praktikabel sind. Natürlich überlebten sie als Ideale, konnten aber die anhaltenden Probleme der chinesischen Gesellschaft nicht lösen. Die Entwicklung in Japan und anderen Staaten in Ostasien war gekennzeichnet

durch Merkantilismus, Kommerz und heftigen internationalen Konkurrenzkampf. Die Volksrepublik China hat sich für die gleiche Strategie der Entwicklung entschieden und seit dem Beginn der Reformen im Jahr 1979 somit eine ähnliche Wertorientierung gezeigt. Mit anderen Worten, gegenwärtig offerieren konfuzianische und neo-konfuzianische Lehren vor allem die Vorschläge neuer Möglichkeiten, aber keine präzisen Modelle.
Es wird zum anderen deutlich, dass die modernen Konfuzianer erstens einen Philosophiebegriff vertreten, der einige im Westen vertraute Grenzziehungen nicht beachtet – zum Beispiel die zwischen Philosophie und Religion – und dass zweitens im Diskurs des modernen Konfuzianismus sich zwei Ebenen miteinander vermischen, nämlich die Artikulation bestimmter philosophischer Inhalte mit einer den Bereich akademischer Philosophie weit überschreitenden kulturpolitischen Strategie.[3] Das schafft viele Spannungen und Widersprüche im neukonfuzianischen Denken: Immer wieder bestimmt und überlagert nämlich das kulturpolitische, strategische Ziel die philosophische Abstraktion.
Drittens lässt sich der Großteil des neukonfuzianischen Denkens in diesem Sinne eher als moralische Vision begreifen – und damit kann gleichzeitig erklärt werden, warum westliche Interpreten konfuzianisches Denken häufig als theoretisch schwach und ungenügend empfunden haben bzw. zu der Meinung gelangt sind, dass chinesische Denker keine Trennung zwischen Sein und Sollen, Deskription und Präskription durchführen und sich also fortwährend eines schwerwiegenden Kategorienfehlers schuldig machen. Wenn die obigen Ausführungen zutreffend sind, handelt es sich aber nicht um einen Fehler, sondern geradezu um die grundlegende Intention des gesamten konfuzianischen Denkens.
Was viertens an dieser moralischen Vision auffällt – unabhängig davon, für wie erhellend man sie hält – ist der merkwürdige, auf den ersten Blick willkürlich wirkende, tatsächlich aber ganz bewusste Einsatz von Begriffen aus der westlichen Tradition des gesellschaftspolitischen Denkens (z.B. Zivilgesellschaft). Es sind, mit anderen Worten, theoretische Begriffe, welche die Konfuzianer aus der westlichen Tradition übernehmen und in ihren eigenen ‚visionären' Kontext überführen. Es scheint, dass die chinesischen Autoren ihren Texten eine bestimmte Oberfläche zu geben versuchen, indem sie Begriffe benutzen, die Präzision und Prägnanz suggerieren, tatsächlich aber besteht unter der Oberfläche einer wissenschaftlich präzisen und logisch stringenten Philosophie die durchaus bewusste und gesuchte Vagheit der visionären Inhalte.

Literatur

Lackner, Michael (2003) „Philosophie, Theologie oder Kulturwissenschaft? Legitimationen des modernen Neokonfuzianismus“, in: Iwo Amelung et al. (Hrsg.) *Selbstbehauptungsdiskurse in Asien: China – Japan – Korea*, München: Iudicium, S. 275-290.

Li Wenchao (2000) *Die christliche China-Mission im 17. Jahrhundert*, Stuttgart: Studia Leibnitiana, Supplementa, Bd. 32.

Li Wenchao, Hans Poser (Hrsg.) (2000) *Das Neueste über China. G.W. Leibnizens Novissima Sinica von 1697*. Internationales Symposium, Berlin 4. bis 7. 1997, Stuttgart: Studia Leibnitiana, Supplementa, Bd. 33.

Madsen, Richard (2007) „Confucian Conceptions of Civil Society”, in: Daniel A. Bell (Hrsg.) *Confucian Political Ethics*, Princeton University Press, S. 3-16.

Makeham, John (2003) „The Retrospective Creation of New Confucianism”, in: John Makeham (Hrsg.) *New Confucianism: A Critical Examination*, New York u.a.: Palgrave Macmillan, S. 25-53.

3 „Kulturpolitisch“ ist hier im weitesten Sinne gemeint: bemüht um das Überleben der kulturellen und politischen Entität „China“.

Marchal, Kai (2011) *Die Aufhebung des Politischen: Lü Zuqian (1138-1181) und der Aufstieg des Neukonfuzianismus*, Wiesbaden: Harrassowitz Verlag.

Song Xianlin (2003) „Reconstructing the Confucian Ideal in 1980s China: 'The Cultural Craze' and new Confucianism", in: John Makeham (Hrsg.) *New Confucianism: A Critical Examination*, New York u.a.: Palgrave Macmillan, S. 81-104.

Tu Wei-ming (1995) „Confucian Dimension in the East Asian Development Model", in Josef Kreiner (Hrsg.) (1996) *The Impact of Traditional Thought on Present-Day Japan*, München: Iudicium Verlag GmbH, S. 31-48.

Tu Wei-ming (Hrsg.) (1996) *Confucian Traditions in East Asian Modernity*, Cambridge, MA: Harvard University Press.

Tu Wei-ming (1998) „Beyond the Enlightenment Mentality," in Mary Evelyn Tucker and John Berthrong (Hrsg.) *Confucianism and Ecology: The Interrelation of Heaven, Earth, and Humans*, Cambridge: Harvard University Center for the Study of World Religions, S. 3-21.

Widmaier, Rita (Hrsg.) (1990) *Leibniz korrespondiert mit China. Der Briefwechsel mit den Jesuitenmissionaren (1689-1714)*, Frankfurt am Main: Veröffentlichungen des Leibniz Archivs.

Tan Mingran

An Evaluation of Confucian Sympathy from the Perspective of Evolutionary Ethics

In this essay, I employ sympathy, kin altruism and reciprocal altruism from evolutionary ethics as a framework reference to examine the origin of Confucian sympathy or humanity (仁 *ren*), and to evaluate the probability of its extension. I do not endorse the idea of filial piety, the prime approach for achieving sympathy, as an innate ability and therefore question the efficiency of promoting filial piety in shaping personality and beautifying custom as assumed by Confucian scholars. Undoubtedly, the promotion of sympathy and filial piety has been of great benefit for Chinese families and society, but it also causes people to put family interests before those of public welfare and can lead to bureaucratic corruption. In addition, this essay discusses the role played by intelligence and habit in the process of moral education and in the formation of a second nature, and points out that the promotion of filial piety and sympathy has not helped people to develop a nature of sympathy that is immune to the distraction of selfish interests.

The Origin of Sympathy

Most scholars studying Chinese culture agree that sympathy (仁 *ren*) is the essence of Confucianism. They follow Confucius' words, that "sympathy is to love human beings" (Yang 1980: 138), and identify these with benevolence and humanity. However, before the Song Dynasty (960-1297), few scholars thought of seeking an ontological explanation for the origin of sympathy. Mencius made an attempt, describing sympathy as an innate ability, but he did not provide any further justification (Chan 1963: 54). As a result, from the time of Confucius to the end of the Tang Dynasty (618-907), people's understanding of sympathy remained at the descriptive level, of loving human beings. Since the Song Dynasty, Neo-Confucian scholars have tried to provide an ontological explanation of sympathy, defining it as the vitality and principle of life, and assuming it was endowed by Heaven (Nature) (Cheng/Cheng 2000: 167, 232).[1] This conclusion is partly based on the interpretation of one sentence in the *Book of Changes*, "The great virtue of Heaven and earth is the giving and sustaining life" (Wang 1998, vol. 1: 579), and partly on empathy, on the belief that other sentient beings have the same survival instinct as human beings. As to how sympathy develops in the human mind, further explanations were not provided. At this point, an evolutionist explanation of the origin of sympathy can serve to fill the gap and act as a reference for the evaluation of its Confucian counterpart.

Like the Confucians who claimed that Heaven has the great virtue of producing and sustaining life, the evolutionist founder, Darwin, also maintained that Nature has a tendency to improve organic beings, and thus acts as the origin of sympathy,

> It may be said that natural selection is daily and hourly scrutinizing, throughout the world, every variation, even the slightest. Rejecting that which is bad, preserving and

[1] From my point of view, Confucianism and Neo-Confucianism are the same in that both place an emphasis on sympathy and the Neo-Confucian understanding of sympathy can therefore be used to further clarify the meaning of sympathy. A comparison of Confucianism with Evolutionism will show that they express the same concern for sympathy and life, which will lead us to an evolutionary concept of sympathy, which in turn will serve as a reference framework to evaluate the Confucian doctrine of sympathy.

> adding up all that is good; silently and insensibly working, whenever and wherever opportunity offers, at the improvement of each organic being in relation to its organic and inorganic conditions of life. (Richards 1999: 130)

When explaining how this natural tendency or selection works, Darwin referred to the way that organisms adapt to their environment in order to survive. He suggested that the habits an animal might adopt to cope with a shifting environment would, during the course of generations, slowly become instincts, that is, innately determined patterns of behavior. Instincts in their turn would gradually modify the anatomy of an organism, adapting the creature to its surroundings (Richards 1987: 94). Later, Elliot Sober and David Sloan Wilson found reason to support this claim, in their research on ivy plants which revealed changes in the internal mechanisms related to the plants' selection for phototropism (Sober/Wilson 1998: 200). Therefore, it may be said that the natural tendency or selection works through organisms' adaptability to their environment and toward the improvement of their fitness, and the origin of sympathy lies in the instinctive power of survival that is aroused by environmental stimulation.

However, the instinctive power of survival is not equal to sympathy. Sympathy is essentially identified with altruism and requires the sacrifice of one's own interests for the welfare of others, while an instinct for survival may cause one organism to harm or kill another. To explain the rise of sympathy or conscience, Darwin further proposed social instincts, and contended,

> Any animal whatever, endowed with well-marked social instincts, would inevitably acquire a moral sense or conscience, as soon as its intellectual powers had become as well developed, or nearly as well-developed, as in man.(Richards 1987: 210)

Since intelligence was understood as "a modification of instinct – an unfolding and generalizing of the means by which an instinct is transmitted", that is "not being opposed to instinct, but rather growing out of it" (Richards 1987: 109), it is safe to say that in Darwin's view, social instincts give rise to sympathy and conscience. Darwin made this clear when he reiterated that the insistent character of social instincts, which formed the very ribs of man's civilized being, should be regarded as equivalent to the moralist's ought (Richards 1987: 119).

With regard to the origins of social instinct, Darwin assumed that the habits conducive to the common good, such as, ingrained habits of parental nurture, mutual aid, and group defense would be adopted and developed into social instincts, while habit-satisfying individual desires would gradually fade out over generations. When an individual then came to proscribe actions or judge what ought to be done in a particular situation, the criterion of the common good would recommend itself (Richards 1987: 210). Hence, Darwin maintained that conscience ultimately derives from a persistent social impulse.

Some scholars have argued that social instincts or altruistic habits will be unattainable since the inherent pleasures and advantage are not conferred on their agent but on their recipient (Richards 1987: 121). This may not be true. In order to survive, organisms, especially weak ones, need mutual aid and group defense. In such a situation, their altruistic behaviors will also benefit themselves, as Elliot Sober contends,

> Altruism is naturally defined as a pre-disposition to act so as to benefit others at a cost to oneself. But this definition applies only to interactions between a pair of individuals. In a population, altruistic behavior by many may result in benefits to many, including the altruists. (Sober/Wilson 1998: 86)

Moreover, if the survival and reproduction of one's child is regarded as the copying and continuance of one's own genes, unselfishness can arise from selfishness even at the individual level.

In conclusion, by tracing the origins of sympathy to social instinct, in particular, the ingrained habits of parental nurture, mutual aid, and group defense, we can gain a clearer understanding of sympathy from the evolutionist perspective, This understanding will serve as a reference for the discussion and evaluation of the Confucian doctrine of sympathy which focuses on the function of filial piety and fraternal love. Since some Confucian scholars tend to explain sympathy from the perspective of kin altruism, it is necessary to differentiate between kin altruism, reciprocal altruism and filial piety, in order to illustrate the nature of the Confucian version of sympathy.

Altruism and Sympathy versus Self-interest

Generally, altruism and sympathy are identical in terms of morality. Altruism is naturally defined as a pre-disposition to act so as to benefit others at a cost to oneself, while sympathy is the natural capacity of being pleased at the pleasures, and pained at the sufferings of others (Sutherland 1974, Vol. 2: 19). The question is, in what sense do altruists have irreducible other-directed ends? This requires a distinction to be made between kin altruism and reciprocal altruism.

Kin altruism is mainly taken to refer to parental care, such as the mother's patient tenderness, the father's desperate valor in defense of the home, and the daily care of parents for their little ones. It is seen as deriving mainly from the survival instinct of organisms, which also explains why animals kill other animals in order to feed their own offspring. From this aspect, kin altruism is limited to parents, and appears to be selfish behavior to those outside the kin group. However, since human beings and other social animals may share the same feelings and desire with regard to survival, they are likely to extend their parental care to those who urgently need it, if this does not entail endangering their own existence or that of their family. As Alexander Sutherland pointed out,

> They who love a child because it is their own may have by far their warmest fervour of devotion only for their own offspring, yet they will experience a certain predisposition to tenderness towards children in general; and thus feeling indeed overflows the bounds of the species, giving rise to a certain compassionateness towards the young of all animals, so that we are conscious of a peculiar melting emotion before the lamb, the duckling, the kitten, or the kid. (Sutherland 1974, Vol.1: 353).

This could explain why Mencius said that the king would find it unbearable to see the ox's death (and also why people will try to save a child that is about to fall into a well) (Yang 1988: 14, 79). It may be true, as Darwin said, that nudged by a social instinct, a man would jump into a river to try to save a drowning child, literally without giving a thought to his own safety (Richards 1987: 211). However, the interference of intelligence and reason can serve to restrict kin altruism. A mother may give up trying to save her child if the situation is beyond her control or may give up her own life in the attempt. For example, a sheep will not fight for its young against a wolf, and a mother will probably not jump into deep water to save her child if she does not know how to swim.

If kin altruism takes the welfare of others as the ultimate goal, reciprocal altruism is a balance between the interests of the self and group welfare. Social instincts develop among a group because such instincts can improve every member's chance of survival, particularly during tribal warfare and difficult times, because group-living „offers immense advantage in locating food and avoiding predators", as well as in producing offspring (de Waal 2006: 4). For this reason, Edward Wilson insists that reciprocal altruism is both genetically and psychologically selfish. As a necessary compromise between individual and group welfare, man has adopted implicit social contracts (Richards 1987: 602). Thompson clarifies this notion when he elucidates the survival-enhancing effect of reciprocal altruism. In his view, the basis for this social contract arises from the essential features of Neo-Darwinian fitness for survival, that is, a propensity for self-preservation: evil is the attempt to enhance one's own individual fitness at the expense of the short or long term perpetuation of the population to which the individual belongs. The expense ultimately reduces one's own fitness since population collapse thwarts the perpetuation of the individual's lineage along with everyone else's (Thompson 2002: 246). As reciprocal altruism is one of the most important elements that can enhance one's survival in group competition, it will spread widely in a relatively just and fair social atmosphere within a group, but if the implicit social contract is broken, and the agent realizes his altruistic behavior, far from bringing any gain, results in his being taken advantage of by others, he will become more selfish and reserved.

In this case, although Darwin might be right in contending that social instincts give rise to morality and altruism, particularly when a species needs a strong feeling of solidarity during a hard struggle for existence, tension will always exist between individual interests and group welfare after sufficient intelligence has appeared. It is a common phenomenon that, within a family, there is more affection between brothers and sisters, more mutual forbearance, hopefulness and trust in everyone in difficult times, than in easier times when conflicts are more likely to arise because help from others seems unnecessary. It is very likely due to their low intelligence that ants and bees still follow their social instincts and act in a completely altruistic manner. Humans, as intelligent beings, will always seek to balance their altruistic behavior with their self-interest and prefer reciprocal altruism, although they may still act completely altruistically under the stimulation of passion or moral indoctrination.

The Extension of Sympathy

After the relation between altruism and self-interest has been clarified, people will extend their sympathy in two ways. The first is the overflowing of parental care, as Sutherland (1974) suggested. Many Western and Chinese thinkers have repeatedly described the mechanism of this extension. Aristotle believed that the natural sociality of human beings and other political animals is an extension of parent-child bonding. The various forms of friendly feeling that unite human beings as individuals, as fellow citizens, and as members of the human species, radiate out from the natural affection that exists between parents and offspring, that human beings share with other animals whose offspring require intensive and prolonged parental care. Hume shared Aristotle's belief, stating that the natural moral sentiments (parental care) that bind people in families can extend in principle to all members of the human species (Arnhart 1998: 72f). Similarly, Mencius insisted:

> Treat with reverence the elders in your own family, so that the elders in the families of others shall be similarly treated; treat with kindness the young in your own family, so that the young in the families of others shall be similarly treated. (Yang 1988: 16)

The second refers to the expansion of reciprocal altruism in a just society in which people act in accordance with the implicit social contract. Although Darwin was optimistic about the extension of parental care, he also admitted that "only gradually and with great difficulty does human moral concern expand to include those outside one's own group" (Arnhart 1998: 75). Wilson flatly denies the probability that kin altruism can reach beyond blood relatives, insisting that as a necessary compromise between individual and group welfare, human beings have adopted implicit social contracts, to become reciprocal altruists (Richards 1987: 602). As everyone weighs his own interests when interacting with others, it can be said that reciprocal altruism, rather than kin altruism, is the foundation of morality.[2] With the support of religious and political indoctrination, enforced by legal and just measures, reciprocal altruism expands widely and binds a society together with its implicit social contract.

The question remains as to where Confucianism belongs, to the overflowing of parental care or to reciprocal altruism, because also promotes the extension of sympathy. It will not be surprising to find that many people regard Confucianism as a morality that is based on the extension of kin-love, such as filial piety and fraternal love, since Confucius points to these as the basis for achieving sympathy, but we should make it clear that filial piety and fraternal love are different from parental care. Parental care derives from the social instinct to feed and protect the offspring, while filial piety is the conscious return that a child gives his/her parents in exchange for their parental care, and fraternal love is simply the child's love for its parents being extended to its siblings. A dialogue between Confucius and his disciple, Zai Wo, offers a clear illustration of this characteristic of filial piety.

> Zai Wo asked about the three years' mourning for parents, saying that one year was long enough. The Master (Confucius) said, "This shows that Yu (Zai Wo) is not benevolent. It is not till a child is three years old that it is allowed to leave the arms of its parents. And the three years' mourning is universally observed throughout the empire. Did Yu enjoy the three years' love of his parents?" (Yang 1980: 200)

Obviously, Confucius realized the importance of parental care for children's survival and growth, particularly during the child's first three years of life.[3] However, the extension of parental care is not his main concern; instead he asks children to repay the parents' love, by observing three years' mourning for a parent's death. If a person fails to do this, he/she will be regarded as unsympathetic. To some extent, the three years' mourning can be seen as a reimbursement for the parents' three years' of care and, in this sense, filial piety is a reciprocal altruistic act.

Browsing through the *Analects*, we will not be surprised to find that reciprocal altruism is the theme of Confucius' discourse. Confucius is famous for his golden rules, for the realization of benevolence or sympathy: "Do not do to others what you do not want them to do to you."(Yang 1980: 130, 176). "A man of humanity, wishing to establish his own character, also establishes the character of others; and wishing to be prominent himself, also helps others to be prominent" (Yang 1980: 68). Obviously, all these are based on reciprocity. Confucius' followers have continued this tradition and applied reciprocity to various human relationships. They require: kindness on the part of the father, and filial duty on that of the son; gentleness on the part of the elder brother, and obedience on that

---

2 Actually, Darwin also implied the necessity of reciprocal altruism when he said "As the evolution of mind reached a pitch where individuals of different societies and nations would begin to recognize each other as brothers, members of the same global tribe, then quite automatically social sympathy would also be mutually extended" (see Richards 1987: 217).

3 Confucius asks to extend parental care, saying "In regard to the young, treat them tenderly" (Yang 1980: 55). But this is not the theme of his doctrine.

of the younger; righteousness on the part of the husband, and submission on that of the wife; kindness on the part of elders, and deference on that of juniors; with benevolence on the part of the ruler, and loyalty on that of the minister (Wang 1998, vol. 4: 559; Legge 1885: 379f). We can therefore conclude that the Confucian extension of sympathy is basically a reciprocal process. This reciprocity helped to create the democratic atmosphere and high morality of early imperial Chinese society, but things changed after the rise of Neo-Confucianism, which placed an emphasis on submission to one's superiors.

The Problem of the Confucian Extension of Sympathy

One may wonder why Confucius did not extend sympathy to parental care, but to filial piety. One explanation may be that Confucius realized that in human society, parents often love their offspring more, but children tend to pay back less. And it is a common phenomenon in the animal world that the grown-up young will leave their aged parents unattended. In order to promote sympathy, instead of giving children excessive parental care, their feelings of gratitude should be cultivated. In fact, as many one-child family cases in China have proven, if a child always receives parental care and is not taught to repay this, he/she will become very selfish and self-directed. For this reason, Confucius, like Aristotle, used art to complete what nature cannot complete, rather than to enhance what nature had achieved. In this way, Confucius elevated human beings above animals and made them a civilized species. Later, Wang Fuzhi (1619-1692) clearly indicated this elevation as assisting Heaven (相天 *xiangtian*) with human effort and highly praised the role played by human intelligence in the social and natural process.

One further question is whether filial piety is an efficient way of extending sympathy. If it is reciprocally altruistic rather than innate, how can it overflow to other people, as in the case of parental care? Confucius did not provide any clear evidence that filial piety is innate although he believed that filial piety can be extended, for example, to the way that one behaves towards one's superiors in government. However, almost all Confucian scholars since Mencius have claimed that filial piety and fraternal love are innate abilities, and can be extended universally. As Mencius said,

> The ability possessed by men without their having acquired it by learning is innate ability, and the knowledge possessed by them without deliberation is innate knowledge. Children carried in arms all know to love their parents. As they grow, they all know to respect their elder brothers. To have filial affection for parents is humanity, and to respect elders is righteousness. These feelings are universal in the world, that is all. (Chan 1963: 80)

Lu Jiuyuan (1139-1192) also shared this view,

> As a person, your ears are naturally keen, your eyes are naturally bright. Therefore, you are naturally filial when serving your father; you are naturally respectful when treating your brother. (Lu 1980: 399)

These Confucian scholars aimed to show that filial piety and fraternal love have a natural and unquestionable foundation, and to persuade everyone to extend sympathy by means of practicing filial piety and fraternal love, the assumption being that filial piety will, like parental care, overflow to other people. The extension is achieved through abiding by the principle of differentiated love, which becomes weaker and weaker as it passes from parents, brothers, relatives and neighbors to strangers.

It could be argued, however, that filial piety derives from reciprocal altruism, rather than from a social instinct, such as parental love, and that filial piety develops from a child's dependence and closeness to his/her parents. Children who are raised by adoptive parents are likely to develop filial affection towards them instead of towards their biological parents. Moreover, filial affection is strongly influenced by social interactions that occur during a child's growth. Generally, if a child develops feelings of gratitude and a balanced sense of give and take, he/she will develop filial piety. If a child experiences more taking and less giving and becomes selfish, he/she will develop filial piety to a correspondingly lesser extent. Once the balance between giving and taking has been broken and a person has become selfish, moral education is hardly able to exert any influence that can lead to the person's developing filial piety. For this reason, we would suggest that filial piety is an outcome of social education.

As reciprocal altruism with the help of education, filial piety has been widely accepted for thousands of years. The reason for this lies in the agricultural societies of the past, when people were faced with the prospect of having to retire from farming and become dependents in their old age. At this time, filial sons and daughters offered their only hope and therefore every parent in China hoped to have a filial son or daughter. Ancient emperors also demonstrated their belief in Confucius' words, that a filial son would transfer his love for his parents to his king and superiors and that with filial piety, a king would easily be able to achieve good governance. As a result, since the Han dynasty, all emperors without exception have promoted filial piety and fraternal love for regulating households and governing the state.

The promotion of filial piety as a means of extending sympathy gives rise to both positive and negative consequences. Positively, it consolidates the unity of the family and the clan, and helps them to survive in difficult times. In China, it often happens that all family members will pool their resources to help one member succeed in his/her career, and that brothers and sisters will offer each other unconditional support without expecting any return. However, there are also negative consequences of Confucian filial piety. At family level, family members often take for granted the privilege of enjoying the resources and accomplishments of the others, sometimes even taking advantage of other members of the family, which can cause dependence, laziness and even cruelty. For instance, if a son or daughter gains a position as an official or as a scholar, the other family members will renounce their own endeavors to support themselves and wait for the son or daughter to help them instead. Here, in fact, the continuation can be observed of the old Chinese saying, "when a man attains the Dao, even his pets ascend to heaven" (一人得道, 鸡犬升天 *yiren de dao, ji quan shengtian*). At societal level, the extension and promotion of filial piety can lead people to take advantage of other people's sympathy, as Sutherland describes,

> In China, the growth of sympathy, when it first begins to be felt as a duty, is anomalous and ill directed. It appears as a noble quality but with sad perversions, and it has been responsible for the huge predominance of beggars in China. (Sutherland 1974, vol. 1: 402f)

In the 1980s and 1990s when China began its reform process, beggary once again became a profession around the country and some cunning individuals earned a great deal of money by fabricating a pitiful condition and asking for society to help them.

Furthermore, although filial affection is supposed by Confucius to be converted into loyalty to the king and superiors, the transfer has never been truly accomplished in

Chinese history. On the contrary, parental care, filial piety and fraternal love have tended to make the Chinese family or clan a selfish group, and people have always put their family interests before the national or public interest. For example, Confucius would hide his father's acts of thieving (Yang 1980: 147), and Mencius would suggest that the legendary Emperor Shun give up the throne and help his criminal father to flee (ibid.: 317). These facts led Liang Qichao (1873-1929) to lament that, "ninety percent of Confucius and Mencius' teachings are about family value, while less than one percent is about public value" (Liang 1984: 213). Xiong Shili (1885-1968) decried the Chinese family as the origin of all evils, contending that it led Chinese people to be selfish and nearsighted, blind to public welfare and the long-term public interest (Xiong 1996: 336f). From this perspective, it is obvious that China's bureaucratic corruption is ingrained in Chinese culture and in people's bones, because almost everyone secures their families' interests at the expense of public and national welfare. This situation in China could be taken as evidence in support of Edward Wilson's prediction that "hard-core" altruism (kin altruism) is insufficient, and sometimes even detrimental to the organization of societies larger than kin groups (Richards 1987: 602). But China's case is more complex than the one described in Wilson's prediction, since a combination of kin and reciprocal altruism to procure family interest is reigning there.

The Role played by Intelligence and Habit in the Extension of Sympathy

Intelligence plays a critical role in developing social instincts and altruistic behavior into sympathy and setting human beings free from natural selection and cosmic forces. In order to survive, social insects, such as bees and ants, develop strong kin altruism, but due to their low intelligence (probably also because of the efficiency of their division of labor for survival), their altruistic behaviors remain instinctive. This is why ants and bees will sacrifice their lives without hesitation in defense of their nests and hives. However, this does not mean that their parental affections are arrested as Sutherland (1974, vol.1: 295) suggests, but that bees and ants are still at the mercy of natural selection.

The higher the position of the social animal on the scale of intelligence, the more rational and less instinctive it is. Different methods will be adopted towards different enemies. For example, a goat, other than the always altruistic ants and bees, will stand and face a deer in order to protect its kids, but flee from a wolf. Intelligence decreases the intensity of sympathy or altruism, but enhances the individual's fitness to survive.

However, rather than abandon their implicit social contract (reciprocal altruism), human beings have sufficient intelligence to effect a compromise between their self-interest and group welfare. They are well aware that their happiness and chances of survival will be greatly reduced without the support of their relatives, friends and countrymen; they choose to comply with the implicit social contract in order to secure their welfare. This is what Darwin referred to as the origin of morality: man compared an unsatisfied social instinct with a more powerful feeling, such as hunger, fear, or the sexual urge, based on his past and future actions and motives, and then approved the former but suppressed the latter (Richards 1987: 211). Consequently, human beings are specifically guided by reason to extend their sympathy, by balancing their self-interest against public welfare. Under normal circumstances, people will neither be as altruistic as ants and bees, nor as selfish as a psychopath, although their social instinct may prevail in some cases. This explains why altruism is not identical with morality.

At this point, it is clear that, with the development of a person, intelligence will win over instinct and habit. Unlike instinct and habit, intelligence renders the agent more flexible and responsive to environmental contingencies and cosmic forces. As Morgan states,

> Once human brains achieved the plasticity of rational response, they could adjust to their environment without the necessity of those adaptations being carved into the nervous system. Rationality relieved the selective pressures on human beings to alter their physiology to accommodate new situations. (Richards 1987: 396)

This flexibility enables human beings to shape both their environment and behaviors, instead of listening passively to the play of cosmic forces. This is demonstrated in the ability of human beings to form a second nature.

According to Darwin, habit, guided by intelligence, would come to mold the conduct of individuals, so that acting in accordance with the wishes of the community, even in matters of small moment, would contribute to the formation of a second nature. (Richards 1987: 208) This can be viewed as justifying moral education on the grounds that it changes and rebuilds human nature in all societies. In Chinese culture, "habit" and "practice" share the same signifier, *xi* (习), which can be seen as an indication that, even long ago, the Chinese believed that an act could become a habit through practice. Although Confucius did not clearly endorse the notion that habit could become part of human nature, he acknowledged its significance in the formation of personality, "human beings are close in nature, it is habit that separates them far from each other" (Yang 1980: 192). Later, Neo-Confucian scholars proposed the formation of a new personality/nature with good habits, suggesting that this could be achieved with consistent moral practice by following Confucian principles. In this context, Wang Fuzhi claimed that, "habit joins the formation of human nature, and human nature is formed along with the completion of habit" (Wang 1998, vol. 2: 299), and "it is only habit that makes a person incorrigible after it has changed him" (Wang 1998, vol. 2: 492).

Nevertheless, if habit truly exerts such a powerful influence upon human nature, sympathy and filial piety, after being promoted in China by Confucian scholars for thousands of years, should have become second nature to the Chinese long ago. Why have so many Chinese people become free-riders since 1980, given that the market economy has been in existence for only thirty years? This shows that not all habits will be molded into a second nature. In light of the fact that nature is similar to instinct, acting without deliberation, it may be easy for an animal with low intelligence and less knowledge to mold a habit into nature. However, with higher intelligence and more knowledge, people will tend to go with the flow. Laozi argued that the promotion of knowledge and humanity led people to become competitive for profit and unsympathetic. In order to achieve good customs and allow people to enjoy their lives, a ruler should abandon sageliness and humanity, and discard wisdom and righteousness (Chan 1963: 149). This does not mean that Laozi abandoned human civilization, but rather demonstrates his perspicacity with regard to finding a balance between knowledge (intelligence) and altruism, artificiality and nature. This echoes Sutherland's view that the rule of cultural transmission – "imitate the most successful individual in your group" – would be disastrous for group selection because it would be sensitive only to relative fitness within groups (Richards 1987: 150).

In short, there is no doubt that social instincts and ingrained habits help to extend sympathy. But without adequate intelligence, the extension does not go beyond blood relatives. With sufficient intelligence, higher animals and human beings can extend sympathy to their own kind, and even to other living things, but the intensity of sympathy decreases, the more they are concerned about their own welfare. As people become more intelligent and complex along with the development of civilization, they also become more skillful in procuring their self-interest in the guise of and by the use of altruism and morality. This may explain why many philosophers look for their ideal society in the remote past while condemning present society. Laozi opposed the promotion of sympathy and wisdom because he knew that "when the people of the world all know beauty as beauty, there arises ugliness; when they all know the good as good, there arises evil"(Chan 1963: 140). It is not that beauty and good turn into ugliness and evil; it is because they will be used as instruments to procure selfish interests and disturb social custom. For this reason, both Laozi and his follower, Zhuangzi (365-290 BC), suggested that with less knowledge and fewer desires people would be simple and have true sympathy.

Conclusion

Confucian fever is sweeping China and a critical evaluation of Confucianism is urgently required to show the place of Confucianism and its legacy in the process of globalization. This essay, by means of a comparative study on Confucianism and evolutionism, tries to indicate the nature of Confucian sympathy and filial piety as a kind of reciprocal altruism, instead of the assumed kin altruism. In this way, I have placed Confucian sympathy and conscience back on a rational foundation, and made up for the insufficiency of the Chinese emphatic tradition which assumes that everyone shares the same conscience and sympathy and acts in the same way. I have continued to analyze the promotion of filial piety in Chinese society, along with its strong and weak points. Finally, since the roles of wisdom (intelligence) and habit are highly valued in the development of human nature and sympathy in Confucianism, I have further explored the double-edged function of intelligence in the development of habit and sympathy, and my findings show that a subtle balance must be maintained between self-interest and group welfare in order for people to achieve a high level of morality and sympathy. In short, this comparison of Confucianism with evolutionism has made manifest the strong and weak points of Confucianism, while at the same time seeking a path for the renewal of Confucian ethics.

References

Arnhart, Larry (1998) *Darwin Natural Right: the Biological Ethics of Human Nature*, New York: SUNY Press.

Chan, Wing-tsit (1963) *A Source Book in Chinese Philosophy*, Princeton: Princeton University Press.

Cheng, Hao 程顥 and Cheng, Yi 程頤 (2000) *Er Cheng Ji* 二程集 [The Collection of the Cheng Brothers] Shanghai: Shanghai Guji Chubanshe.

De Waal, Frans (2006) *Primates and Philosophers: How Morality Evolved*, Princeton, NJ: Princeton University Press.

Laozi 老子 (1990) *The Laozi* 老子, Shanghai: Shanghai Guji Chubanshe.

Legge, James (trs) (1885) *The Sacred Books of China, The Texts of Confucianism, Part III, the Li Ki*, I-X, Oxford: the Clarendon Press.

Liang, Qichao 梁启超 (1984) *Liang Qichao Xuanji* 梁启超选集 [Selected Works of Liang Qichao], Shanghai: Shanghai Renmin Chubanshe.

Lu, Jiuyuan 陸九淵 (1980) *Lu Jiuyuan Ji* 陸九淵集 [A Collection of Lu Jiuyuan's Writings], Beijing: Zhonghua Shuju.

Maienschein, Jane and Ruse, Michael (eds) (1999) *Biology and the Foundation of Ethics*, UK: Cambridge University Press.

Richards, Robert J. (1987) *Darwin and the Emergency of Evolutionary Theories of Mind and Behavior,* University of Chicago Press.

Richards, Robert J. (1999) „Darwin's Romantic Biology: The Foundation of His Evolutionary Ethics", in: Maienschein/Ruse 1999, pp. 113-153.

Sober, Elliot and Wilson, David Sloan (1998) *Unto Others: The Evolution and Psychology of Unselfish Behavior*, Cambridge: Harward University Press.

Sutherland, Alexander (1974) *The Origin and Growth of the Moral Instinct*, Vol.1 and Vol. 2, New York: SUNY Press.

Thompson, Paul (2002) „The Evolutionary Biology of Evil", in: *The Monist*, April, V.85, Issue 2, pp. 239-259.

Vicedo, Marga (1999) „Laws of Inheritance and Rules of Morality", in: Maienschein/Ruse 1999, pp. 225-256.

Wang, Fuzhi 王夫之 (1998) *Chuanshan Quanshu (CSQS)* 船山全書, vol. 1-16 [Complete Works of Wang Chuanshan] Changsha: Yuelu Shushe.

Xiong, Shili 熊十力 (1996) *Xiandai Xin Ruxue De Genji – Xiong Shili Xin Ruxue Lunzhu Jiyao* 现代新儒学的根基 – 熊十力新儒学论著辑要 [The Foundation of Modern New Confucianism – A Concise Collection of Xiong Shili's New Confucian Works], Beijing: Zhongguo Guangbo Dianshi Chubanshe.

Yang, Bojun 楊伯峻 (1988) *Meng Zi Yi Zhu* 孟子譯注 [The Mencius: Translation and Annotation], Beijing: Zhonghua Shuju.

Yang, Bojun 楊伯峻 (1980) *Lun Yu Yi* Zhu 論語譯注 [The Analects: Translation and Annotation], Beijing: Zhonghua Shuju.

Gu Zhengkun

Confucian Family Values as Universal Values in the 21st Century Family – Nation – World

This paper aims to answer a challenging question: what sort of values are held to be relatively more acceptable and valid than others in the 21st century? In my opinion, the best choice is the Confucian value system, which, derived from the traditional family-like society, is the most universal moral guide for mankind that has ever been offered by any society in the past. The paper begins with the startling argument that Confucius is not the originator of Confucianism. I contend that Confucianism is mainly the result of the combined efforts of many of the cultural elites of ancient China and that Confucianism, historically, as a complete set of values, is a necessary and natural ideological product of the ancient Chinese family-like societies. I then provide a comparative study of family-nation vs. state-nation, power through examination vs. power through democracy and many other values, both Western and Chinese. There is a discussion on the values established in the *Rites of Zhou* which I see as a family contract dating back to the ancient Chinese nation. Confucius' main contribution to Confucianism is carefully revalued according to the facts. Needless to say, the family-like social structure which is bound to encounter modernity is also given some necessary reflection. Finally, I suggest that the values of Confucian worldism should be placed above other sorts of values, such as the values of interest groups and "The world should be structured as one family." My aim is to prove that the Confucian family value system provides the most valuable experiences that can be used by human beings to return to an excellent family-like social structure and value system. This most ideal social structure and value system can be summarized in three words: family – nation – world.

Who is the Originator of Confucianism?

Confucius (551-479 BC) is widely held to be the originator of Confucianism, but this belief is not based on solid facts. Confucianism has been accepted in various academic and non-academic circles as a doctrine with a complete set of Confucian terms, such as 仁义礼智信 (*ren yi li zhi xin* benevolence, righteousness, rites, knowledge, and integrity) but it was not advanced or constructed by Confucius himself.

My denial of Confucius' authorship of Confucianism is backed up by Confucius' own confession: "I do not voice my own original ideas but just narrate and expound the ideas of the ancients whom I like most and have deeply believed in" (*Lunyu: Shu´er*).[1] In voicing these sentiments, Confucius was not being modest or self-effacing. After all, he was one of the most honest among the ancient Chinese scholars. Around 1,600 years after Confucius made the above statement, Zhu Xi (1130-1200), the great and representative Confucian scholar in the Southern Song Dynasty, offered convincing annotations in praise of Confucius' modesty, characterizing a morally perfect person (圣人 *sheng ren*) "whose sense of humility grows with the progress of his moral improvement" (Zhu 1992).[2] Zhu maintained that Confucius "did not advance any new ideas of his own but

1 《论语.述而》： "述而不作，信而好古。" 朱熹《论语集注》，卷四述而第七: "述，传旧而已，作，则创始也。"

2 朱熹《论语集注》卷四述而第七： "盖其德愈盛而心愈下。"

just disseminated the old ideas of ancient emperors though he indeed edited the *Book of Odes*, emended the *Book of Rites* and the *Book of Music*, explained the *Book of Change* and expurgated the *Spring and Autumn Annals*" (Zhu 1992)[3] and that Confucius was too modest to rank himself among the worthy scholars who had preceded him (ibid.). In other words, since Confucian ideas had been in circulation long before Confucius was born, he could hardly be seen as the source of these ideas.

This however begs the question: Why didn't Confucius advance new ideas? Did he decline to be an originator? Was it because he lacked the ability to produce original ideas? No. The true reason is that Confucius was too erudite to deny the fact that ideas concerning politics and moral values had already been developed by his predecessors to such a high degree that later scholars, such as he, had little chance to add or detract or outshine. This immediately brings to mind the biblical saying that there is nothing new under the sun, and the remark made by Johann Wolfgang von Goethe (1749-1832) to the effect that we can only repeat in different ways what the ancients have already said.

This does not mean that Confucius had nothing to do. After all, not all his contemporaries were really able to understand the meanings of these ancient ideas. The historical documents were written in glyphs that challenged even the learned scholars of the time and there was a need for modernized versions, popularized interpretations, more systematic classification and organic integration. And it is precisely here that Confucius saw his mission: as the most erudite scholar of the age, when the system characterized by the *Rites* had been totally destroyed, he was the only scholar truthfully qualified to take on the task of dealing with the legacy of collected wisdom that was to be handed down from ancient China. He perceived it as his sacred mission to edit, revise, annotate, interpret, and transmit the ancient culture. The task that the age had entrusted to him of preserving the ancient wisdom was so incredibly compelling that Confucius simply did not have the need or the time to voice his own original ideas. This was a time when scholars were needed to save the old and precious cultural heritage from being lost forever, rather than to construct brand-new theories. Confucius therefore chose to base his narrative on the ancient wisdom and to restrain himself from proposing new ideas, to "transmit, but not to innovate" (述而不作 *shu er bu zuo*) (*Lunyu* 7:1). This was the best strategy for him to adopt for the monumental task of maintaining the cultural heritage and the best attitude, for which the Chinese nation with its treasure of ancient wisdom will forever be indebted. Naturally, Confucius occasionally voiced criticism of others for putting forward so-called original thoughts without aspiring to sure mastery of the ancient cultural traditions. He was proud not to belong among those who randomly published so-called creative ideas, "There are scholars who have invented new ideas without the true knowledge of ancient wisdom, fortunately I am not one of them" (*Lunyu: Shu'er*).[4] This self-knowledge of Confucius is a moral quality that many scholars lack. Contemporary scholars sometimes tend to over-emphasize the importance of being creative and naturally infer that Confucius must have had the same sort of character, with the result that Confucius' words "transmit, but do not innovate" are persistently misinterpreted as words

3 朱熹《论语集注》卷四述而第七："孔子删诗书，定礼乐，赞周易，修春秋，皆传先王之旧，而未尝有所作也，故其自言如此。盖不惟不敢当作者之圣，而亦不敢显然自附于古之贤人；盖其德愈盛而心愈下，不自知其辞之谦也。其事虽述，而功则倍于作矣，此又不可不知也。"

4 《论语·述而》："盖有不知而作之者，我无是也。"

of pure self-abasement or modesty. Originality is indeed seen as praiseworthy in the contemporary world, but this was not necessarily the value that Confucius sought. A good explanation of this point is found in Zhu Xi's *Annotations to the Analects of Confucius*. As Zhu states, in the era in which Confucius lived, a rich accumulation of political systems and theoretical creations was already in existence and Confucius was only required to synthesize and generalize the great and manifold doctrines of morally perfect sages and political leaders in order to bring them all together (Zhu 1992).[5] Zhu suggested that "narration and interpretation" (述 *shu*) may not be less important than original creation. This judgment might seem extreme to the modern ear, but the social conditions of the age when Confucius lived and worked have to be taken into account (ibid.).[6]

Who, then, to be precise, is the originator of Confucianism? This is the question that is naturally asked in the contemporary world, above all, in the West, where it is taken for granted that any theory must be the output of a single theoretician. I do not intend to refute this modern logic, but it is necessary to repeat the question: Who, to be precise, is the originator of Confucianism? Careful study of this question opens our eyes to the fact that several potential candidates present themselves for consideration, rather than only one. The earliest amongst these are the Emperors, Yao and Shun (2357-2208 BC)[7], in the Xia Dynasty, King Wen, and, in particular, the Duke of Zhou (1100 BC)[8] in the Zhou Dynasty (1046-771 BC), because the core of what we call Confucianism today is located mainly in the political, ethical, and economic systems that characterized the Xia, Shang and Zhou Dynasties, which had the *Rites* as their central ideology. Confucius knew of the rites of Xia and Shang but his knowledge was far from sufficient, because of the scarcity

---

5 朱熹《论语集注》卷四述而第七："然当是时，作者略备，夫子盖集群圣之大成而折衷之。"

6 朱熹《论语集注》卷四述而第七："其事虽述，而功则倍于作矣，此又不可不知也。"

7 Yao and Shun are mentioned in many Chinese historical records and articles. Doubts have sometimes been expressed as to their existence, but these have never really been proved valid. Most Chinese scholars, ancient and contemporary, have tended to consider them as true figures in history although statements about their actual roles and activities vary according to the different authors and times. One thing is certain: even if it is finally proved that Yao and Shun did not exist, there is proof that some of the ideas embodied in the later *Rites of Zhou* were in circulation long before the Dynasty of Zhou. Confucius had great admiration for the reigns of Yao and Shun. He stated that their government was run so smoothly and naturally that even if it seemed that nothing had been done, in reality, everything had been done; that the people under their rule could not find sufficient words to describe their virtues, in the same way that they could not find sufficient words to describe Heaven. In the *Analects,* Confucius said: "Great indeed was Yao as a sovereign! How majestic was he! It is only Heaven that is great, and it is only Yao who corresponds to it. How vast was his virtue! The people could find no name for it." (*Lunyu: Taibo*). (Compare《论语·泰伯》："子曰：大哉尧之为君也！巍巍乎，唯天为大，唯 尧则之。荡荡乎，民无能名焉。巍巍乎其有成功也，焕乎其有文章！"）["May not Shun be instanced as having governed efficiently without exertion? What did he do? He did nothing but gravely and reverently occupy his royal seat."]

8 The Duke of Zhou (周公旦 Zhou Gongdan). Ji Dan (姬旦) was the personal name of the Duke of Zhou, who was a great statesman, strategist and thinker of the early Western Zhou Dynasty. He was also one of the sages most admired by Confucius. As the territory conferred on him was called Zhou (present-day northeastern Qishan of Shaanxi) and he was the fourth son of King Wen of Zhou, he was called the Duke of Zhou.

of relevant literature (*Lunyu: Bayi*).[9] He travelled frequently to the states where Xia and Shang had been founded to collect firsthand documents related to the *Rites* but he was unable to collect as much material as he had expected (Sun/Chen 2007: *Liyun*).[10] For this reason, it is difficult to deliver a judgment on the supposition that the rites of Xia and Shang constitute the essentials of later Confucianism. Fortunately, the Zhou Dynasty, and particularly the Western Zhou Dynasty, boasted an abundance of documents about the *Rites* which were rich enough to constitute the essentials of Confucianism as we now understand it. Confucius said: "The *Rites of Zhou* have been enacted on the basis of those of both Xia and Yin (Shang) Dynasties. How rich and brilliant they are! I prefer the *Rites of Zhou*." (*Lunyu: Bayi*)[11] This shows that the *Rites of Zhou* (周礼 *zhou li*), being more systematic, rich and reliable, can be considered the main source of Confucianism (Liu 1990: 103),[12] and the person who enacted the *Rites of Zhou* can be considered to have the strongest claim to being the originator of Confucianism. As we know, this person was the Duke of Zhou, who is usually considered to be the author of the *Rites of Zhou,* which contains the core or the essentials of what we now call Confucianism. It is therefore understandable that Confucius held the Duke of Zhou in high respect all his life. He once complained, in his old age, about his great disappointment that he had not dreamed of the Duke of Zhou for rather long time – this shows how passionately obsessive Confucius was about the Duke of Zhou and his *Rites*. So here there would seem to be reason to say that the Duke of Zhou is the originator of Confucianism as it is known in academic circles.

However, if the Duke of Zhou is taken to be the originator of Confucianism, this immediately gives rise to the challenging facts that 1) the *Rites of Zhou*, although constituted of many creative elements, were after all enacted on the basis of the rites of the Xia and Shang dynasties, and therefore the Duke of Zhou's role as the main originator of Confucianism is dubious; 2) the Duke of Zhou, as a powerful statesman, could have enlisted help or advice from many of his underlings, could have organized many scholars to engage in establishing the *Rites*, and could simply have given many insightful directions for the designing of various rituals, as the state required at the time. It is well-known that this mode of policy-making was often adopted in ancient China and is even found in many countries today.

At this point, I would like to draw the tentative conclusion that Confucianism, as it is currently understood, is actually the resultant achievement of the combined efforts of many (possibly hundreds of) scholars, political leaders, of ancient China, in particular, of the Western Zhou Dynasty. It represents the labors of many collective hands. True, Yao, Shun, King Wen, and the Duke of Zhou, as well as later scholars, such as Confucius, all joined hands to bring Confucianism to fruition to varying degrees, but no single individual is fully entitled to lay claim to being the creator of Confucianism, let alone

9 《论语·八佾》子曰："夏礼吾能言之，杞不足征也；殷礼吾能言之，宋不足征也。文献不足故也。足，则吾能征之矣。"

10 《礼记·礼运》 也记载孔子说："吾欲观夏道，是故之杞，而不足徵也，吾得"夏时" "焉；吾欲观殷 道，是故之宋，而不足徵也，吾得（坤乾）焉。"

11 《论语·八佾》："周监於二代，郁郁乎文哉！吾从周。"

12 刘宝楠《论语正义》引《汉书·礼乐志》："王者必因前王之礼，顺时施宜，有所损益。周监于 二代，礼文尤具，事为之制，曲为之防。故称礼经三百，威仪三千。孔子美之曰，郁郁乎文哉， 吾从周" (Liu Baonan 1990: 103).

Confucius himself. As mentioned above, in ancient China, the most authoritative figure was often the leader, for whom many other scholars worked hard. Emperors, such as Yao and Shun, could be in possession of excellent wisdom themselves, but more often than not they had ministers or counsellors who would work out policies or plans for them. So the ideological products under their names may not necessarily have been completely their own creations. The *Kang Xi Dictionary* (康熙字典 *Kangxi Zidian*), with a total number of 54,350 entries, is held to be the greatest dictionary ever compiled in Chinese history, but it is not really the work of Kang Xi, the Emperor, but the result of the collective efforts of hundreds of Chinese scholars in the Qing Dynasty. The formation of Confucianism underwent a similar process, although over a much longer period of time.

Incidentally, the above discussion can help to explain the problems concerning the identification of the originators of many doctrines and academic achievements in ancient China. In sharp contrast to the question of authorship in Western cultures, where most doctrines, inventions and academic achievements are usually considered to have been created separately by individual persons, such as, Platonism by Plato and Aristotelianism by Aristotle, most traditional Chinese cultural achievements are accepted as the joint efforts of many Chinese creators in different historical periods, for example, Taoism (道学 *dao xue*), Confucianism (儒学 *ru xue*), the *Book of Changes* (易经 *yi jing*), and the *Yellow Emperor's Inner Canon* (黄帝内经 *Huangdi neijing*).

The tentative conclusion that Confucianism represents the combined efforts of many traditional Chinese scholars and political leaders, although reasonable, is still not entirely satisfactory, because it is suggestive of a certain degree of contingency that Confucianism could not have emerged if Yao, Shun, King Wen, the Duke of Zhou and Confucius had not existed.

The next question therefore presents itself: Would Confucianism still have been created without Yao, Shun, King Wen, the Duke of Zhou and Confucius in ancient China? The answer is that this is entirely possible. Even without King Wen, the Duke of Zhou, and Confucius, the complete set of ideas and values that are today known as Confucianism would have been put forward and documented by other scholars and political leaders in ancient China, because particular ideologies are the products of particular thinkers and particular thinkers are the products of a particular type of societies. As long as there are particular types of societies, corresponding particular thinkers will emerge, hence the particular ideologies. Therefore, logically, in a broad sense, Confucianism is the necessary and natural ideological by-product of the ancient Chinese family-like society typical of farming dynasties. For thousands of years, traditional Chinese dynasties were societies precisely modelled on the structure of a family. In other words, given the existence of the family-like society, theories and doctrines such as Confucianism would have occurred in one way or another, even without King Wen and the Duke of Zhou. [13]

---

13 The question might arise here, why other farming dynasties all over the world did not generate similar ideologies. In fact, many of them had some sort of Confucianism, yet with very different degrees of humanitarianism and never up to the ideal of Chinese Confucianism. The latter requires four key conditions to take shape: 1) a closed geographical environment; 2) a relatively long time-span; 3) highly developed farming cultures; 4) family-like social structures with a huge population.

The Western farming culture was relatively weak compared with that of the East, and its family-like social structures disintegrated early in the times of ancient Greece and Rome. The later social structures were mainly based on interest groups, that is, groups representing military, economic, and political interests. Oriental farming cultures were also relatively developed. However, they were also more

Again why? The reason is simple. In a family-like society, all ideas or values ranging from politics, economy and ethics to law and art must meet the practical needs of its members. In the Zhou Dynasty, for example, society consisted of a huge tribe-like extended family, in which all ideas and values concerning politics, economy, ethics, law, religion and even art had to be in agreement with the nature and characteristics of the family. Obviously anti-family characteristics, such as, competitiveness and bellicosity, had to be naturally excluded. Through years of consultation and compromise among family members, and also through the response on the part of family as a whole to the challenges posed by the geographical and social environment, all the ideas, systems and values were collected together to form something like a family contract. This was, of course, different from Rousseau's "social contract"; here in the case of the Zhou Dynasty, the individual elements crystallized into what are now known as the *Rites*.

The *Rites,* as a collection of regulations and principles that function as political, moral and economic governing systems, can be seen as the necessary choices and the outcome of a family-nation which has to face the challenges posed by the specific environmental conditions, geographical as well as social. They take the form of policies or contracts for all the members of the family-nation to establish how interests shall be divided among them; they are values that are generated and cherished by the members of society and are employed to harmonize the personal relationships within the family-nation. The necessary choices are made by the nation. In order for the family-like society to continue to exist, it must produce the appropriate values, policies, and strategies. And it does not matter at all whether these are called Confucianism or Taoism.

Once again, I would like to emphasize the point that the family-like society holds the key to understanding the formation of Confucianism, which as a value system, has a history reaching back over more than 3000 years, and also to understanding traditional Chinese culture. In fact, I would maintain that Confucianism with its values is great because 1) it epitomizes the wisdom of hundreds or even thousands of morally perfect ancient personages who were usually also highly intelligent; 2) it is the essential and natural ideological product of the ancient Chinese family-like society; 3) it offers a highly pragmatic approach towards harmonizing the personal relationships within a huge extended family-like society.

---

exposed geographically, thus easier to invade or influence, and their social structures vulnerable. Other oriental countries and regions, such as Egypt, Babylon, Africa, and India were highly developed farming dynasties. But they either lacked the favorable geographical conditions, or were vulnerable to alien attacks or easily influenced by foreign ideologies. Ancient India, to some extent, fulfilled the last three conditions of the four, and this generated Buddhism, which is very similar to Confucianism in the sense of morality. As for ancient China, it was guarded by high mountains in the West, deserts in the North, seas and oceans in the East and South. For thousands of years, its culture and social structure were relatively safe from attacks or external intruders. Its family-like social structure developed to such a high degree that Confucianism had to be set up to meet the demands of this gigantic family. True, the neighboring nations, such as Mongolia and Manchu, once ruled China, but these two nations themselves, once they had entered the Central Plains, soon abandoned their own cultures and ideologies and adopted Confucianism as values valid throughout China. Other countries, such as Japan, Korea, Vietnam, Singapore, Malaysia accepted Confucian values for a long time. Japan, for example, adopted Confucianism as its national doctrine for nearly 2000 years. For detailed discussions, please see Gu Zhengkun 2004.

Why Are the Values Derived from a Family Best in Terms of Morality?

Of all human relationships, kinship is the most intimate. Therefore, the most reasonable and natural human relationships are found in the kinship-based family. Although there are also unavoidable conflicts over benefits, intimacy, love and devotion among family members, such relationships are without doubt unrivalled by any other form of human relationship. Therefore, the values generated within a family are the most natural, reasonable, moral, virtuous and also the most ideal values. A logical inference is that a family-like social structure will give rise to the most ideal system of values. And it is this ideal that should be the ultimate goal of human kind. Could we find any other group or community within which all the members love and care for each other as sincerely and truthfully as they do in families? Members of a group or a social community can also love and care for each other. Not unconditionally as in the case of family members, because kinship and blood ties, after all, lead to stronger bonding than any other relationship. That is why people who have close friendly relationships with each other are described as being as close as if they belonged to the same family. For thousands of years, the Chinese people have been keenly aware that all people in China are the descendants of one ancestor, of one family, of one kinship.[14] For this reason, the traditional Chinese society has naturally modelled itself on the structure of a family and consequently offers corresponding systems and ideologies concerning morality, politics, economy, religion, art, and other social phenomena. In contrast to this, Western society has mainly modelled itself on the structure of an interest group, as I have already explained (Gu 2004). And it is this essentially factual difference, in my opinion, that sharply distinguishes traditional Chinese society and culture from Western society and culture. This is the key to understanding the manifold differences between China and the West in the context of culture.

The Family Contract of the Ancient Chinese Nation: The Values Found in the *Rites of Zhou*

The *Rites of Zhou* constitute the essential elements of Confucianism. The discussion about the *Rites* is the discussion about Confucianism. The values are the core of the *Rites*. As a set of norms of conduct; the *Rites* are composed of regulations and values. Values in this case are mainly of a moral nature, and they can be summarized into 15 Chinese characters (concepts): love/benevolence (仁 *ren*), righteousness/justice (义 *yi*), civility/rites (礼 *li*), wisdom (智 *zhi*), honesty (信 *xin*), gentility (温 *wen*), kindness (良 *liang*), humility (恭 *gong*), frugality (俭 *qian*), obedience (让 *rang*), reconciliation (恕 *shu*), loyalty (忠 *zhong*), filial piety (孝 *xiao*), the sense of shame (廉耻 *lian chi*), and courage/bravery (勇 *yong*).

---

14 This statement is possibly suggestive of a kind of modern Chinese nationalism, but Chinese nationalism is different in the sense that it is benign. It maintains that a nation should live in peace and harmony with ten thousand other nations. As the *Book of History* says about Emperor Yao: "When the hundred clans had become illustrious, he harmonized a myriad of nations." (Compare 《尙書: 尧典》: "曰若稽古，帝尧曰放勋，钦明文思安安，允恭克让，光被四表，格于上下。克明俊德，以亲九族。九族既睦，平章百姓，百姓昭明，协和万邦，黎民于变时雍。"). According to Toynbee, so-called modern Chinese nationalism is actually the result of Chinese reactions to foreign aggressions that happened ever since the Opium Wars (Toynbee/Daisaku 1985: 280).

Love/Benevolence (仁 ren)

It must be conceded that when taken alone, the two great value systems, Chinese and Western, both appear reasonable, because they can be seen as representing the strategic values produced by the two societies in response to the specific challenges posed by their specific environments. However, if we compare them point by point, they have different qualities to them. Above all, among all the values above, the two societies have different emphases.

So what is so special about Confucian values? It is the order of them which is essential. Which one is in the foreground, which is put in the middle, which is put at the end? That means a lot. Take *ren* (仁) for example. That it takes the lead in the list is surely not an accidental arrangement, because in a family, love comes first. However, love, in this context, does not only refer to sexual love but to the love between parents and their sons and daughters, love between husbands and wives, love between children, love between relatives, love between neighbors, love between community members, and finally love between people all over the world, even between enemies. *Ren* as love is to be extended to all human beings. It is the core of the cores. In the Chinese family-like society, benevolence is taken as the top priority and all the other values are placed underneath it. The original meaning of the character 仁 (*ren*) is 1) two human beings and 2) love; benevolence means love between human beings. Mencius (孟子 372-289 BC), explained that "The one who is benevolent must love people" (*Mengzi ·Lilou*).[15] The *Doctrine of the Mean* (中庸 *zhong yong*) states, "*ren* means humane" (Han Yu 1988).[16] The Confucian scholar, Han Yu (韩愈 768-824), also explained *ren* as "love extended to all human beings and things" (Han Yu 1988: *Yuandao*).[17] Benevolence is human-centered and love-centered. This concept appears to be the same as humanism in the West, but there are differences between *ren* and humanism. For instance, sexual love is very much in the foreground in humanism but in *ren,* it takes second place, coming after the love between parents and their offspring. *Benevolence*, as the supreme guideline for the governing of a country, is without doubt the most humanitarian principle. It is undoubtedly the most reasonable and ideal principle, no matter whether rulers are able and willing to adhere to it or not. Since the Chinese nation is structured like a huge family, this principle was emphasized in the political system of ancient China. The family is the nation in miniature, while the nation is the extension of the family. The love between family members, such as parents, brothers and sisters, naturally evolves or is sublimated into the love between all the members of society and it was therefore natural for Confucius to appeal to the members of society to "love the populace extensively and stick closely to the kind and upright men" (*Lunyu: ·Xue´er*).[18]

Righteousness and Justice (义 yi)

Righteousness and justice can also be achieved to some extent in other kinds of human relationships, but it is only in the family-like social structure that the maximum degree of

15 《孟子·离娄下》："君子所以异于人者，以其存心也。君子以仁存心，以礼存心。仁者爱 人，有礼者敬人。爱人者，人恒爱之；敬人者，人恒敬之。"

16 《中庸》第二十章："仁者，人也，亲亲为大。"

17 韩愈《韩昌黎集·杂著部》"原道"："博爱之谓仁。"

18 《论语·学而》："子曰：弟子，入则孝，出则弟，谨而信，泛爱众，而亲仁。行有馀力，则 以学文。"

righteousness and justice can be obtained, because in light of morality and obligation, every member of the family-like society has to recognize other members as relatives or family members. Ideally, the distribution of benefits among relatives or family members is fair. Moreover, the highest authority within a family structure is always held by the parents, the oldest, or the most prestigious, who, compared with other members in the family or in other social structures, show a greater degree of impartiality in dividing property, distributing power, or mediating conflict between family or clan members.

It should be noted that the more a family-like society expands and the more complex the social situation gets, i.e., the more people have to share its rights and benefits, the degree of attainable fairness will definitely decrease. However, as long as the family members acknowledge that they all belong to the same family, the advanced values originating from family relationships can be extended and further developed within the society. Only within the family-like social structure do opportunities arise for values to emerge, such as harmony, obedience, rapprochement, collaboration, loyalty, cosiness, peace, gentility, accommodation, auspiciousness, reconciliation, and moderation. When the family-like society is faced with problems such as dividing and sharing benefits, distributing power, and mediating conflicts, comparatively less conflict arises. The leader of the family-like society should try to show impartiality and behave in the same way as a father would towards his sons and daughters, even if this is never entirely possible. Interestingly, officials used to be referred to as parent-like (officials) (父母官 *fumuguan*) while the citizens were referred to as son-like (common people) (子民百姓 *zimin baixing*).

The interest-group (the military group, political group and economic group) social structure found in the Western world also has its characteristics and limitations. In a society that is controlled by different interest groups and governed by the majority (democracy), justice is determined only by the strength of interest groups. The most powerful (both politically and financially) group is able to decide the basic standard of justice. In the interest-group (military group) social structure, the different interest groups invariably emphasize their different interests, and the ensuing conflicts have to be resolved. The most common solution is to obtain ruling status by means of a war or an election, and then pass laws to promote or at least protect the winning group's own interests. The sanctification of law is the necessary cultural consequence when interest groups clash (and are reconciled) with each other in order to snatch and protect benefits. It is inevitable that such a social structure will give birth to a value system which attaches great importance to bravery, intelligence, abstinence, righteousness, cautiousness, freedom, democracy, self-reliance, and individualism.

Courage (勇 yong)

The Western world has been dominated by four important moral values, the four cardinal virtues of "Prudence", "Courage (or Fortitude)", "Temperance", and "Justice". The Christian Church has added "Faith", "Hope", and "Charity", expanding the system into the "Seven Cardinal Virtues". Taking any of these virtues alone, each of them is good. However, when they are compared with the traditional values in China as mentioned above, we have to admit that the values in China are better. For example, in the West, prudence and courage are regarded as the most important virtues, and they are therefore prioritized, while in the Chinese culture, the most important values are benevolence and justice.

As mentioned earlier, when extended from a family to the whole society; the universal values of benevolence and love in China are undoubtedly a far better moral pursuit for human beings compared with wisdom and courage – the most important moral standard in the west. Of course, the Western virtue of prudence is also important, but it is desirable only when guided by good will. In addition, courage, without proper restrictions, as in reckless courage, is not desirable. In China, foolhardiness is even derided. In the Taoist doctrine of China, the quality of bravery is dismissed. Laozi maintained that those who behave in an excessively rash and reckless manner always come to a disastrous end. In his opinion, "courage, when exceeding a reasonable degree, induces death" (Gu 1995: *Daodejing*).[19] Of course, the quality of courage is not altogether excluded from the traditional values of China. It is one of the fifteen virtues in Confucianism as mentioned above. Courage/bravery, however, is deliberately placed at the bottom of the list, because it is not a value that needs emphasis for family members. Courage/bravery can certainly be good if it helps one to do something well, but it can also have a negative quality, if it instigates reckless actions. Competition and wars between opponents and enemies call for courage to be shown, but, ideally, family members are neither opponents nor enemies. Courage is indeed desirable, but only when based on justice. In contrast to the Western culture, where an emphasis is placed on courage, Confucianism tends to weaken its significance.

Altruism and Self-centered individualism

Altruism, in China, is widely esteemed as the first principle and is often placed next to *ren*. According to this principle, one's own interests take second place. This other-centered principle, compared with the self-centered individualism found in the West, is without doubt superior. Traditional Chinese values advocate a family-like structure for the world, with peace and reconciliation. According to the prescribed standard of morality, the strong should be restrained a little and the weak should be helped a little, aggression should be prohibited and war, opposed. In contrast, traditional Western values advocate competition; the principle of natural selection, and the survival of the fittest is widely propagated and bellicosity has become a pattern. If we compare the two systems of values, it goes without saying that Confucian values, at this level, are relatively superior. The three additional values in the Christian Church, of faith, hope and charity, might sound very good, but unfortunately they are not strongly emphasized by Westerners. "Charity" is similar to the Chinese "benevolence", but it does not seem to hold sway in the Western world. There was even a period when the value of charity was criticized by some Western scholars and it was a shock to the Chinese mind to hear it said that alms-giving and engaging in charitable conduct simply encourages laziness in a society.[20]

Obligations and freedom

The Western value system gradually came to the concept of freedom. Freedom as a value has been emphasized in different ways in the West for more than two thousand years. In ancient Greece, for instance, the unceasing pursuit of freedom was accompanied by

19 老子《道德经》第73章："勇于敢，则杀。"

20 See the English *Statute of Artificers* of 1563 and the *Scottish Act* of 1663. Also, the ruling of Stitchill the baronial court in 1698, forbidding the giving of alms or house-room by any in the barony except to "those allenarly that shall be listed" (Cited in: Gunn 1905: 135).

developmental ideas of freedom that varied in particular situations and times (Bury 2011: 9). Hegel's definition of history is also of interest here:

> The history of the world is none other than the progress of the consciousness of freedom.[21] The Eastern nations knew only that one is free, the Emperor, the Pharaoh. The Greek and Roman world thought that only some are free. In Christianity, according to Hegel, there is the consciousness that everyone is free, even if he sits in jail. (transl. from Zhao Yafeng 2008: 50)

But Rousseau's dramatic line on freedom has a more familiar ring: "Men are born free, but everywhere they are in chains" (Rousseau 1762: I Ch.1). I would like to use this citation as representative of the emphasis on the value of freedom in the West. Rousseau might stand out in his rigor, but he still is a representative example of many other Western scholars, ancient and modern: he attributes the highest value to freedom, whereas in China, freedom, traditionally, has never been given much emphasis. Rousseau proposed this concept in his renowned *Social Contract*, and thousands of scholars have cited it. Freedom as a value in today's world has almost become a sacred creed. The pursuit of freedom itself as an ideal is, of course, a good thing. However, people tend to forget that an ideal is simply that: an ideal. And as Rousseau asserted, in reality, freedom is everywhere confined. If freedom is only emphasized without the relevant conditions being stated, it becomes an empty, meaningless and misleading slogan. By relevant conditions, I mean certain aspects, for example, how can a society protect its citizens under various circumstances, and how can society ensure the people's well-being and provide the basic means for their survival. If a person constantly faces the risk of unemployment, or the risk of illness without being able to afford hospital treatment, or if a person is of average intelligence but is deprived of all opportunities for a better education, or if a person with a large family cannot afford an apartment to live in: even if he or she has the freedom to curse and swear in the streets and to criticize the authorities in the media, what is the benefit of freedom for him or her? For the empty stomach, bread is more important than freedom. Of course, some aspects of freedom in association with other values, such as many initiatives regarding human rights in modern Western society, are worth learning from.

Traditional Western values take freedom as an end in itself, seeing it as an abstract sort of individual freedom, while Chinese traditional values place a greater emphasis on the obligations that arise in one's everyday life. Obligations and freedom do not totally contradict each other, but it is very difficult to achieve a balance in reality. In other words, a man has to take on duties and responsibilities, but would prefer to indulge in a carefree life without any obligations. Rousseau's proposition is too vague and it is safe to say that men are actually not "born free". In my opinion, since people are unable to choose the place and time of their birth, they are destined to be un-free even before they are born. If born into an aristocratic and official family, for instance, a person stands a chance of being privileged all his life, whereas if born into a poor and common family, it is likely that hunger and misery will accompany him all his life. In rural China, when a child is born, he or she is almost destined to become a farmer; only a small percentage of the rural population may be offered an opportunity to become something other than a

21 „Die Weltgeschichte ist der Fortschritt im Bewusstsein der Freiheit." For the original text, see: Georg Wilhelm Friedrich Hegel (1837) *Vorlesungen über die Philosophie der Geschichte*, published by Dr. Eduard Gans, Chapter 1.

peasant. And a man born in America or in developing countries will obviously experience different opportunities, better or worse, in his career. It is therefore useless to talk about freedom without being specific. People are not born free; they are born without freedom and with the burden of having to fulfil their obligations! People have the obligation to adjust themselves to the environment they are born into. They are born with the obligations that are imposed by the environment and they have to deal with these throughout their lives. For instance, they have to support their parents, obey their elders, care for the young and the old, fulfil all the duties that are imposed by society and they have to become sufficiently self-reliant to be able to contribute to their own brothers and sisters' livelihoods, etc. Only a completely selfish person would consider these essential obligations as shackles and seek to indulge in a carefree lifestyle without any responsibilities. In fact, in his/her view, freedom is an escape from one's obligations to the world.

True, freedom is a kind of pleasure, but it is conditional, and conditions always impose restrictions. I would suggest, however, that these very restrictions give a true meaning to freedom. Only when we understand this point, will we be able to understand why the ancient Chinese had a set of rituals to regulate their behaviour. Each individual's obligations and duties were systematically regulated and these were carefully prescribed in the Chinese rites (礼 *li*, or the norms of social conduct). The practice of freedom could only be carried out in accordance with the regulations set up in the rites; it is under such conditions that freedom attains its particular value and significance. Many Western literary works, poetry in particular, that sing the praises of shaking of the yoke, bring to mind the image of the naughty and perverted child who is desperately trying to obtain everything they want, such as toys and food. Yet only modest obligations and modest freedom are desirable; over-indulgence in freedom will harm others and lead to one's own self-destruction. Even the birds and beasts of the jungle know that they have to care for their offspring! Extremes, of course, should be avoided; extremes are dangerous. If a society over-emphasizes the obligations, it will become too rigid and harsh, intentionally or unintentionally, and basic human rights will be affected in one way or another. All this should be taken into consideration when pondering the value of freedom.

Confucius' Main Contribution to Confucianism

We have been talking about Confucianism without Confucius. In saying this, I would like to reiterate that I do not mean to belittle Confucius, who was the most authoritative and the most qualified spokesman for Confucianism. No one in Chinese history has done more than Confucius in advocating ancient Chinese ideas – Confucian ideas. Confucianism, after all, bears the name of Confucius. Meanwhile, Confucius is also universally accepted as one of the greatest scholars and greatest educators in the world.

To be more specific, the main contribution of Confucius is his rediscovering, editing and expounding of those parts of traditional Chinese political and moral systems, particularly the *Rites of Zhou,* which are now called Confucianism. Confucius discovered that the ideology represented in the *Rites of Zhou* were particularly suited to traditional Chinese society as political, moral and economical systems and made a tremendous effort to expound the above systems, in particular, Confucian values, based on the rites.

Confucius lived in a time when the system of rites was almost totally corrupted. Throughout his life, he preached what he called "克己复礼" (ke ji fu li), which means that everyone should do his bit to try to restore the *Rites of Zhou* by morally restraining oneself, by conforming to the rites in everything (*Lunyu: ·Yan Yuan*).[22] He believed that the world would return to its original state of benevolence and love if people really acted in accordance with the principles laid down in the rites, even for one single day (ibid.).[23]

Confucius tried in every way to help to restore the political and cultural system of the Zhou dynasty. He travelled a great deal, in the hope that the kings and lords of various states would be persuaded to restore the *Rites of Zhou*. He almost succeeded in realizing his ideal when he was appointed prime minister of the State of Lu, but unfortunately he fell out of favour with the king and had to relinquish his efforts. Nevertheless, he continued to encourage his disciples to follow his example in trying to persuade other kings and lords.

Confucius set up the first private schools, now regarded as the first kind of university in the world, where he lectured upon the rites and asked his students to put the rites into practice. The university was open to all men whether rich or poor, and is said to have received about 3,000 students, among whom 70 were considered to turn out worthies. At the time, this was also the largest training centre for political statesmen in the world.

As is known again, Confucius collected, revised and edited many documents closely related to the *Rites of Zhou*, the *Book of Odes*, the *Book of History* (尚书 *shang shu*), the *Book of Change*, the *Spring and Autumn Annals*, etc. He made the most appropriate illustrations of Confucianism and elucidated principles from the *Rites of Zhou* in such a way that the ordinary people of his time were able to understand them.

Finally, Confucius set an excellent example of how the ancient values from the rites could fashion the ideal personality and character that was required by a family-like society. He has been acclaimed as a perfect person, in terms of both morality and intelligence, whom nearly all traditional Chinese people would willingly follow all their lives. He is renowned as a "sage" (圣人 *shengren*). This is considered a mark of the highest esteem by people all over the world.

The Family-like Social Structure: Encounter with Modernity and Further Reflection

Many Chinese scholars have discussed, to varying degrees, the issue of the family-like social structure in China. Unfortunately, most have criticized the family structure, in negative terms, as a backward social structure. This criticism has a history of almost one hundred years in China: beginning with many articles by scholars, such as Chen Duxiu and Hu Shi, particularly with regard to a scathing short story entitled *A Madman's Diary* by Lu Xun (1881-1936) in 1918. According to the author, the story was "meant to expose the maladies of the family system and the Neo-Confucian Orthodoxy" (Lu Xun 2002).[24] The entire traditional history of China is described through the eyes of a madman in terms of a man-eating society. Since then, "man-eating" (吃人 *chi ren*) has become a pet phrase for many Chinese people to define the nature of any sort of traditional Chinese culture. In doing this, people have disregarded that fact that Lu Xun's short story is only a fictional creation, a completely non-academic narration, a product of artistic imagination. The hero of the story, a madman, utters a great deal of nonsense, how could academic circles

22 《论语·颜渊》："子曰： 非礼勿视，非礼勿听，非礼勿言，非礼勿动。颜渊曰：回虽不敏，请 事斯语矣！"

23 《论语·颜渊》："颜渊问仁。子曰：克己复礼为仁。一日克己复礼，天下归仁焉！为仁由 己，而由人乎哉？"

24 鲁迅《且介亭杂文二集》"《中国新文学大系·小说二集》序"："但后起的《狂人日记》意在 暴露家族制度和礼教的弊害。"

assume that this nonsense is true? This pet phrase is like a curse placed upon Confucianism. It has been repeated thousands upon thousands of times in numerous articles, poems, monographs and in all Chinese primary, middle school and college textbooks. Marxist theorists found it a pertinent label for marking the essential nature of Confucianism and the feudal societies in Chinese history. They have launched countless, aggressive attacks against what they call "Confucian Store" (孔家店 *kongjiadian*). All the Confucian family values, such as love/benevolence, righteousness and justice, civility, wisdom, honesty, gentility, kindness, humility, frugality, obedience, reconciliation, loyalty, filial piety, the sense of shame, courage/bravery have been subjected to merciless and absurd attacks.

Once more, I would like to call the attention of the reader to the following fact: arising in direct response to their different geographic environments, the different social structures in China and the West have a flesh-and-blood correspondence with Chinese and Western cultural structures. This is why I emphasize the fact that the family-like social structure is one of the key factors for gaining an understanding of the traditional mainstream Chinese culture, and the interest-group (military group) social structure is also one of the key factors for gaining an understanding of the traditional dominant Western culture. In other words, the family-like social structure in China has a complex and pervasive connection with traditional Chinese philosophy, politics, economics, ethics, aesthetics, law, architecture, medicine, sport, etiquette, and even military affairs. The doctrine of Taoism is also the necessary outcome of the family-like social structure in China. This holds true even in the case of some imported doctrines, such as Buddhism (particularly the Mahayana branch). The reason why Buddhism is widely accepted in traditional Chinese society is that its doctrines conform to the family-like social structure and Confucian values of ancient China. Likewise, the interest-group (military group) social structure in the West also has a complex and pervasive connection with Western philosophy, politics, economics, ethics, aesthetics, law, architecture, medicine, sport, etiquette, and even military affairs. For instance, the doctrine of rationalism and the fetishes of science and technology are the necessary choice of the Western interest-group (military group) social structure. This holds true even in the case of some foreign doctrines, such as Christianity, which has its origins in the east. The reason why it is widely accepted in traditional Western society is that its basic principles, after slight modifications, agree with the interest-group (military group) social structure and the cultural structures of the west.

Comparison and Contrast:
Family-Nation vs. State-Nation and Examination vs. Democracy

While I take note of the fact that the dominance of the farming culture of China inevitably restrains commerce and emphasizes agriculture, and sets great store by peaceful values such as living and working in peace and contentment, I also take note of the fact that the dominance of the trade and business culture in the West inevitably suppresses agriculture and emphasizes commerce, and puts an emphasis on aggressive values, advocating military force and the plundering of other lands' resources. In an agriculturally-based society, living and working in peace and contentment, small families will inevitably develop into big families, big families into extended families, and then into the establishment of a country, and later into 家国 (*jia guo*), the family-nation, which will inevitably have its corresponding political systems and governments. Similarly, regular mobility and commercial risk will inevitably lead to the disintegration of the primitive family-tribes, which will then be replaced by interest factions that will finally foster bigger interest factions, which leads to the formation of a country, the 邦国 (*bang guo*), the nation-state, which will inevitably have its corresponding political systems and governments.

The family-nation political system embodies the values of clans or tribes. This form of government is incompatible with the Western government based on the political party system. Confucius once said: "Gentlemen unite the masses without forming a clique (Party) to pursue selfish interests" (*Lunyu: Weilinggong*)[25], which can be taken as hinting that villains form a clique to pursue selfish interests without uniting the masses. This thinking actually reflects the family-nation political system in ancient China.

In a large family, members will be nurtured by the values of *ren* (benevolence) and *ai* (爱 love) as the guiding principle of behaviour. As time goes on, their behaviour gradually evolves into a set of ethics and rituals known as the rites. Thus the traditional political system in China is a family-nation system guided by ethics and rites. The family-oriented values, under different circumstances, will exhibit two characteristics: first, since all members of the society will universally identify themselves with one family and they share ancient genetic relationships, under the government of a family-nation system guided by ethnics and rites, they will naturally have a strong sense of equality. Too much sense of equality in turn makes people prone to a mindset based on self-righteousness. And this self-righteous attitude, under certain conditions, will weaken the cohesive force of the government, and lead to a lack of cohesion in the government in times of peace.

Second, in times of crisis, members embracing such family-oriented values will show the same high degree of national unity as a large family, which will result in strong nationalism. To prevent such a messy situation, this form of government needs to strengthen its cohesion, to strengthen its legitimacy. Moreover, since the government is subordinated to the characteristics of the family, in order to prevent an over-concentration of feudal power, the society must self-regulate itself by inducing adherence to a code of strong moral ethics among its family members (the people). Hence the idea that "since the people are the foundation of the nation, if the people live and work in peace and contentment, the nation will stand firm"[26] (*Shangshu: Wuzizhige*) will be propagated by traditional elite groups of intellectuals. This is in accordance with Mencius' idea of government for the people (民本 *minben*). The idea of government for the people, in this respect, is a Chinese-style democracy. It is not organized and implemented by competitive elections but by relying on the highest level of virtues being possessed by the ruling group. The persons of the ruling group must go through very strict imperial examinations to test the capabilities as well as the moral quality of all the candidates. Every citizen in the country has the right to take part in these fair examinations. Only those who are both morally intelligently perfect can enjoy the power at the imperial court. One may call this Chinese-style democracy "a government mainly ruled by virtue" (德主政体 *dezhu zhengti*).

The traditional political system in the West is a nation-state system armed with religion (God) and laws. It is quite different from the traditional Chinese political system based on family values. The political system of the nation-state is the embodiment of the values put forward by its various interest groups. In this form of government, different interest groups agree on compromises in order to govern the nation. As time goes on, the values of individualism (oriented toward the individual) will gradually form a set of rules and

25 《论语•卫灵公》："子曰：君子矜而不争，群而不党。"

26 《尚书 ·五子之歌》：民为邦本，本固邦宁。

regulations, guiding and protecting the interests of the individuals, this is called the "law". Hence the traditional Western political system can also be described in terms of nation-states that are ruled by law. These individual-oriented values, under different circumstances, will exhibit different characteristics: in the nation-state system, large family structures have long been disintegrated. The sense of family has been weakened, and the members of this society no longer possess a strong sense of belonging to a family. Thus, each member now places an emphasis on his or her autonomy and independence. If this is taken to an extreme, selfishness will be seen as a natural value.[27] This selfish attitude will again rationalize the competitiveness among the different people.[28] Which, finally, becomes legalization. Legalization requires a sound set of regulations to ensure fairness in competition. To this end, the nation-state is forced to govern by law, rather than by virtue. Meanwhile, the universal competition, particularly the commercial competition, leads to the formation of intense interpersonal relationships between individuals in the society. The loss of family-oriented values leads Westerners to invite the introduction of religion as a substitute for the loss of family-based ethics in order to relieve the tensions that derive from the conflict between individuals. For instance, the Christian idea of "brotherhood" is a religious technique for forming an artificial bond among the members of any group in the nation-state's society. To a certain extent, this regulates interpersonal relationships. Therefore, it is an inevitable choice for Western mercantilism to appeal to Christianity. To a certain extent, individual-oriented values inevitably form interest groups or factionalism, and encourage the formation of various parties. The competition among individuals reflects the competition between different groups and parties. This sort of competition will cause the decentralization of power by contract. Decentralization by contract aims at protecting various interest groups (including royal interests), while it also limits the royal power. The conflict of interests within the government plays a crucial role in bridging the interests among different nations. The ruling party is, in fact, not all the people but just a few, or a majority of the people at best, that is 帮 (*bang* a clique, a party, or parties and groups). [29] The leader of a

---

27 While selfishness has always been severely attacked by the mainstream traditional Chinese ideologies, it often seems to be defended in one way or another in the West as having a positive function. Naturally, if one is over-egocentric, one is estranged from other people. In the end, an extremely selfish person tends to find only enemies amongst other people.

28 The idea of "laissez-faire" and the sense of competition based on selfish greed was highly justified and popularized by Adam Smith, the great Scottish philosopher and economist who stated in *An Inquiry into the Nature and Causes of the Wealth of Nations*: *"As every individual, therefore, endeavors as much as he can both to employ his capital in the support of domestic industry, and so to the direct that industry that its produce may be of the greatest value; every individual necessarily labours to render the annual revenue of the society as great as he can. He generally, indeed, neither intends to promote the public interest, nor knows how much he is promoting it. By preferring the support of domestic to that of foreign industry, he intends only his own security; and by directing that industry in such a manner as its produce may be of the greatest value, he intends only his own gain, and he in this, as in many other cases, led by an invisible hand to promote an end which was no part of his intention. Nor is it always the worse for the society that it was no part of it. By pursuing his own interest he frequently promotes that of the society more effectually than when he really intends to promote it"* (1776, VI, ii: 456).

29 The recent "Occupy Wall Street"-movement taking place in the United States obviously voices the indignation of the downtrodden who see the United States as only technically an electoral democracy and criticize it as an actually entrenched plutocracy that dominates most political decisions. Democracy

political party or group could be the president, or leader of a government if the party came to power. The Chinese characters 民主 (*minzhu*) are translated from the English term "democracy". This is, to some extent, a mistranslation of the foreign term, because in Chinese, 民 (*min*) means inclusively all of the people, while 主 (*zhu*) means to rule or to be the leader/master. 民主 (*minzhu*) thus means "the people are the ruler" or "ruling by all the people"; this does not mean that a representative of the majority or a certain party, having won the election in the West, is to be the ruler (the president, for example). In Chinese, the expression, to rule by all of the people (民主) sounds like a very attractive proposition, but few realize that it is self-contradictory both in logic and in the Chinese wording. The people are in no way to be the rulers. The ruler has to be just one single person or a small group of people. The people or the majority of the people usually are the ruled. Thus the Chinese term 民主 (*minzhu*) is as ridiculous as saying that "the ruled is the ruler". In contrast, the family-like government in ancient China had an emperor from one family, but the thousands of officials were mostly common people who had obtained the positions through fair examinations; there was even one prime minister who was a beggar before he went through the Imperial Examination system and became a doctor (进士 *jinshi*). I am inclined to think that this method of selecting officials from among the people through strict examinations that are designed to test the moral quality and wisdom of each candidate is superior to that employed in Western democracies, which is mainly carried out by means of elections for the various interest-parties or groups.[30] The Chinese Imperial Examination System of selecting officials from the common people was conducted for about 1,300 years in China. The system was the realization of the Confucian value that "The one who is both morally and intelligently superior should be an official" (*Lunyu: Zi Zhang*).[31]

Conclusion: Toward a Confucian Family-like World

I hope the illustrations and comparison above will serve to explain that the Confucian value system, despite the fact that it contains some elements that call for further refinement and improvement in the new era, is the world's most advanced value system to date. This value system is both humane and rational, because it is the product of the collective efforts of millions of family members who cherished the idea of love and peace arising from their natural needs rather than some other compulsory requirements. Arnold Toynbee, the well-known British scholar, thought highly of the "humanism characterizing the Confucian view of the world" and the "rationalism characterizing both Confucianism and Buddhism" (transl. from Toynbee/Daisaku 1985: 277). These values, as part of the cultural heritage of East Asia, can help to unify the world. Toynbee further maintained that "in the future it is China rather than European countries that will possibly unify the world" (transl. from ibid.: 278) and stated that we need not feel surprised that "Nobel prize winners have suggested that if mankind is to survive it must go back 25 centuries in time to tap the wisdom of Confucius" (Marnham 1988). Therefore, to some extent, we may conclude that as far as its general orientation is concerned, the system of moral values based on Confucianism is now the most ideal for all mankind. Marx identified

---

in their eyes is only a political system governed by wealthy people, the wealthy group.

30 The Chinese Imperial Examination System of selecting officials is usually considered to have begun in 598 AC in the Sui Dynasty and to have been abolished at end of the Qing Dynasty in 1905 after a history of 1307 years.

31 《论语・子张》："子夏曰：仕而优则学；学而优则仕。"

primitive society as communist because it was almost always structured like a family. In such a social structure, the members of the family produce food together, manage the labour together, and consume the goods together, without possessing any personal property. The only drawback of the communist society in the primitive stage is that, due to low productivity, the society is unable to yield sufficient material wealth. Reasoned in this way, when a society has enough capacity to produce sufficient material wealth and make the wealth circulate, mankind should reconsider returning to the family-like society. Toynbee had a clear idea of the excellent qualifications of the spiritual legacy of the Chinese civilization. He predicted that China would be the center of the world for mankind in the future:

> The unity of the world is a way to avoid human beings committing mass-suicide. And now the nation that gets prepared well in this respect is China since it has cultivated its unique way of thinking for more than two thousand years. (transl. from Toynbee/Daisaku 1984: 284)[32]

Again,Toynbee argued that:

> China has maintained a unity for almost two thousand years and thus is qualified for the leader of the future world. And China will play a very significant role in unifying the whole world in the future. (transl. from ibid.: 283)

Toynbee's viewpoint is very interesting. And I would further add that the origin of the excellent qualifications of the spiritual legacy of the Chinese civilization is actually closely related to the family-like social structure of the ancient Chinese. In accordance with what was said earlier, a series of values born out of the social structure of the large Chinese family is destined to play an important role in pursuing the highest form of world culture in the future.

All humanity should be seen as members of one family. And modern genetic research is increasingly working to convince us that human beings actually are members of one family. If all humanity are members of one family, the use of family-oriented values in a society is inevitably a good choice.

Let us embrace the ancient Confucian idea of cosmopolitanism, the so-called "worldism"[33]. We should combine the concept of the descendants of the Yan and Huang Emperors with the story of Adam and Eve and human genes taken from modern technology to expand the view of family-nation to the view of family-world, to the view that all human beings are members of a family in which *ren* is worshiped as the supreme principle to harmonize all personal relations.

These expressions may seem only high-sounding words, but the intention is good and logical. If the world remains in separate parts and groups, values derived from interest groups may work well, but if the world considers itself a family, the values derived from the traditional family society may work better. Fortunately, globalization is now

32 The Toynbee quotations here and further below are translated by the author from the Japanese edition (Toynbee/Daisaku 1984), part II, Chapter 4: "One World". Other Japanese versions are also available, in which the respective chapter contains six sections: (1) *International Currency*; (2) *East Asia's Role*; (3) *China and the World*; (4) *Japan's Contribution to the Future*; (5) *From Bipolarity to Multipolarity*; and (6) *World Unification*. Interestingly enough, in the English version (Toynbee/Daisaku 1976), the same chapter contains only five sections with the section (3) *China and the World* seemingly deleted.

33 The word "worldism" is not a synonym for "globalism". Globalism often implies the unifying effect of economic power while "worldism" here mainly emphasizes culture-oriented influences.

developing in an intensified manner that may help to sharpen our awareness of the fact that human beings are on an earth that is too small for them to forget that they live in the same earth-village. They should not split into cliques and groups; they should reunite into one family, no matter how large.

Therefore, I would suggest that the world should replace the values of interest groups with the concept of "the world as one family" (天下一家 *tian xia yi jia*). And for this, it is evident that the Confucian-family value system provides the most valuable experiences and serves for human beings returning to the excellent family-like social structure and value system with, of course, adequate modifications.[34] This excellent social structure and value system can be summarized in three words: family – nation – world.

References

Ban Gu 班固 (2007) *Hanshu* 汉书 [The History of the Han Dynasty], Beijing: Zhonghua shuju.

Bury, John Bagnell (2011) *Siwang ziyou shi* 思想自由史 [A History of Freedom of Thought], Changchun: Jilin renmin chubanshe.

Gu Zhengkun 辜正坤 (1995) *Laozi Yingyi* 老子英译 [The Book of Tao and Teh], Beijing: Beijing Daxue chubanshe.

Gu Zhengkun 辜正坤 (2004) *Zhongxi wenhua bijiao daolun* 中西文化比较导论 [A Comparative Study of Chinese and Western Cultures], Beijing: Beijing Daxue chubanshe.

Gunn, Clement B. (1905) *Records of the Baron Court of Stitchill,* Edinburgh: Scottish History Society.

Han Yu 韩愈 (1988) *Han changli wenji xiaozhu* 韩昌黎文集校注 [Collation and Annotation of Han Changli Prose Collection], Shanghai: Shanghai guji chubanshe.

Hegel, Georg Wilhelm Friedrich (1837) *Vorlesungen über die Philosophie der Geschichte*, Berlin: Verlag von Duncker und Humblot.

Liu Baonan 刘宝楠 (1990) *Lunyu Zhengyi* 论语正义 [Correct Meaning of the Analects], Beijing: Zhonghua shuju.

Lu Xun 鲁迅 (1973) *Qiejieting zawen erji* 且介亭杂文二集 [Essays from the Qiejie pavilion, vol. 2], Beijing: Renmin wenxue chubanshe.

Lu Xun 鲁迅 (2002) *Kuangren riji* 狂人日记 [A Madman's Diary], Beijing: Renmin wenxue chubanshe.

Lu Xun 鲁迅 (2003) *Zhongguo xin wenxue daxi xiaoshuo erji* 中国新文学大系 小说二集 [Sequel Selections of Novels in The Great Series of the New Literature], Shanghai: Shanghai wenyi chubanshe.

Lunyu 论语 [Confucius, the analects] (2007), ed. by Liu Shengli 刘胜利, Beijing: Zhonghua shuju.

Marnham, Patrick (1988) „Nobel winners say tap the wisdom of Confucius" in: *Canberra Times*, Canberra, Australia, 24, January, 1988.

Rousseau, Jean Jacques (1762) *The Social Contract*, Amsterdam: Marc-Michel Rey.

Shangshu 尚书 [Book of History] (1999), ed. by Kong Yingda 孔颖达, Beijing: Zhonghua shuju.

Smith, Adam (1776) *An Inquiry into the Nature and Causes of the wealth of Nations*, Idion: München.

34 By modifications, I mean, for example, more freedom should be given to family members so that they are not torn by too much duty and collective spirit should be brought into play in such a way that egoistic pursuits are not completely suppressed.

Sun Xidan 孙希旦 and Chen Xiaohuan 沈啸寰 (2007) *Liji jijie* 礼记集解 [Annotations to the Rites], Beijing: Zhonghua shuju.

Toynbee, Arnold and Ikeda Daisaku (1975) *Nijūisseikie no taiwa* 二十一世紀への対話 [Forecast of the 21st. centery], Tokyo: bungei shunjū.

Toynbee, Arnold and Ikeda Daisaku (1984) *Nijūisseikie no taiwa* 二十一世紀への対話 [Forecast of the 21st. centery], Tokyo: seikyô shinbunsha.

Toynbee, Arnold and Ikeda Daisaku, Richard L. Gage (ed.) (1976) *Choose Life. A Dialogue*, London: Oxford University Press.

Toynbee, Arnold and Ikeda Daisaku; transl. by Gou Chunsheng 苟春生 Zhu Jizheng 朱继征 Chen Guoliang 陈国梁 (1985) *Zhanwang 21 Shiji* 展望 21 世纪 [Forecast of the 21st. centery], Beijing: Guoji wenhua chuban gongsi.

Wang Guoxuan 王国轩 (2006) *Daxue Zhong Yong* 大学中庸 [Doctrine of the Mean], Beijing: Zhonghua shuju.

Zhang Wenxiu 张文修 (ed.) (1995) *Mengzi* 孟子, Beijing: Beijing Yanshan chubanshe.

Zhao Yafeng (2008) *Deutsche Philosophen*, Beijing: Foreign Languages Press.

Zhu Xi 朱熹 (1992) *Lunyu jizhu* 论语集注 [The Confucian Analects Annotated by Zhu Xi], Jinan: Qilu shushe.

Hans van Ess

Der Konfuzianismus und die globale Weltkultur: Überlegungen bei der Lektüre der Konfuzianismuskritik im frühen 20. Jahrhundert

In China redet man seit längerer Zeit über die Wiederbelebung der ostasiatischen Zivilisation. Im Vordergrund steht dabei die Frage, wie man den Konfuzianismus und das kulturelle Erbe Chinas für die Zukunft Chinas und sogar der ganzen Welt nutzen kann. Vor hundert Jahren hat der Reformer Kang Youwei in seinem *Buch von der Großen Einheit*, dem *Datong shu*, schon einmal eine Utopie entworfen, wie eine gemeinsame Weltzivilisation auf der Basis chinesischer und westlicher Ideen entstehen konnte. Man hat ihn damals allerdings weder im In- noch im Ausland, wo Teile des *Datong shu* entstanden, wirklich angehört. Zwar war Kang Youwei ein berühmter Mann, aber der Widerstand gegen die konfuzianischen Ideen in seinem Buch war in seinem eigenen Land zu groß.

Vielleicht sind die Bedingungen heute besser: Vor hundert Jahren war China ein schwaches Land, dem niemand etwas zutraute – in den USA und in Europa interessierte man sich kaum für moderne Ideen aus diesem fernen Land. Heute hingegen ist China erstarkt und hat eine Stimme in der Welt. Gleichzeitig ist der Westen erstaunlicherweise ausgerechnet zu dem Zeitpunkt seines größten Triumphes in eine Krise geraten: Nach dem Zusammenbruch des osteuropäischen Sozialismus 1989 hatte Francis Fukuyama in seinem 1992 erschienen Buch *Das Ende der Geschichte* noch ganz siegessicher verkündet, dass nun der Kommunismus keine politische Alternative mehr sei und die freie Marktwirtschaft die einzige Lösung für die Welt darstelle. Im gleichen Jahr reiste Deng Xiaoping nach Shenzhen, und nur zwei Jahre später wurde die „sozialistische Marktwirtschaft" in der chinesischen Verfassung verankert, was damals höchste Verwunderung im Westen auslöste, denn die Vereinigung von Sozialismus und Marktwirtschaft in einem Ausdruck schien ein Widerspruch in sich selbst zu sein. Dennoch wurde dies als ein Schritt Chinas auf die westliche Welt zu gefeiert. Doch wie wir in den letzten Jahren erfahren mussten, hat das westliche Modell einer immer freieren Marktwirtschaft seit diesen Ereignissen gewaltige Probleme bekommen. Vielleicht muss man sich vor diesem Hintergrund um das Fortbestehen der chinesischen Kultur angesichts eines übermächtigen westlichen Einflusses keine Sorgen machen: Die Dominanz des Westens ist nicht mehr so groß. Der Kapitalismus funktioniert nicht mehr so gut wie vor 1989, als es in Europa und der Sowjetunion noch einen Sozialismus gab. Da erscheint es richtig, dass nun umgekehrt wir Europäer uns nach neuen Modellen und Lösungen umschauen sollten. China und seine Kultur bieten sich dafür an. Die Frage ist allerdings, was denn die chinesische Kultur überhaupt ist, die als Vorbild dienen soll.

Renaissance des Konfuzianismus im gegenwärtigen China

Der Konfuzianismus wird heute gerne als ein Modell angepriesen. Ein regelrechter Hype um Konfuzius ist ausgebrochen: „Die Gespräche des Konfuzius sind entflammt, Konfuzius ist heiß", so schreibt Li Ling im Vorwort zu seiner Ausgabe der *Gespräche* (Li Ling 2007: 1).

In den 1980er Jahren wollte kein chinesischer Student mehr etwas von Konfuzius wissen – die konfuzianischen Klassiker waren noch unbeliebter als Marx und Lenin, von denen mir meine Kommilitonen in Shanghai immer sagten, dass der Unterricht zum einen Ohr hinein- und zum anderen wieder herausginge. Man lechzte nach moderner westlicher

Berliner China-Hefte/Chinese History and Society 41 (2012), pp. 63-71

Philosophie. Heute ist genau das Gegenteil der Fall: Kurse über die Gespräche des Konfuzius sind an den Universitäten so voll, dass sie in mehrere Klassen aufgeteilt werden müssen, und populäre Versionen wie diejenige der Fernsehprofessorin Yu Dan erreichen Millionenauflagen.[1] Mit Konfuzius kann man als Autor plötzlich reich werden, und die Tatsache, dass das Symposium, im Rahmen dessen der diesem Aufsatz zugrundeliegende Vortrag gehalten wurde, an einem Konfuzius-Institut stattfand, spricht natürlich ebenfalls Bände. Hu Jintao spricht seit seinem Amtsantritt als Staatspräsident von „Harmonie", einem Schlagwort, das jeder Chinese als konfuzianisch versteht. Konfuzius soll Probleme lösen. Mancher Kollege in China sagt übrigens, dass dies mehr mit den sozialen Gegensätzen, die es in China gibt, als mit dem Konfuzianismus zusammenhängt – und die vor 23 Jahren an einem 4. Juni schon einmal zu einem tragischen Ausbruch kamen. Vielleicht ist der Konfuzianismus heute mehr ein innenpolitisches Schmiermittel, das verhindern soll, dass es noch einmal zu einer solchen Entladung kommt wie damals, auch wenn er uns natürlich auch außenpolitisch dazu auffordern soll, harmonische anstelle von aggressiven Lösungen für die Weltprobleme zu suchen.

Doch ich glaube nicht, dass es leicht sein wird, konfuzianische Ideen als Beitrag zu einer neuen Weltkultur einzuführen, auch wenn es immer wieder Sinologen gegeben hat, die von diesem Gedanken begeistert waren. Von einer einigen Welt, in der der Kulturaustausch leicht funktioniert, sind wir noch sehr weit entfernt, und die allermeisten Europäer und Amerikaner wissen über China viel zu wenig, um alte chinesische Ideen einfach verstehen und dann auch noch adaptieren zu können. Meistens gibt es im Kulturaustausch doch unglaubliche Missverständnisse, über die sich der Sinologe wundern muss, aber die den anderen Beteiligten nicht selten gar nicht auffallen. Der Hauptgrund, warum ich glaube, dass noch einige Probleme beseitigt werden müssen, bevor das Ausland vom Konfuzianismus zu überzeugen ist, ist aber ein ganz anderer, nämlich der Antitraditionalismus in China selbst. Zu Beginn des Jahres war auf dem Tian'anmen Platz eine Konfuziusstatue aufgestellt und als neue Touristenattraktion angepriesen worden. Bis ins Frühjahr stand sie da, doch dann hat man sie eines Nachts in den Hof eines nahegelegenen neu eingerichteten Museums gestellt. Vielleicht war das alles von vorneherein so geplant gewesen – aber vielleicht war es auch einfach so, dass es Personen gab, die meinten, ganz so prominent sollte Konfuzius dann doch nicht dastehen. Wer regelmäßig chinesische Zeitschriften liest, der weiß, dass es Gegner des Konfuzius in China nach wie vor gibt. Dies alles erinnert sehr stark an das, was man schon vor hundert Jahren und dann mehrmals im zwanzigsten Jahrhundert beobachten konnte.

Konfuzianismuskritik bei Chen Duxiu

Als Kang Youwei seine Ideen von einer konfuzianischen Staatskirche in der Zeit des ersten Präsidenten der jungen chinesischen Republik, Yuan Shikai, vorantreiben wollte, wurde er von modernen Intellektuellen massiv dafür kritisiert. Wahrscheinlich der erste, der ihn aus inhaltlichen Gründen angriff, war Yi Baisha, der im ersten und zweiten Jahrgang der Zeitschrift *Xin Qingnian*, der *Neuen Jugend*, einen Aufsatz mit dem Titel „Kritische Beurteilung von Kongzi" veröffentlichte (Yi Baisha 1916a, b). Viel berühmter aber ist natürlich Chen Duxiu (1879-1942) geworden, einer der geistigen Väter des Ikonoklasmus der Vierten Mai-Bewegung 1919, der im zweiten Jahrgang dieser Zeitschrift mehrfach den Konfuzianismus angriff. Ein besonders wichtiger Aufsatz trug dabei

1 Yu Dan 2006. Erste Auflage im renommierten Zhonghua shuju-Verlag, im Februar 2010 erschien bereits der 41. Nachdruck, mit 5.100.001-5.150.000 Exemplaren.

den Titel „Die Lehre des Konfuzius und das moderne Leben" (Chen Duxiu 1916). Chen Duxiu schreibt in diesem Aufsatz, dass er und viele andere junge Intellektuelle Kang Youwei zuerst sehr bewunderten, weil er versucht hatte, den Konfuzianismus und auch China zu modernisieren. Man sei dann aber enttäuscht worden, denn Kang Youwei sei so konservativ geworden, dass er nur noch dem alten konfuzianischen Prinzip gefolgt sei, nur das Alte hochzuschätzen und das Neue gering zu schätzen (贵古贱今 *guigu jianjin*, ebd.: 345). Der Konfuzianismus aber lasse sich nicht mit den Idealen der französischen Revolution, „Freiheit", „Gleichheit" und „Demokratie" – er benutzt den chinesischen Begriff *minquan* 民权 anstelle von „Brüderlichkeit" – vereinbaren. Chen Duxiu fragte sich dann, ob der Konfuzianismus überhaupt Werte habe, die man in der Gegenwart noch befolgen könne. Er wies darauf hin, dass Lehrmeinungen gesellschaftlich bedingt seien und umgekehrt: „Eine Lehrmeinung kann eine Gesellschaft hervorbringen, aber eine Gesellschaft kann auch eine Lehrmeinung hervorbringen."[2] (ebd.: 346). Und: „In einer zivilisatorisch fortschrittlichen Gesellschaft hängt der Aufstieg oder Fall einer Lehre immer mit den Veränderungen der gesellschaftlichen Lebensumstände zusammen"[3] (ebd.: 346). Das Verhalten von Europäern und Amerikanern sei ja auch nicht mehr von Aristoteles und Kant bestimmt, da könne Konfuzius für ein zivilisiertes China auch nicht mehr so wichtig sein: „Der Weg ändert sich mit den Zeiten!"[4] (ebd.: 346)

Das ist interessant, denn es widerspricht auch dem, was in der modernen westlichen interkulturellen Literatur immer wieder zu lesen ist: Der Westen sei so, wie er ist, weil wir alle von der christlichen Kultur geprägt seien – ich habe einige Sympathie für die Argumentation Chen Duxius: So einfach ist die Sache nicht. Auch Mao Zedong hat in seinen Sprüchen gesagt, dass das chinesische Volk ein unbeschriebenes Blatt sei.

Kang Youwei hatte den Konfuzianismus besonders deshalb als eine Lösung vieler Probleme benannt, weil er nicht wie Christentum oder Buddhismus eine Religion sei, in der es darum ginge, die Welt zu verlassen und sein Heil in einer anderen Welt zu finden, sondern weil er die menschlichen Beziehungen und die tägliche Praxis zum Gegenstand habe (Chen Duxiu 1916: 346). Chen Duxiu antwortete, dass diese Beobachtung richtig sei, dass aber genau deshalb der Konfuzianismus keine Religion sein könne. Ich glaube übrigens, dass ein Grund dafür, dass in China gerade der Konfuzianismus für besonders attraktiv gehalten wird, auch heute noch der ist, dass viele Menschen sagen, er sei nicht auf das Jenseits ausgerichtet, sondern vor allem eine praktische Lehre (ebd.: 347).

In der zweiten Hälfte seines Aufsatzes spricht Chen Duxiu dann nur noch über die menschlichen Beziehungen. Er sagt zunächst, dass die Lebensader des modernen Lebens die Wirtschaft und die persönliche Unabhängigkeit seien. Das sei in der Ökonomie das Hauptprinzip des Produktionsprozesses, das auch die Ethik beeinflusse. Ethischer Individualismus und ökonomische Unabhängigkeit des Einzelnen hingen also miteinander zusammen (ebd.: 347 f). Im Konfuzianismus aber seien Hierarchien das Entscheidende: Kinder und Frauen hätten gegenüber Eltern und Ehemännern keine Unabhängigkeit. Kang Youwei habe behauptet, dass einzelne Sätze aus dem *Buch der Riten* und anderen konfuzianischen Texten zeigten, dass schon Konfuzius die Bedeutung der Unabhängigkeit des Einzelnen erkannt habe. Er zitiert hier insbesondere die Sätze: „Die Witwer und

2 Im chinesischen Originaltext heißt es: 一种学说可产生一种社会，一种社会亦产生一种学说.

3 Im chinesischen Originaltext heißt es: 文明进化之社会, 其学说之兴废, 恒时 时 其社会之生活状态为变迁.

4 Im chinesischen Originaltext heißt es: 道与世更!

Witwen, die Waisen und Alleinstehenden werden ernährt“[5] (*Liji. Liyun*) und die so genannte Goldene Regel: „Was ich nicht möchte, das ein anderer mir antue, das werde auch ich nicht jemand anderem antun“[6] (公冶长 *Lun-yu* 5.12). Das sei aber falsch. Zwar könne man hier durchaus die Ideen von Freiheit und Gleichheit erkennen, aber die negativen konfuzianischen Prinzipien der Pietät, als der bedingungslosen Kindesliebe, und der Bruderliebe löschten diese positiven Ansätze gleich wieder aus.

Der Rest des Aufsatzes spricht fast nur noch von dem Problem, das die Stellung der Frau im Konfuzianismus für die moderne Gesellschaft darstellt. Dass Frauen nach dem Tod ihres Mannes nicht heiraten dürften, wie das *Liji* sagt (*fu si bu jia* 夫死不嫁), ist das größte Problem. Das sei im Westen viel besser. Und auch dass Männer und Frauen in der Öffentlichkeit nicht zusammensein dürften, sei nicht mehr zeitgemäß. Die Moral des Konfuzius sei eine feudalistische Moral[7] (Chen 1916: 349).

Die Konfuzianismuskritik des zwanzigsten Jahrhunderts hat eigentlich niemals etwas anderes gesagt, als das, was man schon bei Chen Duxiu lesen kann: Die Hauptkritikpunkte waren immer, dass der Konfuzianismus erstens einen Glauben an Hierarchien fordere, der für eine moderne Gesellschaft schädlich sei, zweitens, dass besonders die Stellung der Frau im Konfuzianismus mit modernem Denken nicht vereinbar sei, und drittens, dass der Konfuzianismus aus einem feudalistischem Zeitalter komme. Die Kritiker haben den Konfuzianismus also immer vor allem als ein soziales System verstanden, nicht als eine philosophische oder gar religiöse Lehre, die Werte enthielt, die man für eine moderne Gesellschaft fruchtbar machen konnte.

Als ich in den 1980er Jahren in Shanghai studierte, da war diese Kritik noch überall zu hören. Besonders berüchtigt war der Satz, dass hungers sterben eine sehr kleine Angelegenheit sei, während es eine sehr gravierende Sache sei, wenn man von der Tugend abkomme[8] (Cheng/Cheng 1981: 22 B, 301). Dieser Satz findet sich in den *Gesammelten Worten der Brüder Cheng Hao und Cheng Yi*, und er steht am Ende der Antwort zu der Frage danach, ob eine verwitwete Frau wieder heiraten dürfe. Cheng Yi sagt dazu, dass es diese Frage doch nur gebe, weil Frauen Angst davor hätten hungers zu sterben und deshalb wieder heiraten wollten, nicht etwa deshalb weil die Heirat für sie einen echten inneren Wert bedeute.

Konfuzianismusrezeption bei Otto Franke und Richard Wilhelm

Schon kurz nachdem Chen Duxiu den Konfuzianismus angegriffen hatte, kamen auch neue wissenschaftliche Erkenntnisse hinzu. Die Strömung der „Zweifler am Altertum“ (*yigupai* 疑古派) machte sich daran, die alten konfuzianischen Texte zu untersuchen und fand heraus, dass vieles, was man dem Herzog von Zhou oder Konfuzius zugeschrieben hatte, gar nicht von diesen Männern geschrieben worden sein konnte, sondern viel später war. Den Klassikern wurde damit ein Teil ihrer Autorität genommen. Das gab der Konfuzianismuskritik weiteren Auftrieb, der so stark war, dass auch westliche Sinologen der festen Überzeugung waren, dass der Konfuzianismus in China tot sei. Der berühmte deutsche Sinologe Otto Franke sagte 1929, dass der Konfuzianismus in der chinesischen Krise dieser Zeit sicherlich keine Rolle spielen könnte.

---

5 Im chinesischen Originaltext heißt es: 鳏寡孤独废疾者皆有所养.

6 Im chinesischen Originaltext heißt es: 我不欲人之加諸我也，吾亦欲無加諸人论语.

7 Im chinesischen Originaltext heißt es: 孔子生長封建時代所提倡之道德封建時代之道德也.

8 Im chinesischen Originaltext heißt es: 餓死事極小，失節事極大.

> … Oder höchstens: die eines Verstorbenen in einem zusammengestürzten Hause. Wer glaubt, den Konfuzianismus aus den Trümmern des alten China retten zu können oder zu sollen, der muss sich bewusst bleiben, dass er einen Leichnam trägt. Der mit Konfuzius und dem Konfuzianismus getriebene Kultus, der unter dem Einfluß ungeschichtlicher Vorstellungen im Abendlande vielfach Mode geworden ist, wird in China teils mit Erstaunen, teils mit einem Lächeln beobachtet. (O. Franke 1929:83, zit. in: W. Franke 1958:156)

Otto Franke hatte natürlich auch Max Weber gelesen, der gesagt hatte, dass konfuzianische Gesellschaften zur Modernisierung unfähig seien. Worauf Weber abzielte, das war natürlich der Konfuzianismus, von dem man in Europa gehört hatte, nachdem Männer wie Adam Smith, die im Gefolge des Kolonialismus nach China gekommen waren, das Urteil Hegels bestätigt hatten, dass China ein Land des ewigen Stillstandes sei. Was man damals für Konfuzianismus hielt, das waren gesellschaftliche Hierarchien, strikte Familienordnung, Untertanengeist und ein Loyalitätsgedanke, der nur Gehorsam bedeutete und jede Eigeninitiative erstickte. Konfuzianismus galt als fortschrittsfeindlich, nicht nur, was die Entwicklung von Technologien anging, sondern auch in Bezug auf den Handel. Das hatte natürlich auch mit der Praxis der Ming- und der Qing-Dynastie zu tun, die den privaten Kaufleuten eine Reihe von Einschränkungen auferlegten. Dass es einen „konfuzianischen Unternehmer“ (*ru shang* 儒商) geben könnte, konnte sich niemand vorstellen. Diese westliche Einschätzung hatte in China viele Anhänger. Deshalb kam in den zwanziger Jahren auch erstmals das Schlagwort von der vollständigen Verwestlichung (*quanpan xihua* 全盤西化) auf, die man durchführen müsse, um China zu modernisieren.

Ein anderer bekannter Sinologe, Joseph Levenson, hat in seiner Trilogie *Confucian China and its Modern Fate* Ende der 1950er Jahre die These aufgestellt, Konfuzius sei zwar nicht tot, doch habe China ihn ins Museum entsorgt. Man gehe mit ihm freundlich um – aber einen Einfluss auf die Gegenwart habe er nicht mehr (Levenson 1965: 76-82). Das war eine These, welche eine Gruppe von chinesischen Neukonfuzianern auf den Plan brachte, die nach der Machtübernahme durch die Kommunistische Partei das Land verlassen hatten und nach Hongkong bzw. Taiwan ausgewandert waren. Sie verfassten gemeinsam ein Manifest, mit dem sie die Welt darauf aufmerksam machen wollten, dass der Autoritarismus in China nicht gottgegeben bzw. kulturimmanent, sondern dass die konfuzianische Kultur nach wie vor lebendig sei und viele Elemente eines Humanismus enthalte, von dem die westliche Welt viel lernen könne.[9] Diese Auffassung ist auch heute in China weit verbreitet. Auch wenn sie häufig von sehr klischeehaften Vorstellungen ausgeht, wie sich die menschlichen Beziehungen im Westen gestalten,[10] propagiert sie doch mit großem Selbstbewusstsein Ideen davon, wie die eigene Kultur aussehe und dass der chinesische Humanismus dem westlichen überlegen sei.

Auch dies ist allerdings ein Punkt, der schon zu Beginn des zwanzigsten Jahrhunderts verbreitet war. Ein weiterer deutscher Sinologe ist in diesem Zusammenhang zu nennen: Richard Wilhelm, der ursprünglich als Theologe zur Mission in die deutsche Kolonie Qingdao gegangen war, dann aber vom „rechten Pfad“ abkam und immer größere Sympathien für die chinesische Kultur äußerte.

---

9 Eine englische Version des Manifests, das ursprünglich in der Zeitschrift *Minzhu pinglun* 民主評論 erschienen ist, findet sich z.B. als Appendix in: Chang 1958, 1962.

10 S. z.B. den in China heute sehr populären Autor Nan Huaijin 南懷瑾, (1996), der sich in seinem Buch Lunyu biecai 論語別裁 überaus kritisch, aber eben auch sehr klischeehaft, mit den amerikanischen Familienwerten auseinandersetzt.

Otto Franke, der zu Beginn des 20. Jahrhunderts viele Jahre in China gelebt hatte, schrieb die oben zitierten Worte wahrscheinlich gar nicht nur, weil er meinte, dass man in China viel über Konfuzianismus diskutierte, sondern weil ein Jahr zuvor, 1926, Richard Wilhelm sein berühmtes Buch *Die Seele Chinas* veröffentlicht hatte, in dem er immer wieder auf die Bedeutung von Konfuzius für China eingegangen war. Auch Wilhelm hatte zwar gesehen, dass der Konfuzianismus zu dieser Zeit nicht mehr in derselben Weise lebte wie unter der Qing-Dynastie, an deren Ende er nach Shandong gekommen war, aber er glaubte, dass es eben doch innere Werte gebe, die China beeinflusst hätten. Er schrieb:

> Aber wenn auch das Sterbliche an Kungtse in dieser neuen Welt sich auflösen wird: das Ewige an ihm, die große Wahrheit von der Harmonie zwischen Natur und Kultur, wird bleiben und wird der neuen Weltanschauung und Menschengestaltung einen starken Antrieb geben. Hierin ist er ewig. (Wilhelm 1926: 67)

Und:

> Konfuzius schafft ein Gebäude geistiger Kräfte, das imstande ist, die Kultur auf Jahrtausende hinaus zu tragen und zu umschließen... Was er auf der anderen Seite erstrebte, war Harmonie zwischen Natur und Kultur. Die Kultur sollte die Natur des Menschen nicht vergewaltigen oder verzerren, sondern verklären und läutern. So begründete er die Sippe als Grundlage der Gesellschaft. Innerhalb der Sippe leben natürliche Gefühle der Zuneigung. Eltern und Kinder lieben einander aus freiem Instinkt, ebenso Mann und Frau und die Geschwister untereinander. Diese Nächstenliebe ist kein schweres Muss, sondern reiner selbstverständlicher Naturtrieb. Es gilt nur, diese Triebe zu formen, dass sie harmonisch ineinandergreifen, dass bei aller Gemeinsamkeit des Gefühls Ordnung und Zucht gewahrt bleibt. Es entspricht dem Namen Vater, dass er seine Liebe dem Sohn gegenüber anders gestaltet als der Sohn dem Vater gegenüber. Der rechte Vater hat eine zärtliche Fürsorge für seinen Sohn, der rechte Sohn einen verehrungsvollen Gehorsam gegen den Vater. Der rechte Gatte übt eine gütige Rücksicht gegen die Gattin, die rechte Gattin weiß sich ihrem Gatten in Grazie zu fügen. Der ältere Bruder hilft seinem jüngeren Bruder und schützt ihn, der jüngere ordnet sich unter und gibt nach. So gestaltet sich die Familie zur Harmonie ihrer Beziehungen, und die Liebe wird verklärt durch die sanfte Leitung der Sitte. Von der kultivierten Natur der Sippe ist dann der Übergang nicht schwer zur natürlichen Kultur des Staates. Das Gefühl der ehrfurchtsvollen Liebe zum Vater, der freundschaftlichen Unterordnung unter den älteren Bruder wird zur Pflicht der Treue gegenüber dem Fürsten und der Unterordnung unter die Vorgesetzten und umgekehrt. So wird die Pflicht zur erweiterten Liebe und der Staat zur erweiterten Familie. Aber der Blick bleibt bei keinem begrenzten Gebilde haften. Wie sich der Himmel allgegenwärtig über die Erde schützend breitet, so bleibt die letzte Einheit der Kultur die Menschheit, harmonisch geordnet durch die Auswirkung letzter Ideale. (Wilhelm 1926: 223)

Wenn man diese Worte liest, dann hat man den Eindruck, dass Richard Wilhelm den Konfuzianismus mehr liebte als die meisten Chinesen seiner Zeit. Doch das stimmt nur halb: Es gab natürlich auch in China Denker, die andere Ansichten hatten als Chen Duxiu. Einer der wichtigsten von diesen war Feng Youlan, der den Konfuzianismus ja auch in den 1950er und 1960er Jahren verteidigte, indem er sagte, dass die Werte des Konfuzius universal gültig seien und nicht nur auf eine gesellschaftliche Schicht bezogen seien. Er sprach damals nicht über konkrete Forderungen des Konfuzianismus, wie sich jüngere gegenüber Älteren und Frauen gegenüber Männern zu verhalten hätten, sondern über die wichtigste Tugend des Konfuzianismus, nämlich die Menschlichkeit. Diese ist unabhängig von Hierarchien. Doch gehörte Feng Youlan zu einer Minderheit, und er hat für diese

Meinung schon vor Beginn der Kulturrevolution eine Selbstkritik schreiben müssen (Staiger 1969: 43, 50, 108).

Fazit

Es hat im zwanzigsten Jahrhundert also zwei Strömungen gegeben: Auf der einen Seite eine Gruppe, die den Konfuzianismus vor allem als eine Soziallehre ansah, die einen schädlichen Einfluss auf die Gesellschaft ausübte, weil sie Hierarchien befürwortete und damit Teile der Gesellschaft zur Unterordnung zwang. Auf der anderen Seite standen Diejenigen, die den Konfuzianismus eher als eine Philosophie verstanden, die dazu da ist, Konflikte in der Gesellschaft auszugleichen. Mit anderen Worten: Neben dem Konfuzianismus als hierarchischer Sozialstruktur gibt es auch den Konfuzianismus mit einem allgemeinen positiven Menschenbild. Man kann die Hierarchien deshalb positiv und negativ auffassen.

Nachdem in China die Kritik an Konfuzius lange Zeit sehr stark gewesen ist, ist in den letzten Jahrzehnten aus verschiedenen Gründen das Bedürfnis gewachsen, wieder an die Tradition anzuknüpfen. Das bringt mit sich, dass man sich weniger auf den Konfuzianismus als soziale Organisationsform konzentriert, bei dem es eine Reihe von Problemen gibt, wenn man ihn konkret auf die heutige Gesellschaft anwenden möchte. Stattdessen konzentriert man sich wieder mehr auf das konfuzianische Menschenbild. Doch das Problem des Antikonfuzianismus ist damit noch nicht gelöst.

Ich denke, dass das Problem heute ist, dass beide Seiten recht haben. Zwar gibt es im Konfuzianismus universell gültige Ideen, die für die Welt interessant sein können. Aber gleichzeitig gibt es natürlich auch die negative Seite. Wenn man liest, wie positiv Richard Wilhelm im Zitat oben über die Fünf Beziehungen schreibt, dann könnte man meinen, dass die chinesische Gesellschaft aufgrund des Konfuzianismus immer von Harmonie gekennzeichnet gewesen wäre. Jeder weiß aber, dass das so nicht stimmt. Natürlich haben Menschen zu recht gegen die rigiden Moralvorstellungen des Konfuzianismus rebelliert, und natürlich ist die Stellung der Frau im Konfuzianismus ein echtes Problem.

Viele Dinge, die der Konfuzianismus lehrt, sind gar nicht verschieden von dem, was man im Westen auch glaubt. Aber es gibt auch Dinge, die im Westen auf Unverständnis stoßen. Wenn ich in Vorträgen zum Beispiel Bilder von den 24 Vorbildern der Kindespietät zeige (Doré 1919: 469, 500), dann müssen westliche Zuschauer meistens lachen, weil sie sich gar nicht vorstellen können, dass dies ernst gemeint sein könnte. Wenn ein Kind seine Oberbekleidung abnimmt, damit es selbst von den Mücken gestochen wird und nicht seine Eltern, dann erscheint dies für einen durchschnittlichen Europäer wie eine groteske Übertreibung. Früher kannte ich solche Bilder nur aus alten Büchern, die westliche Missionare im neunzehnten Jahrhundert verfasst hatten. Als ich in den 1980er Jahren in China studierte, konnte man sie nirgendwo sehen – der chinesische Ikonoklasmus des beginnenden 20. Jahrhunderts fand sie genauso lebensfremd wie der durchschnittliche Europäer. Heute aber finden sich Darstellungen der 24 Vorbilder der Kindespietät an vielen öffentlichen Plätzen, und man kann jetzt allenthalben in China auch wieder kleine Büchlein kaufen, in denen diese Bilder abgebildet sind.

Es gibt sehr viele ähnliche Dinge, die uns Europäer in China überraschen, weil sie auf den ersten Blick so unglaublich unmodern anmuten: Da ist zum Beispiel ein kleiner Lehrtext aus dem achtzehnten Jahrhundert, der den einfachen Titel *Schülerregeln* trägt (*Dizi gui* 弟子規). In Europa kennt ihn sicherlich kaum jemand und bis vor kurzem war er auch in der Volksrepublik China nicht weit verbreitet. Doch jetzt wird er in China immer häufiger zu Unterrichtszwecken verwendet. Auch dies weckt im Westen großes Erstaunen, weil man sich gar nicht vorstellen kann, dass die Inhalte dieser Texte die Menschheit weiterbringen können. Die Tugenden, die sie verbreiten – Ehrfurcht vor den Eltern, Gehorsam, Disziplin, Rücksichtnahme – erscheinen zu einfach.

Auf das politische System des Konfuzianismus, in dem ein Untertan dem Herrscher Gehorsam schuldet, möchte ich hier nicht eingehen. Dies ist eine sehr schwierige Frage, denn natürlich ist die Vorstellung davon, wann man im Konfuzianismus gehorsam sein muss und wann nicht, von vielen konfuzianischen Denkern im Laufe der Jahrhunderte unterschiedlich beantwortet worden. Doch ein kurzes Beispiel für die Komplexität des Sachverhalts sei dennoch angesprochen.

Als in den 1980er Jahren die Diskussion um die asiatischen Werte begann, da sagten Singapurs Staatspräsident Lee Kuan Yew und der malaysische Ministerpräsident Mahathir, dass bestimmte autoritäre Formen erlaubt sein müssten, und dass sie mit asiatischen Werten vereinbar seien. Exemplarisch wurde einem jungen Amerikaner die Prügelstrafe verabreicht. Hier interessierten die Vertreter der asiatischen Werte also auch die sozialen Aspekte, die mit der alten Tradition verbunden war – dabei war es gar nicht so wichtig, dass die Prügelstrafe in Singapur ursprünglich von den Briten eingeführt worden war. Sie ist also, obwohl es sie in China auch gab, natürlich nichts Konfuzianisches. Dennoch zeigt der Fall, dass asiatische Werte gebraucht wurden, um zu beweisen, dass der Staat das Recht haben soll, Individuen zum Gehorsam zu zwingen. Ob dies mit Konfuzianismus zu vereinbaren ist, über diese Frage kann man als Konfuzianer aber gewiss streiten.

Auf jeden Fall ist es aber gerade im politischen Kontext wichtig sich daran zu erinnern, dass es zwar solche unmodernen Praktiken wie die Prügelstrafe gibt, die mit traditionellen Werten begründet wurden, dass aber die Antitraditionalisten wie Chen Duxiu genauso wie Staatsoberhäupter, die die Tradition für ihre eigenen Zwecke befürworten, nicht alle Teile des Konfuzianismus bedacht haben. Jeder, der etwas vom Konfuzianismus versteht, der wird bei der Erwähnung des Schlagworts von der Harmonischen Gesellschaft an die wichtige Stelle im dreizehnten Kapitel des *Lunyu* denken, in der es heißt: „Der Edle ist harmonisch, macht sich aber nicht gemein, der Geringe macht sich gemein, ist aber nicht harmonisch“[11] (*Lun-yu* 13.23). Diese Stelle zeigt – zumindest wenn der Satz wie hier übersetzt wird – dass die konfuzianische Harmonie etwas ganz anderes ist, als es sich viele Menschen im Westen, aber vielleicht auch in China denken. Es geht bei ihr nicht darum, dass man Konflikten aus dem Weg geht, sondern darum, dass man mit Konflikten so umgeht, dass beide Seiten Freunde bleiben können. Europäer meinen häufig, dass man sich in China nicht traue, zu sagen, wenn man eine andere Meinung hat. Aber das Ideal eines jeden Konfuzianers der chinesischen Tradition ist es gewesen, Widerspruch zu leisten, wenn er meinte, dass in der Politik etwas Falsches geschah. Der Satz des Konfuzius über die Harmonie des Edlen ist die Grundlage für diese Idee. Damit ist natürlich auch gemeint, dass der Konfuzianismus meint, dass dem Einzelnen das Recht auf Widerspruch zusteht und dass er nichts zu befürchten haben sollte, wenn er einem Vorgesetzten widerspricht. Konfuzius-Institute in aller Welt sollten deshalb Orte sein, an denen man unterschiedliche Standpunkte zu China in Freundschaft vertritt.

Vor allem glaube ich, dass es wichtig ist, sich klar zu machen, was die traditionelle Kultur Chinas eigentlich bedeutet, wenn man sie wiederbeleben möchte. Mit anderen Worten: Ich glaube, dass es zwar wichtig ist, wenn man traditionelle Werte wie die Harmonie pflegt, aber dass man gleichzeitig das Thema der Hierarchien und der Gleichberechtigung

11 Im chinesischen Originaltext heißt es: 君子和而不同，小人同而不和.

der Frau nicht übergehen darf. Neben der Harmonie hat es natürlich in der chinesischen Gesellschaft immer auch den Widerspruch gegeben. Man sollte an dieser Stelle keine Lücken lassen oder Tabus haben, sondern man sollte diese Dinge ansprechen und sagen, wie man mit ihnen umgehen möchte. Erst wenn man befriedigende Antworten darauf gegeben hat, wird es gelingen, die Skeptiker in China zu überzeugen. Ich habe viele Frauen in China getroffen, die den Lehren des Konfuzius gegenüber zurückhaltend sind, weil sie befürchten, dass sie für sie selbst von Nachteil sein können – ganz wie das Chen Duxiu zu Anfang des 20. Jahrhunderts sagte. Für „Konfuzianismus global" wird es notwendig sein, diese Probleme zu lösen und die gegensätzlichen Positionen zu vereinen.

Literatur

Chang, Carsun (1958, 1962) *The Development of Neo-Confucian Thought*, London/New York: Greenwood Press.

Chen Duxiu 陳獨秀 (1916) *Kongzi zhi dao yu xiandai shenghuo* 孔子之道與現代生活, [Die Lehre des Konfuzius und das moderne Leben] in *Xin Qingnian* 新青年 2.4, S. 345-351.

Cheng Hao 程颢 und Cheng Yi 程颐（1981）*Ercheng quanshu, Yishu* 二程全书·遗书二十二 [Gesammelte Worte von Cheng Hao und Cheng Yi, Nachlass 22], 4 Bde., Beijing: Zhonghua shu ju.

Henan Cheng shi yishu 河南程氏遺書, enthalten in Cheng Hao und Cheng Yi (1981).

Doré, Henri (1919) *Recherches sur les superstitions en Chine. IIIème partie*, Shanghai: Imprimerie de T'ou-sè-wè.

Franke, Otto (1929) „Das Konfuzianische System und sein Ende", in: *Zeitschrift für Missionskunde und Religionswissenschaft*, 44. 3, S. 65-85.

Franke, Wolfgang (1958) *Das Jahrhundert der chinesischen Revolution*, München: Oldenbourg.

Fukuyama, Francis (1992) *The End of History and the Last Man*, New York, NY: Free Press.

Levenson, Joseph (1965) *Confucian China and its Modern Fate. A Trilology,* Bd. 3, Berkeley: University of California Press.

Li Ling 李零 (2007) *Sang jia gou. Wo du Lunyu* 丧家狗- 我读《论语》 [Ein streunender Hund – Wie ich das „Lun yu" lese], 2 Bde., Taiyuan: Shanxi Renmin Chubanshe].

Li Yuxiu 李毓秀 (18. Jh.) *Dizigui* 弟子规 [Schülerregeln].

Lun-yu. Gespräche. Übersetzt und herausgegeben von Ralf Moritz. Leipzig: Philipp Reclam jun. 1982.

Nan Huaijin 南懷瑾, (1990, 1996) *Lunyu biecai* 論語別裁 [Ein anderer Zuschnitt für die Gespräche des Konfuzius], Shanghai (zuerst Taibei 1976).

Staiger, Brunhild (1969) *Das Konfuziusbild im kommunistischen China: die Neubewertung von Konfuzius in der chinesisch-marxistischen Geschichtsschreibung*, Wiesbaden: O. Harrassowitz.

Wilhelm, Richard (1930) *Li Gi. Das Buch der Riten, Sitten und Gebräuche*. Jena 1930. Neuauflage: Diederichs Gelbe Reihe Bd. 31.

Wilhelm, Richard (1926) *Die Seele Chinas*, Erstauflage, Berlin: Reimar Hobbing.

Yi Baisha 易白沙 (1916a), „Kongzi pingyi shang 孔子平議上" [Kritische Beurteilung von Kongzi, Teil 1], in *Qingnian zazhi* 青年杂志 1.6, S. 571-576 (Nachdruck Tokio 1970).

Yi Baisha 易白沙 (1916b), „Kongzi pingyi xia 海孔子平議下", [Kritische Beurteilung von Kongzi, Teil 2], in *Xin qingnian* 新青年 2.1, S. 25-30.

Yu Dan 于丹 (2006) *Lunyu xin de* 論語心得 [Konfuzius im Herzen], Peking: Zhonghua shuju.

Jens Damm

The Multiculturalization of Taiwan: From a Unified Han-Identity to the "Four Great Ethnic Groups"

There is no doubt that in Taiwan today the concept of multiculturalism is "celebrated [...] as a way of resolving ethnic differences within complex societies" (Simon 2009)[1] and applauded by the mainstream political parties as well as by most of the ethnic groups. In the West, however, the term "multiculturalism" is often subject to criticism, rejected on the grounds that it is only a euphemism for the alleged unwillingness of immigrants to integrate in a host society and often connoted with an uncritical view of cultural relativism (Joppke 2004; Koopmans 2005; Vertovec and Wessendorf 2010). This paper examines the ways that political developments have helped to shape Taiwan's multicultural policies during recent decades as well as the discursive influence that these multicultural policies have had on the image and the self-perception of the "four great ethnic groups," which are now widely perceived as "essentialized" and as possessing a long and objectively verifiable history. Taiwan's "four great ethnic groups" (*Taiwan si da zuqun* 臺灣四大族群) (Ngo and Wang 2011: 3) are the Hoklo (*fulao* 福佬), the Hakka (*kejia* 客家), the Mainlanders (*waishengren* 外省人) and the Aboriginal peoples (*yuanzhumin* 原住民). Issues related to identity politics and the contributions that the various groups have made to the discourse are also investigated. In addition, it will be argued that this broad new spectrum, which includes the division of Hoklo, Hakka and Mainlanders into separate ethnic groups, questions the standard formulation of a homogeneous Han ethnicity and that this discourse, originally introduced by DPP leaders to limit the dominant influence of the Hoklo and to provide an alternative to differentiating between the Taiwanese and the Mainlanders on the basis of their "origin," has gained popular support within Taiwanese society and the various ethnic groups, probably with the exception of the Mainlanders. Interestingly enough, although the rather deliberate construction of these ethnicities has been sharply criticized by various sides in the political discourse, the legal regulations and self-organization of various groups followed precisely those lines (Ngo and Wang 2011: 3) and while certain nuances still survive, the existence of ethnic groups, even within a Han ethnicity that was formerly assumed to be unified, is generally accepted in Taiwan.[2]

The paper is structured as follows: first of all, there is a general overview, which also serves as an introduction to the notion of multiculturalism, with a particular emphasis on the international discourse and its translation into the specific context in Taiwan,

---

1 The strong and usually un-reflected criticism in Western countries that is leveled against any policy of multiculturalism is usually directed against the "youngest" group of migrants, that is, the former guest workers and refugees. In Taiwan, these groups are (still) rather small; only since the 1990s have foreign workers been arriving in Taiwan, but they do not have the right to permanent residence and this limits their opportunities to claim specific multicultural or intercultural rights. This situation has, however, slowly begun to change. As Corcuff said: "In Taiwan, multiculturalism is thus usually understood as the celebration of cultural and linguistic specificities of the island's 'original' populations" (Corcuff 2002: 163). – The research for this paper was partly funded by a grant from the National Science Council, Taiwan: NSC 99-2410-H-309-012.

2 In contrast to Mainland China, the term Han 漢 is seldom used for the Chinese language, which is called Hanyu 漢語 in Mainland China, and either Zhongwen 中文 or Huayu 華語 in Taiwan. When referring to the ethnicity, the term Huaren 華人 is now most often used.

Berliner China-Hefte/Chinese History and Society 41 (2012), pp. 72-89

including various policy measures. After this first section, the different perceptions and self-perceptions of the four ethnic groups are identified and examined within the framework of multiculturalism in Taiwan. The material employed in this paper includes published official statements, newspaper articles, academic texts and examples of the ethnification discourses found in the new media. The key questions dealt with here are the ways in which political changes have influenced the idea of multiculturalism and the way that various ethnic groups have reacted to these changes, even if these ethnic groups have actually been "constructed during this political process"; the underlying reasons for the differing reactions of the various ethnic groups are also discussed. Finally, there is the question of whether the notion of multiculturalism is linked to the creation of a particular Taiwanese political identity to counteract the all-embracing Chinese identity that prevailed in the state-led discourse during the first decades of the ROC on Taiwan.

From Multi-Racialism to Multiculturalism: The Political Developments from Sun Yat-sen to Taiwan's Democratization

The current popularity of "multiculturalism" (*duoyuan wenhua zhuyi* 多元文化主義) in Taiwan can be seen as the continuation of earlier developments and also as a counter-reaction to these, that has its roots in the history of the early Republic of China (ROC) and the related formation of a Chinese nation, the Sinification policy of the Kuomintang (Guomindang/KMT) after 1949 in Taiwan, the dramatic processes of transformation that took place in Taiwan after 1987 and were accompanied by ethnic tensions, and finally the shift in identity-building in the late 1990s and the new millennium which was aimed at overcoming ethnic cleavages.

Sun Yat-sen, in the "Three Principles of the People" (*Sanmin zhuyi* 三民主義) specifically mentioned that the "Chinese nation" could be seen as built on five "races" (Manchus, Han, Mongols, Muslims, and Tibetans) (Duara 1993: 24). The *theoretical concept* of the ROC (including the ROC on Taiwan after 1949) was therefore based on the idea of a "multiracial" nation, which was embedded in the official ideology of the KMT, for example, Article 5 of the 1947 constitution stated: "There shall be equality among the various racial groups in the Republic of China. Despite the fact that the "notion of a unified Han nationality *(minzu* 民族*)* that occupies 91.96 percent of China's population" (Gladney 1994: 98-99; 2004)[3] had only arisen during the late 19th century, doubts about the unity of the Han ethnicity were not allowed. That is to say, the various Han groups, no matter how different in language, customs and history, were seen as one unified group. In 1949, therefore, when the KMT moved the central government to Taipei, the Mongolian and Tibetan Affairs Commission (*Zhonghua minguo Meng Zang weiyuanhui* 中華民國蒙藏委員會)[4], which did not have any relevance whatsoever for

3 Gladney commented: "The use and perhaps invention of the term Han minzu [漢民族] was a brilliant attempt to mobilize other non-Cantonese, especially northern Mandarin speakers, and the powerful Zhejiang and Shanghainese merchants, into one overarching national group pitted against the Manchu and other foreigners threatening China during the unstable period following the Unequal Treaties. … The 'imagined' Han majority nationality and derivative minority nationalities that were created. (and) led to the invention and legitimization of the Han" (Gladney 1994: 98-99).

4 After the founding of the Republic, and as early as April 1912, the Commission was established as the "Mongolian and Tibetan Affairs Agency" (Meng Zang gongzuochu 蒙藏工作處) and some months later was renamed as the "Bureau of Mongolian and Tibetan Affairs" (Meng Zang shiwuchu 蒙藏事務局). In 1914, it became the "Mongolian and Tibetan Affairs Yuan" (Meng Zang yuan 蒙藏院) directly under the control of the Northern government. In 1929, it was finally named the Mongolian and

the regions remaining under control of the KMT, was also transferred to Taiwan, but none of the various ethnic Han Chinese groups in Taiwan (such as the Hakka, for example, who had long since formed a specific ethnic group) were perceived as possessing their own cultural roots (Constable 1996; Yang 1993) and the Aborigines were even denied any official representative body. The behavior and the *actual policy* of the KMT, at that time, did not leave any room for doubt with regard to the supposed superiority of the Han culture and the underlying implicit idea that China (that is, including Taiwan) was a pure Han Chinese state (Chou 2006; Phillips 2003; Wang 2005b).

Taiwan was regarded as part of the Chinese nation which was essentially seen as dominated by the Han Chinese. Language, cultural policy and a nation-state discourse were formulated according to the concept of a homogeneous Taiwan that formed part of the larger imagined construct of the Republic of China within the borders as they were drawn in 1949. This could be seen in the language policy, which focused on promoting an alien language, the North Chinese dialect, and enforcing its use in Taiwan as the national language (Mandarin/*guoyu* 國語). The North Chinese culture and religious beliefs were also given preference over local customs: the December 1952 KMT edict, for example, banned the use of the still widely-popular Japanese language in Taiwan's government, schools and printed media and also instituted measures to repress the Japanese influence on customs and religious beliefs (Hsiau 1997). An even stronger Sinification campaign was launched with the Cultural Renaissance Movement (*Zhonghua minguo fuxing wenhua yundong* 中華民國文化復興運動) in 1966: Taiwan's Aboriginal people were now told that their culture was worth less than the Chinese culture and that a project was being set up to help to "civilize" them (Stark 2009: 119). In this way, despite official references to other ethnic groups, Taiwan was seen as a monolithic Chinese society and Taiwan's historical roots were not recognized as being different from those of China. In addition, the KMT at that time exercised colonial rule over Taiwan with the aim of constructing Taiwan as a Chinese model province (Phillips 2003: 14). Ironically, these policy measures showed that Taiwan, during that period, was not a homogeneous nation, but a combination of various ethnic groups: the instruments of martial law were only used to sinicize every group that was seen as "un"- Chinese. While paying constant lip service to Sun Yat-sen, the Sinification of Taiwan was undertaken in such a way that little space was left for any multicultural policy or for the acceptance of difference (Wei 2008). Taiwan, as a centuries-long migration destiny for the Han Chinese from Fujian and Guangdong, after having been settled for thousands of years by Austronesian Aboriginals, was now, by means of strict authoritarian policy measures, to be developed into a "China en miniature" possessing, in particular, the features of the Northern Chinese culture. Nevertheless, two distinctions were made between the so-called Mainlanders, *waishengren* (外省人), the group who arrived with Chiang Kai-shek in 1945 and in greater numbers, in 1949, and the *benshengren,* or "Native Taiwanese" (本省人) (Corcuff 2011b; Wu 2011). These distinctions were, first of all, the so-called "provincial origin"

Tibetan Affairs Commission (Meng Zang weiyuanhui 蒙藏委員會). In January 2013, however, the Commission will be re-organized and will become part of the "Mainland Affairs Council of the Executive Yuan" (Xingzhengyuan dalu weiyuanhui 行政院大陸委員會) under the name of "the Mongolian and Tibetan Bureau" (Menggu, Xizang shiwuchu 蒙古、西藏事務處).
See <http://www.mtac.gov.tw/epages.php?lang=5&page=131>, accessed 1 May 2012, see also <http://www.mtac.gov.tw/> and the Wikipedia entry <http://zh.wikipedia.org/wiki/%E4%B8%AD%E8%8F%AF%E6%B0%91%E5%9C%8B%E8%92%99%E8%97%8F%E5%A7%94%E5%93%A1%E6%9C%83>, accessed 1 May 2012.

(*shengji* 省籍), this being the origin of two contrasting identities (Corcuff 2002) and, secondly, the language issue. The new government, composed only of officials who were fluent in Mandarin (or Chinese languages not commonly found in Taiwan), punished generations of children for speaking Japanese, Hoklo, Hakka or any of the Aboriginal languages, which created further feelings of difference between the "islanders" *benshengren* and the "Mainlanders" *waishengren*. With regard to political representation and the civil service recruitment process, 85 per cent of the people of the original "Taiwan province" were given only 5 per cent of the representation (Ngo and Wang 2011: 3), that is to say, most posts were given to the Mainlanders, which led to increasing alienation among the Hoklo who regarded themselves as a discriminated-against majority. During the early years of the rule of Chiang Ching-kuo,[5] the son of Chiang Kai-shek (Jiang Jieshi) and, at that time, the President of the ROC/Taiwan, Taiwan's cultural policy was still focused on promoting (ROC) Chinese nationalism and on homogenizing culture in the sense of Sinification; right up until the end of Chiang Ching-kuo's rule, Taiwan continued to be regarded as a monolithic Han Chinese dominated area: "The KMT was bidding to be 'more Chinese than China' – the exiles keeping alive the authentic cultural traditions" (Wang 2005b: 1). Things slowly began to change in the late 1970s, when the Taiwanese started to play a greater role in the government and the first signs of Taiwanization began to emerge in society after the global community had largely shifted its official recognition to Beijing. Chiang Ching-kuo now introduced a policy which admitted the particularities of Taiwan and also increased the number of Taiwanese in his government and the civil service. Cultural and linguistic affairs were subsumed under the mandate of the Executive Yuan Council for Cultural Affairs (CCA) from 1982 onwards. Jiang Jingguo's broad-based attempt

> to indigenize or localize the ROC state apparatus within the territorial confines of Taiwan in the aftermath of its expulsion from the United Nations was also the point of departure for his attempt to defuse the longstanding conflict between the Mainlanders and the Taiwanese. His famous declaration that he was Taiwanese, despite his thick Zhejiang accent and obvious Mainland origins, had important ramifications for the meaning of ethnic indigenization and the process of Taiwanization in particular (Chen 2007: 9).

However, the mid-1980s through to the late 1990s were then characterized by the democratization processes and the rapid liberalization of society, including the increasing influence of the Taiwanese independence movement (Taidu 台獨) as well as a broader process in culture and literature known as nativization (*bentuhua* 本土化) (Hsiau 2005; Jacobs 2005; Makeham 2005; Makeham and Hsiau 2005; Yoshihisa and Damm 2011). Clashes occurred more and more frequently between the old ROC inclined forces which considered Taiwan to be part of a homogeneous Han Chinese nation, and the adherents to a Taiwanese identity who wanted to see the "alien and foreign" ROC nationalism replaced with primordial Taiwanese nationalism; this nativization process involved the replacement of one form of nationalism with another (Neder 2003) as well as increasing awareness that Taiwan was multicultural. Even as early as 1987, however, due to influential social movements, the DPP had stated in the party program that bilingual education should be provided and that there should be a focus on Taiwanese history and

5 Chiang Ching-kuo became President three years after his father's death in 1978, and remained President until his death in 1988.

culture, which they recognized as a native culture parallel to a Chinese culture (Ho 2005). And it is no wonder, then, that only two years later, in 1989, the newly established Democratic Progressive Party (DPP) started to employ the anthropological concept of the ethnic group (*zuqun* 族群) (and not a racial concept) to describe Taiwanese society as composed of the Hoklo, Hokkien, Mainlanders and Aborigines, "Taiwan's Four Great Ethnic Groups." This usage of ethnicity emphasized the cultural differences between the groups, and also their common historical experience of being on Taiwan rather than in China (Rudolph 2004: 98).[6] This pluralization of Taiwanese society is hardly imaginable without the political and democratic transformation which started with the founding of the Democratic Progressive Party (DPP), the first opposition party to be tolerated, in 1986, when the state of emergency and the end of the prohibition on founding other parties was lifted by decree of Jiang Jingguo. From 1986 to 1996, Taiwan completed the formal transition to democracy, marked by political reforms in the ruling KMT, constitutional reforms, and a power shift to the DPP at various administrative levels, for example, when Chen Shui-bian became Mayor of Taipei in 1996, another milestone was reached on the road to changing the dominance of the Mainlanders' rule. The KMT later gave official recognition to the value of Taiwanese culture, but only as a sub-culture or "local culture" within Chinese culture (Wang 2003a: 96-97). The former President, Lee Teng-hui (Li Denghui), of the KMT, spoke of "a community of 21 million with a shared fate" composed of "the new Taiwanese" (Chen 2001; Lee 1999; Li 1999; Zheng 1988). In 1993, still under the guidance of Lee Teng-hui, the government began to offer official support to local "integrated community development" projects emphasizing Taiwan's multicultural nature. In addition, democratization and liberalization were accompanied by the intensive process of Taiwanization from below (that is, indigenization and localization, but not necessarily de-Sinification) and a focus on the cultural and ethnic diversity of Taiwan. The first official claims, at national level, that Taiwan was a multicultural country derive from 1997, when Lee Teng-hui was still President (Wang 2003b: 1); the idea of multiculturalism then spread rapidly during the late 1990s and achieved an even greater momentum with the election of Chen Shui-bian as the first successful presidential candidate of the oppositional Democratic Progressive Party (DPP). With Chen Shui-bian as President, multiculturalism was announced as the official policy: Chen stated firmly that the ROC on Taiwan was a multi-ethnic and multi-cultural country, that multiculturalism would be the basic national policy (Wang 2003b: 301) and defined Taiwanization in terms of enabling "Taiwan's own cultures to interact naturally with Chinese cultures and world cultures" (ibid). After 2000, in particular, a raft of measures was introduced under the rubric of "multicultural Taiwan" and since then, the Taiwanese discourse on multiculturalism has focused mainly on the four ethnic groups mentioned in the official discourse in today's Taiwan. In addition to this, a top-down, state-sponsored definition of ethnic groups has been set up for the specific purpose of empowering the marginalized groups, while ethnic identities and multiculturalism are reflected in the more self-reflexive and interactive parts of the new media which play such an important role in creating and preserving cultural diversity. International developments played a certain role, for example, the UN, with its focus on Aboriginal peoples (Loa 2007), and the UN

6 The term zuqun 族群 is also interesting. While the term "ethnic nation" or "nation" was usually referred to as minzoku in Japanese or minzu 民族 in Chinese, the Taiwanese anthropologist, Xie Shizhong, in 1989, used the term zuqun to describe an ethnic group focusing on the self-perception of the specific group (Rudolph 2003: 207).

General Assembly's adoption of the Declaration on the Rights of Indigenous Peoples was referred to by the DPP and by the representative of the Aboriginal peoples (Wang 2003b: 96-97).[7] Of course, political considerations within the DPP government played an important role during the rule of Chen Shui-bian and these considerations were behind the Aborigines being attributed a crucial role: first of all, they were regarded as the only non-Han minority in Taiwan and, secondly, since they had been settled in Taiwan for at least 6500 years, they served as "proof" that Taiwan was different from China, as Lin Chiang-yu, the Director of the Planning Department at the Council for Indigenous Peoples, said:

> The Gezaixi (歌仔戲, an opera performed in Hoklo) of the Fulo [Hoklo] or the Ping-Opera of the Mainlanders, both came from Mainland China. When Taiwan's cultural groups perform in other countries, people will feel that Taiwan is similar to Mainland China. Taiwanese culture is similar to Chinese Culture. Only Taiwan's Aboriginal culture can present Taiwanese culture as different to Chinese culture. (quoted in Wang Li-jung 2003: 167)

The policy under the new President, Ma Ying-jeou (Ma Yingjiu), who came to power in 2008, and was re-elected in 2012, has generally followed the already existing policy of multiculturalism, but some contradictions have been observed which derive, to some extent, from the KMT's previous emphasis on a unified Han race/ethnicity. In his inaugural speech in 2008, Ma Ying-jeou talked of promoting "harmony among sub-ethnic groups," but, in 2010, he described the people on the two sides of the Taiwan Strait as "ethnic Chinese" and "descendants of the legendary emperors, Yan and Huang".[8] Other remarks also showed a new ambivalence, so that the positioning of Ma Ying-jeou with regard to the relation between Taiwanese culture and Chinese culture remains unclear, for example, when talking about 100 years of ROC celebration, Ma defined Taiwan's culture as "Chinese culture with Taiwanese characteristics," while the DPP legislator, Chen Ting-fei (陳亭妃), stressed that "Taiwanese culture is Taiwanese culture and Chinese culture is Chinese culture," adding that "Taiwan has its own culture and it is brand new. There is no such thing as a Greater China culture here" (Ko 2010). Nevertheless, there does not seem to have been any dramatic change in the actual policy: the Hakka Basic Law was enacted on 27 January 2010 and under the terms of this new legislation, the Hakka affairs administration has been incorporated into the national public servants' examination. In addition, any townships, cities and communities in which the Hakka account for over 33 per cent of the population will be listed as key Hakka culture development districts where the Hakka language will serve as one of the official languages (n.a. 2010b).[9] And while the question of unification or independence plays a role in party politics, the "imagined community has shifted from a Taiwan that embraced a vast population and hinterland, to the island of Taiwan" and "that all major political, economic and social developments should be undertaken in the interest of this island and its populace" (Ngo and Wang 2011: 7).

---

7 For the global influence, and, in particular, the influence of Europe, see Damm 2012.

8 English translation of the inaugural speech made by the President of the Republic of China, Ma Ying-jeou, on 20 May 2008, <http://www.teco.org.au/ATL May 08.ht=-wA2QAX> m. President Ma Ying-jeou's National Day Address "Taiwan's Renaissance," 10 October 2010, Focus Taiwan News Channel, <http://focustaiwan.tw/ShowNews/WebNews_Detail.aspx?ID=201010100004&Type=aIPL>, accessed 15 November 2010.

9 The full text is available at <http://www.glin.gov/download.action?fulltextId=246943&documentId=227543&glinID=227543>, accessed 10 January 2011.

In addition to political discussions and measures, the Taiwanese academic discourse on multiculturalism and ethnic groups also exerted a tremendous influence on the positive evaluation of multiculturalism. Although this discourse tends to show support for the DDP, it has also gained far-reaching support within the traditionally more KMT-inclined Hakka and Aborigines representatives in academics research centers. The Taiwanese academic discourse falls under three main headings: firstly, the translation of the works of Western authors, in particular, those dealing with Canada, the discussion of these works in universities and colleges, and the possibility of adapting and employing multicultural policies in Taiwan.[10] Secondly, the deconstructivist discourses which have analyzed the conceptual development of ethnic groups and denied the essentialist understanding of fixed ethnic boundaries. Thirdly, the wide range of mainly empirical studies that focus on specific groups: these studies have often been based on an essentialist ethnic discourse and have mirrored popular nationalist ideas, such as those put forward by Anthony Smith, who claimed that modern nationalism builds on the pre-existing kinship, religious and belief systems of ancient primordial ethnic groups (Smith 1987, 1995, 2001).

The Taiwanese deconstructivist discourses, which deal with the construction and politically motivated boundaries of ethnic groups in Taiwan, are sometimes supportive of the new policy, as in the case of Wang Fuzhang, a sociologist at the Academia Sinica. Starting from the early settler days and progressing through to the present, Wang Fuzhang examined the ways in which ethnicities have been constructed in Taiwan, and how the focus of the general census during the Japanese era, the early period of KMT rule and today, has shifted between the de-Sinification of origin, languages, ethnic descriptions, and race, creating and deconstructing forms of belonging (Wang 1998, 2002, 2005a, 2008). Nevertheless, Wang Fuzhang, and Zhou Wanyao (Chou Wan-yao) (Chou 2006), probably the best known academics in Taiwan writing on multiculturalism and ethnic groups in Taiwan, emphasize the fact that popular sentiment has been integrated in the new discourses on multiculturalism and that these have been accepted by the representative organizations of the various ethnic groups which are today independent of the state due to the existence of a strong civil society. This differs from earlier periods when a state-led discourse was enforced with harsh legal restrictions, as happened, for example, during the Kominka, the Japanization movement after 1933 and the Chinese Cultural Renaissance Movement of the 1960s. Other authors, such as Shih Chih-yu (Shi Zhiyu) (Shi 1999, 2003, 2004, 2005b, 2006), a political scientist at the National Taiwan university, and Yih-jye Hwang (Huang Yizhi) (Hwang 2006, 2007) described Taiwan's multiculturalism as a purely discursive construction of identity, and while not denying the significance of some historical factors, argued that Taiwanese identity, in ontological terms, exists only in discourse and cannot be taken as fixed, essential, or permanent. They voiced strong criticism of what they called underlying political inclinations while, at the same time, (particularly in the case of Shih Chi-yu, who is a well-known commentator in the mainstream press) taking a pan-Chinese (Han) identity for granted. They accused the so-called indigenous wing of the KMT of "constructing the impression that the Taiwanese are not Chinese" (Shi 2003: 489) and argued that pro-independence leaders in Taiwan were deliberately redrawing ethnic boundaries and rewriting their histories in the hope of generating Taiwanese national consciousness (ibid).

10 For the influence of Western and European discourses, see also Damm 2012.

The third part of the discourse sees ethnic differences as given, and focuses on policy measures, governance and ethnic entrepreneurship, language policy and language practice. This category includes most of the Master's theses written at the newly established Hakka, Aboriginal and Taiwan studies centers, such as the Taiwan Studies Center at the National Chengchi University, the Graduate Institute of Taiwan Culture, Languages, and Literature and the Graduate Institute of Taiwan History at the Taiwan Normal University in Northern Taiwan, the Graduate Study Centers of Taiwan Studies at Chang Jung Christian University and Kaohsiung Normal University in the South, the Aboriginal Study Center at National Songhua University and the Hakka Center at National Central University.

The Four Ethnic Groups: Discourse, Attributed Identity and Self-Identity

A close look at the four ethnic groups mentioned above reveals differences in the particular political discourse, the identity politics, the identity attributed to each of them by other groups, and their self-identity. In addition, the various groups made their own contributions to the discourse to varying degrees.

The indigenous population is made up of the descendants of the Austronesian peoples who arrived in Taiwan some 6000 to 8000 years ago and their number is estimated at 2 per cent of the population, in the official statistics. This segment of the population has certainly made gains in political weight in recent years, but according to strict UN definitions, has still not been granted all the privileges due to a "first nation". Unlike the indigenous peoples of Canada and Australia, whose status as a first nation is unchallenged, the Aborigines still have to compete with the descendants of the early settlers from Mainland China, the Hoklo and Hakka, who also regard themselves as a kind of "first nation" During the 1990s, however, the negative descriptions and pejorative terms that were often used in connection with the indigenous population started to disappear from the media and the political discourse. Before this time, the Aborigines were often referred to as *shu fan* 熟番 ("cooked barbarians") if assimilated, or as *sheng fan* 生番 ("raw barbarians"), if resident in the mountainous regions and non-sinicized; the latter were later also referred to as *shanbao* (山胞), "mountain compatriots" or *shandiren* (山地人), "mountain people". The neutral term, *yuanzhumin* 原住民, meaning Aboriginal people, was officially fixed in 1993, when this term was adopted in the additional articles to the constitution of the ROC (Stainton 2007) and this term, today, is employed almost universally in Taiwan to describe all descendants of the Austronesian peoples, divided into various groups with different languages, social systems and life styles.

Before the introduction of a multiculturalist policy, the official policy of the KMT could be described as follows:

> Before the presidency of Lee Teng-hui [...], the KMT's typical stance towards the island's Aborigines consisted either of ignoring their existence, celebrating their patriotic resistance to the Japanese colonialist, or portraying them as the beneficiaries of assimilatory politics designed to confer 'progress' and the benefits of Chinese culture. (Vickers 2008: 87)

Although in the context of Taiwan's multiculturalist policies, the Aborigines play a decisive role in "proving" that Taiwan differs from China, many Aborigines have indicated that, particularly because of their long-standing local feuds with the Hoklo, they have strong reservations about the policy of the DPP. For this reason, the KMT networks within the Aboriginal communities still function efficiently, with the result that, in elections, the KMT always does well in the Aboriginal areas[11] – despite the fact that the conditions laid down by the United Nations on the rights of Indigenous Peoples have, even today, only partially been fulfilled and the idea of a first nation definitely finds more supporters in the pan green camp. It should also be kept in mind that the Aboriginal identity itself, as an umbrella identity, was a new creation that developed in the 1980s. Before the Aboriginal movement emerged, the tribal identity was more important and, as a matter of fact, one current weakness of the political Aboriginal movement is the great diversity of languages, life styles and cultural expression among the various Aboriginal groups. The case of the Council of Indigenous Peoples' Minister, Sun Ta-chuang (孫大川), Palabang, from the KMT, shows how acceptance of the Han Chinese culture was forced onto the Aboriginal elite. Sun, in all probability, was only able to rise through the KMT ranks because of his China-focused academic achievements: a BA degree in Chinese Literature at National Taiwan University in 1979, and two MA degrees, one in Philosophy at Catholic Fujen in 1983 and one in Sinology at Leuven in 1988. Later on, however, he became involved in Aboriginal cultural issues and, in 1993, founded the literary journal, *Shanhai wenhua* 山海文化. [12]

Another issue is the number of new museums devoted to the Aborigines which is truly amazing, but, of course, the existence of a pure museum culture is not yet sufficient indication of a "real" multiculturalist attitude. Most of the museums only display Aboriginal culture in an ethnographic fashion and seldom take into account the fact that today's Aborigines are aware that they possess a specific identity despite the fact that they do not wear traditional clothing, and often adhere to the Christian religion (Vickers 2008). With regard to ethnic entrepreneurship, Taiwan's Aborigines complain that they have not been given the same preferential treatment in terms of autonomy, hunting rights, language and self-marketing that the indigenous populations have been granted in Australia and Canada. The Aborigines have not profited economically to the same extent as the Hakka from the policy of multiculturalism; while the Hakka govern many prime Hakka tourist spots themselves, the Aboriginal industry remains in the hands of the Hoklo and the Mainlanders. Although PRC Chinese tourists are showing more and more interest in Taiwan's Aboriginal culture, this is presented in such a way that it enhances images of the "uncivilized wild," and could therefore be said to hinder Aborigines from becoming part of the modern nation-building project of Taiwan. PRC Chinese tourism is built on group tourism, with the tourists staying in large hotel chains and being presented with Aboriginal culture in specific Aboriginal centres (n.A. 2009). This is all in stark contrast to the Hakka centers, such as Meinong, which offer a modern kind of tourism, including eco-tourism, cycle paths and bed and breakfast in local farmhouses.

Another symbol of the changed perception of the Aborigines within Taiwanese society is the more recent discussion about the status of the descendants of the Pingpu, that is, the Aborigines who originally resided on the plains of Southern Taiwan. In 1954, the Ministry of the Interior had abolished the Pingpu's status as an ethnic subcategory under

---

11 Of course, some representatives, such as May Chin, the daughter of an Aboriginal mother and a Mainland father (not an uncommon combination), also known as Kao Chin Su-mei, ridicules the independence aspirations of the "Han-native" Taiwanese and seems to favor unification; she is a vehement critic of the Japanese colonial period (probably because of her close affiliation with the blue camp) but ignores the long years of harsh rule suffered by the Aborigines under the KMT (Ko 2005).

12 See the entry 山海文化雙月刊 at <taiwanpedia.culture.tw/web/content?ID=2123>, accessed 1 May 2012. And the entry of Sun Ta-chuang 孫大川 at <www.ey.gov.tw/ct.asp?xItem=59653&ctNode=983&mp=1>, accessed 1 May 2012.

the Aboriginal umbrella, and the Pingpu as a category were removed from the KMT census in 1956, when many of the Pingpu began to register as Taiwanese (Hoklo). In the 1960s and 1970s, only a few Pingpu laid claim to their ethnic identity as Aborigines – which was not particularly surprising, given that the Aborigines were generally being portrayed as inferior to the Chinese majority. Since the turn of the century, however, people have been starting to develop an interest in searching for their ethnic roots, and Lin Sheng-yi, the President of the Alliance of Taiwan Indigenous Cultures, has estimated that 1.5 million people in Taiwan could potentially claim to be of Pingpu origin (Loa 2009).

Nevertheless, various problems between the Aborigines and the Han Chinese continue to exist. There have been frequent complaints that this group has not been granted the rights of indigenous people or First Nations, following the models of Canada or Australia: they do not enjoy full autonomy over their original lands, as evidenced in the on-going disputes over hunting-rights (the Wildlife Conservation Act prohibits the Aborigines from engaging in traditional hunting practices.) versus measures to safeguard the environment in the mountainous regions of Taiwan (Loa 2011; n.A. 2010); other complaints by the Aborigines have focused on the loss of autonomy of the Aboriginal townships in former Taipei county after the 2010 administrative reforms, which combined the former cities of Taipei county to create New Taipei City (Xinbeishi) (Loa 2010).

The next, and largest, ethnic group are the Hoklo (*fulao*). Their language, known under a variety of names, such as Hokkien, Taiwanese, Holo, Holo'oe, Taigi, Taigu, Taioan'oe, and Banlam'oe) is a sub-group of Southern Min. They understand themselves often as "Taiwanese" islanders, de-facto Taiwan's first nation, and since early 2000, their language has been treated as having a legal status that is equal to that of the other languages on the island, which has entailed a shift away from the use of Mandarin. Only after the political liberalization which started in the 1970s and gained force after the lifting of martial law in 1987, were the Hoklo finally allowed to articulate their own interests. In the late 1980s, then, the idea emerged that a Taiwan nation should be built primarily on the Hoklo identity and culture by replacing the alien Mandarin language, the geography lessons which focused on the Yellow River and the Great Wall, the historical focus on the Japanese-Chinese War, and the Beijing opera as representative of culture. This was vehemently opposed, however, by other ethnic groups, such as the Hakka, in the 1998 so-called "return my mother language" movement (*huan wo muyu yundong* 還我母語運動) (Hsu 2010: 171), and by the Aborigines, in their protests against the Wu Feng martyrdom story being included in schoolbooks, a story that tells the tale of a Han merchant in the 17th century who, it was claimed, tried to educate the uncivilized Aborigines but was later brutally murdered by them (Rudolph 2004). These protests led the Hoklo to become supportive of the multicultural discourse, which focused on the equality of the languages and the ethnicities. As Wang Fuzhang, however, said "The Ho lo [Hoklo] do not have a strong ethnic identity since they always define themselves and their language as 'Taiwanese'" (Wang 2003a: 3). This is particularly remarkable, since the ethnic tension between the Hoklo and the Mainlanders was strong: the 228-incident in 1947 led to the slaughter of between 10,000 and 28,000 Taiwanese by Mainlander soldiers, after which the policy of Sinification focused on the Hoklo and particularly restricted the public use of the Hoklo language. Nevertheless, probably due to their large numbers and the prevalence of their language at least in the South, the Hoklo seldom discuss their own identity which is considered to be generally self-affirmative.

One of the most interesting and probably most successful multiculturalist policies in Taiwan concerns the group of the second group of islanders (*benshengren*), the Hakka, not only in the context of state-sponsored multiculturalism, but also in connection with the Hakka's own contributions to multiculturalism and ethnic entrepreneurship. The Hakka people, who number more than four million in Taiwan, form the island's second largest ethnic group after the Hoklo but, for many decades, their identity was downplayed and they were often grouped together with the Hoklo as *benshengren* – "native Taiwanese" (Yang 1993). As a result of the pluralization and democratization of society, however, a Hakka movement which promoted cultural differences emerged in Taiwan and the strong involvement of the Hakka themselves helped to increase the popularity of the political changes. One sign of this new self-awareness is the growing interest in the Hakka language: this language is not only officially recognized in the specific Hakka towns, but is now also taught almost as a discipline all over the Island; since the Ministry of Education started to promote so-called "mother tongue language education," primary school students have to study one of the island's non-Mandarin languages for two hours each week. In trains and public transport, announcements are made in Mandarin, Hoklo and Hakka. The new policy has also led to an emphasis on identification with Taiwan instead of on the Hakka's ancestral links to the "Chinese nobility" (Luo 2009; Yang 1993). As early as 2004, the Hakka Committee Affairs report showed that Chinese identity had declined sharply over the past decade, with only 5 per cent to 11 per cent of the Hakka still identifying themselves as "Chinese" – a ratio that places them between Mainlanders (15 per cent of whom still identify themselves as primarily "Chinese") and Hoklo (4 per cent) (Wang 2005a).

With the introduction of a specific multicultural policy, the government started to offer the Hakka significant support, and since the Hakka formed a large proportion of the population; all political parties were forced to adopt "Hakka policies" in order to win Hakka votes during elections. The main components of the official Hakka multicultural policies entailed, first of all, participation in cultural life and also included Hakka culture promotion, language development and media policy, often with a focus on the localization of Hakka identities (Wang 2007: 877-881). One of the measures that was introduced and warmly welcomed led to the broadcasting of TV and radio programs in Hakka; these became important channels through which people could be reached and through which they could participate in cultural life by sharing and experiencing many different arts and cultures. The newly introduced TV stations deserve particular mention because these, since they were spread by Web 2.0 applications, such as YouTube, were able to attract a much wider audience and also reached Hakka people outside Taiwan. The Taiwan-wide Hakka radio service was also established in 1993, when restrictions were lifted on the use of non-Mandarin languages in broadcasting, and the first Hakka TV Channel worldwide was founded in 2003 (Damm 2008). State-sponsored multi-culturalism has encouraged ethnic entrepreneurship and creative industry, and the Hakka have profited most from this policy. A comprehensive overview of private enterprises and new tourist destinations in Hakka regions that are built on both traditional and modern Hakka culture can be found at the website of the Council for Hakka Affairs, Executive Yuan, ROC <http://www.hakka.gov.tw/> (Chaminade 2006).

The Mainlanders (*waishengren*), as the last of the four grand ethnic groups to be considered here, are a relatively new group which only emerged after 1945-1949, when the new migrants from China who arrived with the KMT formed a distinct group that was shaped by the use of Mandarin as their primary language and also by their different collective memory with regard to the Japanese. The Mainlanders' view of the Japanese was shaped by the atrocities carried out by the Japanese during the occupation of large parts of China and in other parts of Southeast Asia, where the overseas Chinese, in particular, were victims of Japanese aggression; for this reason, their collective historical memory distinguishes them from the other groups on the island, who regard the early Mainlanders as aggressors.[13]

With regard to multiculturalist policies, the Mainlanders, who today form approximately 12 to 15 per cent of the population (Wang 2003b: 8), do not play a significant role and are in some ways the least visible group in Taiwan despite the fact that, for many years, they enjoyed special privileges. While the Hakka and the Aboriginals have been granted specific councils at various levels within the administration, there is no official organization or council for the group of the Mainlanders, and thus no official recognition for the Mainlanders is visible; the publications and statements issued by the Mainlanders also indicate that many of them have a pan-Chinese (Han) identity and that they feel uncomfortable about being described as an "ethnic group" (*zuqun*) (Corcuff 2011a; Corcuff 2011b). A continually recurring issue on the *waishengren* websites is the relation between China, Chinese culture, the Taiwanese and the Mainlanders, and the unresolved questions of "belonging."[14]

Conclusion

It has been shown that Taiwan's policy of multiculturalism that has mostly targeted the "four big ethnic groups" has gained the wide acceptance, in the various political camps, in the civil society and in at least three of the four ethnic groups.[15] However, the politically influential group of the Mainlanders and the largest group, the Hoklo, for different reasons, have been most reluctant to accept the idea of a multicultural Taiwan. The Hoklo, however, who have long considered themselves the most authentic representatives of Taiwan and a Taiwanese identity have increasingly inclined towards accepting the idea of a multicultural Taiwan. The greatest opposition still derives from the Mainlanders, who adhere to the idea of a pan-Han Chinese society and deny ethnic differences within the "Han", partly for political reasons, because they would prefer unification in the long term (Corcuff 2011a; Corcuff 2011b; Li 2002; Marsh 2002).

I would tend to reject the arguments employed by Allen Chun (Chen 2000, 2007), the famous anthropologist at Academia Sinica, and other Mainlanders who claim to have shown that Taiwan's multicultural policy is ineffective. These arguments are based, first of all, on the groups that are excluded and, secondly, on over-emphasizing essentialized claims to ethnicity within the new discourse. In reality, however, the multi-cultural policies employed in Taiwan tend to be more "post-modern" than essentialist, for example, the new system of mother tongue education does not require every individual to learn his/her own mother tongue; instead, each is free to choose any language offered in his/her school to learn more about the other ethnic groups, which includes and does not

13 The Hoklo in Taiwan, however, regarded the Japanese as more or less benign colonizers who had helped to improve the Taiwanese infrastructure and made the Taiwanese people into one of the most educated Asian peoples in 1945; a significant number of Hoklo in the late 1930s even aimed to become Japanese citizens with full rights (Chou 2006).

14 See e.g. <http://tw.myblog.yahoo.com/jw!0ECeB5KcERxPRFIvQiRa12IFjSrB/article?mid=6905>, accessed 20 August 2009.

15 For the exclusion of other groups, see Wang Ngo and Damm 2012 96-97.

exclude members of other groups.[16] Chun maintains, for example, that the various problems confronting multiculturalism in Taiwan derive from its being confined to certain ethnic groups,

> while the embrace of Aboriginal causes and the plight of minority ethnic groups appears to reflect an official recognition of 'multiple identities' and a turn toward 'hybridity' of the kind championed by various flavors of postmodern theory, it is still in essence a multiculturalism that does not include outsiders ("foreigners") or makes no attempt to absorb foreign labor in a way that is by nature blind to ethnicity, which is clearly indicative of transnational movements in an age of disorganized capitalism, where it is driven solely by needs of a global market rather than the interests of global imperialism or national protectionism. (Chen 2000: 14)

Taiwan's multiculturalist policy has certainly been selective but other groups, such as brides and migrants from mainland China, and also non-ethnic minorities, such as women, gays and lesbians, have increasingly been targeted in the interests of multiculturalism and cultural diversity, even if not to the same extent as those ethnic groups which are seen as crucial for the idea of a Taiwanese nation.[17]

In Taiwan, multiculturalism has not only led to ethnicities such as the Hakka and Hoklo enjoying the same rights as the Mainlanders; Taiwan's transformation to a pluralistic and democratic society has been taking place alongside increased globalization, with economic integration within the world economy and China, which has also led to the blurring of spatial borders. These developments, which could be described as the "global dimensions of multiculturalism," could lead us to question whether Taiwanese multiculturalism should be seen as embedded in global developments and transnationalism rather than only as the replacement of Chinese chauvinism by Taiwanese (Hoklo) chauvinism under a new name, as some critics, such as Shih Chih-yu (Shi 2003, 2004, 2005a, 2006), have remarked.

The notion of multiculturalism, however, elicited different reactions from the four main ethnic groups concerned: the Hoklo indicated their acceptance of the idea after a phase of more intense Hoklo chauvinism in the late 1980s and early 1990s. Today, the Hoklo seldom discuss what it means to be "Hoklo" and show more interest in the preservation of the language. The Mainlanders, often for political reasons, try to avoid any "fixed group" understanding. They shun the use of umbrella terms, such as the "new Taiwanese", for the ethnic groups created by the KMT President, Lee Teng-hui, in favor of a more all-embracing Chinese identity within the borders of Taiwan and beyond; the Mainlanders have also voiced objections to being referred to as an ethnic group. The successful implementation of a multiculturalist policy requires this former ruling group to relinquish

16 Malaysia stands as an example of a multicultural system with fixed boundaries. The individual ethnic identity is seen as pre-given and it is not possible to change from one ethnic group to another; in the case of the Malays, even the religious affiliation is proscribed.(Goh 2008).

17 The former President, Chen Shui-bian, also included foreigners and new migrants, to some extent: "President Chen Tries to Appease Aborigines," The China Post, 18 July 2004. Ma Yong-jeou, while he was Mayor of Taipei, emphasized the importance of multiculturalism when referring to groups such as gays and lesbians; see, <http://entour.yunlin.gov.tw/tour_en/10news/10news_02.asp?id=56>2>, see also, <http://www.utopia-asia.com/unews/article_2006_09_19_190352.htm> (all accessed 20 August 2009) On the other hand, it should be pointed out that the former President, Chen Shui-bian, aiming at establishing a new Taiwanese nation, included a variety of groups ranging from the four ethnic groups to the Western cultures (Spain, Netherlands), the Japanese and Chinese cultures, the European and American cultures, and also the Southeast Asian immigrant workers (Wang 2004: 305) in his concept of multiculturalism.

some of its privileges, and this is often interpreted as discrimination. The hypocrisy inherent in this reaction is clear: the language policy, for example, favors Mandarin, and although the other languages are promoted, Mandarin remains the de facto national language. The Mainlanders also continue to hold a dominant position in the current government. The small group of the Mainlanders is still much attracted to the idea that the Taiwanese possess a "Chinese identity with Taiwanese characteristics," and claim an overarching Han identity, assigning the Hoklo and the Hakka to subordinate positions as dialectal subgroups, and differentiating between them only as Han people with different origins.

Finally, it cannot be denied that the notion of multiculturalism has been linked to the creation of a national hybrid Taiwanese identity vs. the all-embracing Chinese identity which prevailed in the state-led discourse during the first decades of the ROC on Taiwan. Now multiculturalism is often related to "constitutional patriotism" (*Verfassungspatriotismus*) and to the question of a national identity and has thus often been seen as posing a threat to a traditional cultural policy based on the Han Chinese culture (Wang 2003b: 2). The issue of multiculturalism has also been employed to gain global legitimacy: Taiwan, despite holding pariah status in the international community and consequently being either ignored or belittled, has nevertheless followed the standards and rules set by United Nations organizations and presented herself as a "good" member of the global state community, for example, with regard to language policy, allowing and promoting the use of various languages and dialects and protecting the rights of the Aborigines. In the future, questions related to the inclusion of the new migrant groups arriving from mainland China, not only as spouses, but also as white-collar workers and students, will require serious consideration. If Taiwanese multiculturalism is perceived only in the context of national identification, it will not be possible for these groups to be included and they will remain a "permanent invisible caste, like Japan's Koreans" (Chen 2000: 15). Multiculturalism in Taiwan can therefore be seen as an appropriate tool for bringing together the various ethnic groups in Taiwan and establishing a Taiwanese identity which is not rooted in the idea of a monolithic ethnic nation, be it the former idea of Taiwan as part of the ROC, or the replacement of a (ROC-) Chinese identity by a Hoklo identity.

References

Chaminade, Christina (2006) Innovation Policy for Asian SMEs: Exploring Cluster Differences, in Working Paper: *Centre for Innovation, Research and Competence in the Learning Economy (CIRCLE) Lund University.*

Chen, Pin-hao (2001) *National Identity and Media: The Taiwanese Case (China)* MA, Pennsylvania State University.

Chen, Yilin (Allen Chun) 陳奕麟 (2000) Grand Illusion: The Long History of Multiculturalism in Taiwan in an Era of Invented Indigenization. Paper presented at the Conference on Remapping Taiwan: Histories and Cultures in the Context of Globalization, <http://www.international.ucla.edu/cira/paper/TW_Chun_Allen.pdf>, accessed 10 Oct 2008, University of California, Los Angeles.

Chen, Yilin (Allen Chun) 陳奕麟 (2007) Ethnic Identity in the Politics of the Unreal in Taiwan, in *Comparative Perspective* 1, pp. 76-86.

Chou, Wan-yao (2006), Between Heimat and Nation: Japanese Colonial Education and the Origins of 'Taiwanese Consciousness', in Fitzgerald, John P. and Sechin Y.-S. Chien (eds), *The Dignity of Nations: Equality, Competition and Honour in East Asian Nationalism*, pp. 115-139 and 231-236.

Constable, Nicole (1996) *Guest People: Hakka Identity in China and Abroad*, Seattle: University of Washington Press.

Corcuff, Stephane (2011a) Liminality and Taiwan Tropism in a Postcolonial Context: Schemes of National Identification among Taiwan's 'Mainlanders' on the Eve of Kuomintang's Return to Power, in Ngo, Tak-Wing and Hongren (Wang Hong-zen) Wang (eds), *Politics of Difference in Taiwan*, pp. 34-62.

Corcuff, Stéphane (2002) *Memories of the Future: National Identity Issues and the Search for a New Taiwan*, Armonk, N.Y.: M.E. Sharpe.

Corcuff, Stéphane (2011b) Taiwan's Mainlanders under President Chen Shui-bian: A Shift from the Political to the Cultural?, in Schubert, Gunter and Jens Damm (eds), *Taiwanese Identity in the 21st Century: Domestic, Regional, and Global Perspectives*, pp. 113-132.

Damm, Jens (2008) The Chinese Diasporic Cyberspace: Cultural Essentialism, Nationalism and Hybrid Identities, in Damm, Jens and Andreas Steen (eds), *Post-modern China* (Berliner Chinahefte/Chinese History and Society 34), pp. 130-148.

Damm, Jens (2012) Multiculturalism in Taiwan and the Influence of Europe, in Damm, Jens and Paul Lim (eds), *European Perspectives on Taiwan*, pp. 84-106.

Duara, Prasenjit (1993) De-Constructing the Chinese Nation, in *The Australian Journal of Chinese Affairs*, 30, pp. 1-26.

Gladney, Dru C. (1994) Representing Nationality in China: Refiguring Majority/ Minority Identities, in *The Journal of Asian Studies*, 53:1, pp. 92-123.

Gladney, Dru C. (2004) *Dislocating China: Reflections on Muslims, Minorities, and Other Subaltern Subjects*, Chicago: University of Chicago Press.

Goh, Daniel P. S. (2008) From Colonial Pluralism to Postcolonial Multiculturalism: Race, State Formation and the Question of Cultural Diversity in Malaysia and Singapore, in *Sociology Compass*, 2:1, pp. 232-252.

Ho, Ming-Sho (2005) Taiwan's State and Social Movements under the DPP Government, 2000-2004, in *Journal of East Asian Studies* 5, pp. 401–425.

Hsiau, A-Chin (1997) Language Ideology in Taiwan: The KMT's Language Policy, the Tai-yu Language Movement, and Ethnic Politics, in *Journal of Multilingual and Multicultural Development*, 18: 4, <http://www.multilingual-matters.net/jmmd/018/0302/jmmd0180302.pdf>, accessed 10 May 2007, pp. 302–315.

Hsiau, A-Chin (2005) Epilogue, in Makeham, John and A-chin Hsiau (eds), *Cultural, Ethnic, and Political Nationalism in Contemporary Taiwan*: Bentuhua.

Hsu, Minna (2010), Forming a Basis for Recognition: The Construction of a Taiwanese Hakka Identity through Government Policy since 2000, in *Taiwan International Studies Quarterly*, 6, 2, 165-193.

Hwang, Yih-jye (2006) Historical and Political Knowledge in the Discursive Constitution of Taiwanese National Identity, in *Perspectives*, 7:3, pp. 110-131.

Hwang, Yih-jye (2007) *Taiwanese National Identity as a 'Discursive Entity'* (unpublished PhD), Aberystwyth: University of Wales.

Jacobs, Bruce (2005) „Taiwanization" in Taiwan's Politics, in Makeham, John and A-chin Hsiau (eds), *Cultural, Ethnic, and Political Nationalism in Contemporary Taiwan*: Bentuhua, pp. 17-54.

Joppke, Christian (2004) The Retreat of Multiculturalism in the Liberal State: Theory and Policy, in *The British Journal of Sociology*, 55:2, pp. 237-257.

Ko, Shu-ling. (2005, 8 April). World War II Veterans Slam May Chin Protest, *Taipei Times*, p. 1.

Ko, Shu-ling. (2010, 15 October). President Touts Chinese Culture, *Taipei Times*, p. 1.

Koopmans, Ruud (2005) *Contested Citizenship: Immigration and Cultural Diversity in Europe*, Minneapolis: University of Minnesota Press.

Lee, Teng-hui (1999) *The Road to Democracy: Taiwan's Pursuit of Identity*, Tokyo: PHP Institiute, Inc.

Lee Teng-hui (Li Denghui) 李登輝 (1999) *Jingying da Taiwan* 經營大台灣 [Managing a great Taiwan], Taipei: Yuanli chubanshe 遠流出版公.

Li, Kuang-chün (2002) Mirrors and Masks: An Interpretative Study of Mainlander's Identity Dilemma, in Corcuff, Stéphane (ed) *Memories of the Future: National Identity Issues and the Search for a New Taiwan*, pp. 102-122.

Loa, Lok-Sin. (2007, 4 September) Minister Urges Faster Review of Aboriginal Legislation, *Taipei Times*, p. 4.

Loa, Lok-sin. (2009, 3 May) Feature: Pingpu Aborigines Heat up Battle for Ethnic Identity, *Taipei Times*, p. 3.

Loa, Lok-sin. (2010, 23 December) Aborigines Protest Township Losses, *Taipei Times*, p. 3.

Loa, Lok-sin. (2011, 2 January) Aborigines Protest ROC Repression, *Taipei Times*, p. 3.

Luo, Lunxin 羅綸新 (2009) Kejia wenhua yu yuyan wanglu ziyuan diaocha [Investigating the resources of Hakka culture and language in World Wide-Web], in: *Jiaoyu ziliao yu yanjiu* (Bimonthly Journal of Educational Resources and Research) 91, pp. 111-130.

Makeham, John (2005) Introduction, in Makeham, John and A-chin Hsiau (eds), *Cultural, Ethnic, and Political Nationalism in Contemporary Taiwan*: Bentuhua, pp. 1-16.

Makeham, John, and A-chin Hsiau (2005) *Cultural, Ethnic, and Political Nationalism in Contemporary Taiwan*: Bentuhua, New York: Palgrave Macmillan.

Marsh, Robert (2002) National identity and Ethnicity in Taiwan: Some Trends in the 1990s, in Corcuff, Stéphane (ed) *Memories of the Future: National Identity Issues and the Search for a New Taiwan*, pp. 1441-1159.

n.A. (2009, 5 December) Chinese Travel Agents to Tour Aboriginal Villages, *Taipei Times*, p. 2.

n.A. (2010, 7 December) Councilor Calls for Return of Traditional Aboriginal Hunting, *Taipei Times*, p. 2.

Neder, Christine (2003) Blut und Boden ('Blood and Soil')? Ideological Tendencies in Taiwanese Literature and its Reception, in Neder, Christine and Ines Susanne Schilling (eds), *Transformation! Innovation? Perspectives on Taiwan Culture*, pp. 101-110.

Ngo, Tak-Wing, and Hongren (Wang Hong-zen) Wang (2011) Cultural Difference, Social Recognition and Political Representation in Taiwan, in Ngo, Tak-Wing and Hongren Wang (eds), *Politics of Difference in Taiwan*, pp. 1-13.

Phillips, Steven E. (2003) *Between Assimilation and Independence: the Taiwanese Encounter Nationalist China, 1945-1950*, Stanford, Calif.: Stanford University Press.

Rudolph, Michael (2003) *Taiwans multi-ethnische Gesellschaft und die Bewegung der Ureinwohner, Assimilation oder kulturelle Revitalisierung?*, Münster [u.a.]: LIT.

Rudolph, Michael (2004) The Emergence of the Concept of „Ethnic Group“ in Taiwan and the Role of Taiwan's Austronesians in the Construction of Taiwanese Identity, in: *Historiography East and West: A multi-lingual on-line journal for studies in comparative historiography and historical thinking*, pp. 86-115.

Shi, Zhiyu (Shih Chih-yu) 石之瑜 (1999) Human Rights as Identities: Difference and Discrimination in Taiwan's China Policy, in Van Ness, Peter and Nikhil Aziz (eds), *Debating Human Rights Critical Essays from the United States and Asia*, pp. 144-166

Shi, Zhiyu (Shih Chih-yu) 石之瑜 (2003) Voting for an Ancestor (Roundtable: Melissa J. Brown's Is Taiwan Chinese? The Impact of Culture,Power, and Migration on Changing Identities), in: *Issues & Studies*, 40:3/4, pp. 488-496.

Shi, Zhiyu (Shih Chih-yu) 石之瑜 (2004, 9 April) *Zuowei waishengren de bei'ai* 作為外省人的悲哀 [The sadness of being a Mainlander], Apple Daily 蘋果日報. Retrieved from <http://tw.nextmedia.com/applenews/article/art_id/846126/IssueID/20040409>, accessed 13 January 2011.

Shi, Zhiyu (Shih Chih-yu) 石之瑜 (2005a) Hainei Huaren? Taiwanren shenfen zhengzhi zhong de zuxian lunshu 海內華人？台灣人身份政治中的祖先論述 (Overseas Chinese at home? The ancestor discourse in Taiwanese identity politics), in Chang, Chi-hsiung 張啟雄 (Zhang Qixiong) (ed) 時代變局與海外華人的族國認同, pp. 71-167.

Shi, Zhiyu (Shih Chih-yu) 石之瑜 (2005b) Hainei Huaren? Taiwanren shenfen zhengzhi zhong de zuxian lunshu 海內華人？台灣人身份政治中的祖先論述 [Overseas Chinese at home? The ancestor discourse in Taiwanese identity politics], in *Quanqiu zhengzhi pinglun* 全球政治評論 Review of Global Politics 10, pp. 141-158.

Shi, Zhiyu (Shih Chih-yu) 石之瑜 (2006) Ma Yingjiu yu Su Zhengchang de zerenguan 馬英九與蘇貞昌的責任觀 [Ma Ying-jeou's and Su Tseng-chang's sense of responsibility], in *Qiaoxie zazhi* 僑協雜誌 OCA Bimonthly 99, pp. 4-5.

Simon, Scott (2009) Multiculturalism and Indigenism: Minority Rights in Canada and Taiwan, in Paper presented at the conference Multiculturalism in Taiwan, National Sun Yat-sen University, Kaohsiung, Taiwan, January 8-10, 2009.

Smith, Anthony D. (1987) *The Ethnic Origins of Nations*, Oxford New York: Basil Blackwell.

Smith, Anthony D. (1995) *Nations and Nationalism in a Global Era*, Cambridge: Polity Press.

Smith, Anthony D. (2001) *Nationalism: Theory, Ideology, History*, Cambridge; Malden, Mass.: Polity.

Stainton, Michael" (2007) Aboriginal Self-Government: Taiwan's Uncompleted Agenda, in Rubinstein, Murray (ed) *Taiwan: A New History*, Expanded Edition, pp. 419-435.

Stark, Deryl (2009) *The Return of the Vanishing Formosan: Filmic and Fictional Representations of the Aboriginal Maiden in Postwar Taiwan as Constructive and Critical National Allegories*. PhD, University of Toronto, <https://tspace.library.utoronto.ca/bitstream/1807/19095/6/Sterk_Darryl_C_200911_PhD_thesis.pdf>, accessed 1 May 2012.

Vertovec, Steven, and Susanne Wessendorf (2010) *The Multiculturalism Backlash: European Discourses, Policies and Practices*, London ; New York: Routledge.

Vickers, Edward (2008) Re-Writing Museums, in Shih, Fang-long, Stuart Thompson and Paul-François Tremlett (eds), *Re-writing Culture in Taiwan*, pp. 86-101.

Wang, Fu-chang 王甫昌 (Wang Fuzhang) (1998) Zuqun yishi, minzu zhuyi, yu zhengdang zhichi: yijiujiuling niandai Taiwan de zuqun zhengzhi 族群意識、民族主義、與政黨支持：一九九〇年代台灣的族群政治 [Ethnic conciousness, nationalism, and party support: Taiwan ethnic politics in 1990's], in *Taiwan shehuixue jikan* 台灣社會學季刊 [Taiwan: A Radical Quarterly in Social Studies] 2, pp. 1-45.

Wang, Fu-chang 王甫昌 (Wang Fuzhang) (2002) Zuqun jiechu jihui? haishi zuqun jingzheng? bensheng minnanren zuqun yishi neihan yu diqu chayi moshi zhi jieshi 族群接觸機會？還是族群競爭？：本省閩南人族群意識內涵與地區差異模式之解釋 [Opportunities for ethnic contact? Or ethnic competition? : Explanation of Bensheng minnan ethnic group consciousness and regional patterns differences], in *Taiwan shehuixue* 台灣社會學 [Taiwanese Sociology] 4, pp. 11-78.

Wang, Fu-chang 王甫昌 (Wang Fuzhang) (2005a) You "Zhongguo shengji" dao "Taiwan zuqun": hukou pucha jibie leishu zhuanbian zhi fenxi 由「中國省籍」到「台灣族群」：戶口普查籍別類屬轉變之分析 [From Chinese Original Domicile to Taiwanese

Ethnicity: An Analysis of Census Category Transformation in Taiwan], in *Taiwan shehuixue* 台灣社會學 [Taiwanese Sociology] 9, pp. 59-117.

Wang, Fu-chang 王甫昌 (Wang Fuzhang) (2008) Zuqun zhengzhi yiti zai Taiwan minzhu zhuanxing zhong de jiaose 族群政治議題在台灣民主轉型中的角色 [The Role of Ethnic Politics Issues in Taiwan's Democratization Transition], in *Taiwan minzhu jikan* 臺灣民主季刊 [Taiwan Journal of Democracy] 5:2, pp. 89-140.

Wang, Fuchang 王甫昌 (2003a) *Dangdai Taiwan shehui de zujun xiangxiang* 當代台灣社會的族群想像 [The etnic imagination in Taiwan's current society], Taipei: Xuejun.

Wang, Lirong (Wang, Li-jung) 王俐容 (2003b) *Towards Multiculturalism? Identity, Difference and Citizenship in Cultural Policy in Taiwan (1949-2002).* PhD, University of Warwick, Warwick.

Wang, Lirong (Wang, Li-jung) 王俐容 (2005b) The Formation of „Transnational Communities" : A New Challenge to „Multicultural Taiwan", in *International Journal of Cultural Policy* 11:2, pp. 171-185.

Wang, Lirong (Wang, Li-jung) 王俐容 (2007) Diaspora, Identity and Cultural Citizenship: The Hakkas in „Multicultural Taiwan", in: *Ethnic and Racial Studies* 30:5, pp. 875-895.

Wei, Jennifer M. (2008) *Language Choice and Identity Politics in Taiwan*, Lanham: Lexington Books.

Wu, Yu-Shan (2011) The Evolution of the KMT's Stance on the One-China Principle: National Identity in Flux, in Schubert, Gunter and Jens Damm (eds), *Taiwanese Identity in the 21st Century: Domestic, Regional and Global Perspectives*, pp. 51-71.

Yang, Guoxin 楊國鑫 (1993) *Taiwan Kejia* 台灣客家 [The Hakka in Taiwan], Taipei: Zheng gang zixun wenhua.

Yoshihisa, Amae, and Damm, Jens (2011) 'Whither Taiwanization?' State, Society and Cultural Production in the New Era, in: *Journal of Current Chinese Affairs* 40:1, pp. 3-17.

Zheng, Yongwei 鄭永維 (1988) Cong nongjing xuezhe dao yiguo zongtong - Li Denghui xiansheng de cong zhengzhi licheng 從農經學者到一國總統 – 李登輝先生的從政治歷程 [From a scholar of agriculture to the President of a country – the politcial CV of Lee Teng-hui], in *Haihua zazhi* 海華雜誌 37, pp. 54-59.

Kimiko Suda

Introduction to Lu Huilin: Migrant Workers in the Process of Urbanization in China

The following essay written by Lu Huilin is going beyond a presentation of academic research results, clearly pushing for urgent policy reforms in regard to migration and urbanization processes and questioning China's current growth model, inter alia referring to Huang Yasheng's critic of high-speed and unsustainable development, which did not increase the GDP of the urban population along with urbanization.

Lu is not alone with his political agenda, but part of an alliance of scholars and public intellectuals[1] from Mainland China and Hong Kong, which has been strongly influencing the public debate about the *new workers* and social justice in recent years.

For example Lu is one of the main investigators of the Foxconn[2] suicide cases[3], in which during a short time in the summer of 2010 thirteen young factory workers died and four were seriously injured after suicide attempts related to mental health problems educed by the factory regime. Together with nine other Chinese sociologists he published an open letter[4] asking for immediate reforms in regard to the policies and regimes causing the victims' living and working conditions, when the series of suicides was actually still continuing.

Lu in addition is co-author of *Dagong Dishang* [大工地上] (2010), a book documenting the difficult living conditions of migrants working on construction sites in China, including many interviews with migrants. The idea of focusing on the main stakeholders' stories, opinions, dreams, in the academic research process, even if they belong to the "lower classes" [底层] and are usually considered voiceless *denizens* in the cities, is shared by other colleagues who are part of the alliance, such as the sociologist Pun Ngai.

His essay can be seen as an important contribution for situating China in the theoretical transnational debates about world, mega or globalized cities, with identifying the production of the social group of "migrant workers" as the specific feature of urbanization processes of the country. The non-existence of literal slums in cities such as Beijing, Shanghai or Shenzhen does, according to Lu, definitely not imply the non-existence of unhealthy living arrangements of the economically disadvantaged population, since such exist everywhere in China's mega-cities, naming factory dormitories and *urban villages* [城中村][5].

---

1 For example he writes regularly on the website *Chengbiancun* (城边村), e.g. about the second generation of migrant workers, <http://www.chengbiancun.com/2010/0803/8823.html>, 12 June 2012.

2 Foxconn (富士康國際控股有限公司) is a Taiwanese multinational electronics manufacturing company, which produces PC components, connectors and cables and runs 13 factories in China, with the one in Longhua, Shenzhen, being the biggest Foxconn-factory in the world.

3 He is co-editor of an in-depth analysis of the Foxconn suicide case (2011) with Pun Ngai, Shen Yuan and Guo Yuhua, scholars who also signed the letter mentioned above. The book includes chapters about students working at Foxconn, the "Dormitory regime", health issues in "the world's factories", the question of workers' rights and representation and one detailed case of a female worker who survived her suicide attempt. It ends with a conclusion: it's time for an "end of the age of world factories".

4 See "Open letter from 9 Sociologists: end the tragedy at Foxconn" (released on May 18, 2010) in English under this link <www.clntranslations.org/file_download/110>.

5 There is no precise definition for *urban villages* in China, but many of them were built on former farmland, which became part of a first-tier city through urbanization. *Urban villages* often consist of

Berliner China-Hefte/Chinese History and Society 41 (2012), pp. 90-91

Within the heated debate about the "second generation of migrant workers", born in the 1980s and 1990s, the generation without land for agricultural cultivation [无土一代], and with no way of return [不归路] and an urban identity ["成为城市人"], Lu does not merely suggest to *improve* the migration regime, with e.g. giving educational training to the migrants to improve their "quality" [素质] as suggested by some Chinese scholars, but to dissolve the social group of *migrant workers* through complete integration into the urban population. Besides Lu, also other public intellectuals such as Yu Jianrong[6], see this particular social group as a potential threat to social stability in a long-term perspective if not getting the well-deserved status of an urban citizen with access to political, civil and social rights.

The importance of critical scholars in the transition process of Chinese society pushing forward public debates on important issues and representing voices probably otherwise unheard, since they lack formal representation, will very likely continue to increase in the next years. Slowly and indirectly they can also influence government decisions through pressure build-up by the public debates and their work in elite universities, which cater as think-tanks of the government. Their strong personal engagement beyond the university campus is somehow still underestimated in "Western" research on migration, urbanization and policy development in urban China.

References

Gransow, Bettina (2007) „Dörfer in Städten" – Typen chinesischer Marginalsiedlungen am Beispiel Beijing und Guangzhou, in Dirk Bronger (Hrsg) (2007) *Marginalsiedlungen in Megastädten Asiens*, Lit Verlag, pp. 343-377.

Pun Ngai 潘毅, Lu Huilin 卢晖临, and Zhang Huipeng 张慧鹏 (2010) *Dagongdi: chengshi jianzhu gongren de shengcun tujing* 大工地：城市建筑工人的生存图景 [The Big Construction Sites: The Existence Picture of the Urban Construction Workers], Peking University Press.

Pun Ngai 潘毅, Lu Huilin 卢晖临, and Zhang Huipeng 张慧鹏 (2010) *Dagongdi shang – zhongguo nongmin zhi ge* 大工地上-中國農民工之歌 [On the Big Construction Sites: the Song of the Migrant Workers], Hong Kong: Commercial Press.

Pun Ngai 潘毅 and Lu Huilin 卢晖临 (2010) "Unfinished Proletarianization: Self, Anger and Class Action among the Second Generation of Peasant-Workers in Present-Day China", in *Modern China* 36:2010, pp. 493-519.

Pun, Ngai 潘毅, Lu Huilin 盧暉臨 and Shen Yuhua 郭于華 (2011) *Fushikang huihuang beihou de lianhuantiao* 富士康辉煌背后的连环跳，商務印書館，香港 [The Suicide Series Behind the Splendid Glory of Foxconn], Hong Kong: Commercial Press.

Yu Jianrong 于建嵘 (2010) *Diceng zhishi qingnian jiang gaibian zhongguo* 底层知识青年将改变中国 [The educated youth of the lower social classes will change China], <http://www.360doc.com/content/10/0409/18/285715_22281212.shtml>, 7 June 2012.

six-floor-buildings of rather poor quality with hardly any space between each of them, rooms are rented out informally for about 450 - 1000 RMB. Hygiene, water and electricity facilities are often substandard. Some urban villages still include traditional buildings and village structures such as temples, village halls and wet markets. See Gransow 2007 for further details about *urban villages*.

6 See Yu 2010.

卢晖临 [Lu Huilin]

中国城市化进程中的农民工问题
[Migrant Workers in the Process of Urbanization in China]

Abstract

The plea for the abolition of the “migrant worker”- regime (制度设计) and the integration of rural-to-urban migrants and second generation migrant workers (新生代农民工) into China’s cities as corporate (企业公民) and social citizens (社区公民) is situated in the center of this essay. Against the discourses about China’s economic growth model and “world cities” (世界城市 *shijie chengshi*), the official statement, that 50% of the population is included in the country’s urbanization is questioned and labeled “fake urbanization” (伪城市化)[1], since migrant workers are only considered as production force to maximize the profit for the nation’s economic boost and not as human beings with the need for reproduction. Subsequent the “unfinished proletarianization” (无完成的无产阶级化) of migrant workers within class formation processes (referring to E.P. Thompson) is discussed and the lack of identity, self-confidence and rights as *workers* [2] identified as harmful consequences. The *dormitory labor regime* (宿舍劳动体制) (referring to Pun Ngai) and its negative impact on the individual is illustrated by the “Foxconn suicide series” (2010) involving young factory workers in Shenzhen. A request that the companies should acknowledge their moral obligation to pay wages as high as they would have to for *urban workers* and the Chinese government to finally take responsibility and provide housing, education, medical care to everyone contributing with their blood, sweat and tears to the economic growth and city life in China, rounds up the essay.

“农民工这样一种制度设计既然这么不合理，这么荒谬，为什么会一直存在？仅仅是认识不到位吗？要回答这一回答，最简单的思路就是问：这样一个制度符合谁的利益？我们认为农民工的存在符合国家追求经济增长与资本追求最大化利润这两个方面的利益。”

“农民工这个制度设计的奥秘是什么？是突破了底线。为什么能突破呢？是因为资本不需要支付一个城市工人的工资，它只需要支付一个农民工的工资，就是比他回去在农村干稍微工资高一点，但是没有办法养活他在城市生活这样一个工资。”

非常高兴有这个机会来跟大家一起讨论农民工的问题。农民工问题到底怎么看？我个人觉得，在当今整个社会上并没有形成一个共识。比如，有人认为今天的农民工几乎不大可能进入城市，其中很重要的原因是农民工没有这种技能和能力，或者还有的人认为今天我们的城市根本没有容纳农民工的能力，城市没有吸纳这么多外来人口的能力。还有人会认为农民工没有相应的素质，比如成为城市人的素质。类似这样的一些看法甚至来自于我们这样一些致力于做农民工研究的学者口中。今天我

1 See article by Ye Tan as part of the discussion about the statement of the Chinese Academy of Social Science issued on 19.12.2011, that 50% of China´s population lives in the cities and is therefore urbanized: <http://www.xinminweekly.com.cn/News/Content/667>, 28.05.2012.

2 The author refers to one of his earlier articles: Pun Ngai and Lu Huilin (2010): “Unfinished Proletarianization: Self, Anger and Class Action among the Second Generation of Peasant-Workers in Present-Day China”, in Modern China 2010/36.

做这个分享会慢慢的回应这样一些具体的问题，实际上是从一个更宏观和结构性的角度来思考农民工的问题。

今天的题目叫“城市化进程中的农民工问题”，城市化意味着农村人口进入城市、由农民变为城市人这样一个过程，可是在中国过去 30 年的经济发展和城市化过程中间，出现了一个特有的问题叫做农民工问题。

改革开放以来，中国经济持续快速增长，这一点无论是从统计数据还是从城市发展本身都能看得很清楚。GDP 平均每年是 10%的增长，30 年的发展，使得中国已经超越日本成为世界上第二大经济体。与此同时，中国的城市化水平也持续稳步的提升，尤其在最近 10 年左右更是快速的提升，从 1978 年的 17.9%上升到 2010 年的 49.7%。此刻，当我们讲这个话的时候，说不定已经超过了 50%。

另外一方面，城市在我们中国整个经济、价值当中的中心地位也越来越明显，可以从去年刚刚闭幕的上海世博会的口号“城市让生活更美好”当中集中地体现出来。我们开会所在地的北京，两年前市委书记刘淇也率先提出要建设“世界城市”的目标。据我所知，最近还有 10 多个城市提出了类似的发展目标，有的叫全球城市，有的叫国际化大都市。从以上谈到的数字、世博会的口号，到一些大城市提出的发展目标，我们都可以看出中国在发展城市化，推进城市化道路上的宏大计划和勃勃雄心。

我们应该如何看待这 30 年的城市化呢？中国的高级官员在总结中国城市化经验的时候，经常非常自豪地提到一个特点：中国城市没有贫民窟。大家知道，比中国的城市化水平高的国家有很多，我们看南美国家，巴西、阿根廷，城市化的水平很高，但是像下面这幅照片里的情况，经常可以在那里看到：现代化的都市，非常漂亮的建筑，可是和这个漂亮的建筑，密集的现代商业人口集中区非常靠近的，可能就是照片上这样的贫民窟地区，卫生条件极差、建筑质量极差，里面居住着一些可能没有办法通过正常的工作来生存的一些人，他们中的很多人需要靠毒品非法交易在这样一些区域生存，这是贫民窟。这样一个大面积的、大规模的贫民窟，在中国的城市确实不常见。所以我们会这样自豪地宣称：中国城市化的亮点是没有贫民窟。

在北京和深圳这样的城市，的确不怎么会看到些贫民窟。可是一些学者研究中国的城市化，发现了一些问题。比如黄亚生研究发现：从 1996-2004 的数据看，中国城市化的特点主要是土地的扩张，而不是人口密度的增加，土地的城市化快于人口的城市化。城市规模越来越扩大，过去的城市就像北京可能就是二环、三环，后来扩展到四环、五环，现在是扩展到五环以外，这是土地的扩张。人口的绝对数当然是在增加，可是人口的密度没有相应的增加，土地的城市化快于人口的城市化。中国的城市化主要是通过通过城市规模的扩大，而不是通过人口密度的增加来实现的。

黄亚生还发现，中国的家庭消费占 GDP 的比例是在大规模的下降，这与经济学的逻辑相悖。按照经济学家的逻辑，城市化必定增加消费在 GDP 当中的比重，可是从中国的宏观数据来看恰恰是相反的，2000 年以后这 10 年城市化步伐加快，可是家庭消费占 GDP 的比例实际上是在下降。这两个现象其实是从不同的方面说一个问题，这个问题就是最近一两年人们热议的“伪城市化”。

回到我们刚才开头的统计数据，我们的城市化水平已经是接近 50%了，可是在被统计为城市人口的人群中间，相当一部分人实际上根本没有办法过上和一般的城市居民一样的生活，没有办法享受到城市各类的公共服务，他们的收入水平、消费模式等都没有办法和一般城市居民相提并论。我们在计算城市人口的统计口径上早已和国际接轨，即采用常住人口概念：只要你在某个城市居住半年以上，就被统计为该城市的常住人口。被统计为城市的人口中，有上亿人实际上是农民工。在我看来，中国城市化的特点不是没有贫民窟，而是它制造了农民工这一庞大的群体，这是一个高度具有中国特色的现象。从表象上看，我们的城市整洁有序，我们的经济也持续增长，可是潜藏的却是农民工问题。

2006 年中央一号文件提出要解决新生代农民工问题。这是农民工引起中央政府、社会各界、新闻界高度关注的一个标志性的时点。农民工已经存在了 30 年,但从改革开放以来，农民工引起中央及媒体的关注竟然是以“农民工问题”的形式。什么叫“农民工问题”呢？一个最简单直观的表述就是农民工自身出了问题。2006 年，我到东莞去做调研，在东莞投资办厂很多年的老板就会说：“现在的农民工出了很多问题。以前的农民工吃苦耐劳，好管理，现在的农民工情绪化，不好管理，经常跳槽。”

所谓“农民工问题”,还表现为一些农民工的个体行为累积而导致的严重社会问题，比如说去年发生的富士康的连环跳事件，还有最近几年经常报道的一些暴力事件,如农民工制造一些爆炸事件来伤害他人等等。一个是向内自我毁灭，一个是向外伤害他人,这些都是个体行为，但累积而导致了严重的社会问题，这是我们讲农民工问题时经常关注到的。还有就是被一些科学研究所证实的农民工的心理健康问题。我读到一篇在公共健康杂志上发表的文章，是针对春节返乡青年农民工的心理调查。这个调查是用一个量表问卷测试他们的心理健康水平，他发现农民工在各项心理健康因子上，阳性项目数据总和高于全国成人常模。这很好理解，我们做体检，一个项目呈现阳性很紧张，你可能要复查。心理健康的指标和项目呈现阳性也说明有异常现象。这项研究发现农民工心理健康方面的主要问题是强迫，然后依次是人际关系敏感、偏执、抑郁、敌对等。这项研究发现农民工的心理状况比一般人要差,这似乎也在支持去年富士康员工自杀跳楼时一些心理学家的分析。

所有这些问题,从现象上看似乎都成立,可能农民工确实不安现状频繁调槽,可能农民工的心理健康确实比一般的成人要差，可能农民工暴力犯罪的比例确实略高，可是如果我们要想得更深一点，这些问题是怎么产生的？它的根源何在？我们就不能仅仅停留在一个现象的层面上。我们需要做一个更深的挖掘。

农民工问题的根源，根据我个人的看法，很直观简单的表述就是“农民工”这三个字。“农民工”这个词最早是由中国社会科学院社会研究所一位社会学家在 80 年代中期提出的。这个词我们已经使用了 20 多年，并被当成非常自然而然的存在了,我们没有觉得多么奇怪,农民工就对应背后一个人群。但认真一想就会发现农民工这个词是多么奇怪和荒谬。早些年，我们和境外的学者进行交流，将农民工直译成 peasant-workers，很多外国学者是不理解的。农民是和土地打交道，从事农业生产，工人和机器打交道，制造工业产品，怎么能够将两者混在一起呢？被我们叫做农民工的人，不管是制造业工人，还是一些从事服务业的人员，甚至包括一些自雇就业的小商小贩，他们早已经不是农民了，他们主要的劳动时间和劳动收入都来自于现有的职业，可我们仍然将他们称作农民工。当然现在我们知道，农民是他的身份，工人是他的职业，他进入城市完成职业上的转换之后，其农民身份仍被保留和维系，以至于他一直无法获得一个完整的工人的身份。很多人说农民工这个词不好，带有歧视的意味，建议改用“工人”或“新工人”等新词。我们在面对农民工这个词的时候虽然倍感刺痛，可是仍然坚持使用，因为农民工背后的实质性歧视不会因为言语上的简单改变而消失。所以，对于农民工本人来说，伤害主要不是来自农民工这个称呼，而是它背后的“制度设计”。

我们在不同场合说农民工是一种“制度设计”。表面看起来，并不存在一个叫做“农民工”的制度，那么我们为什么又说是“制度设计”呢？在社会科学的意义上，制度不仅仅是文本，不仅仅是政策文件、法律法规，而且是现实中实际起作用的一套做法和实践。正是在这个意义上，我们把它叫做“制度设计”。

刚才我提到中国特色的城市化制造了农民工，而农民工本身也是具有中国特色的一种现象。我曾经和潘毅老师合写过一篇文章，叫做《未完成的无产阶级化》，其中讨论到中国资本原始积累的过程。我们知道，资本原始积累就是将农民等小生产者的生产资料、生活资料剥离的过程，因此也是农民等小生产者无产阶级化的过程。农民失去了生产资料和生活资料，不得不进入城市，和机器、工厂结合才能够谋生。工业化催生农民由农村向城市的流动大潮，这不是中国的特色，世界范围内莫不如此，早期的英国、美国，后来的拉美、东亚四小龙都是这样。中国特殊的地方是什么？中国特殊之处是这个无产阶级化过程没有完成：大量的农民从农村进入到城市，职业上发生了转换，可是他们没有获得在城市居住和生活的制度性的安排，缺乏住房、子女教育和医疗保障，他们成了“农民工”。

„未完成的无产阶级化”将农民工置于一个摆脱不了的困境中：农民工劳动力的生产和再生产发生了空间上的分离。什么意思？农民工的劳动力的生产是放在城市，也就是说他们的劳动力被城市雇主使用，可是他们的劳动力的再生产（即劳动力维持和更新）是和城市分离的，很大一部分要依赖农村。在城市不是说没有劳动力再生产，农民工一天劳作下来要休息、要睡觉，第二天还要以同样的体力干活，这种最简单的劳动力再生产当然是在城市，可是更复杂的再生产，如结婚组建家庭，生育养育孩子，就不得不放到老家。而其宏观的后果，就是制造了中国城市化和工业化的分离。我们的工业化非常快，可是我们的城市化，实质意义上的城市化，却大大滞后。从数字上看我们城市化的水平已近 50%，但是看实质，我们说是伪城市化，还有将近 1.3 亿的进城农民工，实际上根本不是一个城市人生活的状态。在这个意义上讲，城市化和工业化是高度分离的。

那么，农民工这一“制度设计”是怎么开始的呢？我们知道，计划经济时代我国施行的是非常严格的户籍管理制度，农民不仅不可以随意到城市工作，甚至不可以随意到城市去走动。但是改革开放之后，随着港资、台资和其他外资进入中国投资办厂，对劳动力的需求大增，在这个情况下国家放松了户口的管制，允许农民工进城，从最初的自带口粮，到后来慢慢的把口子放得更大，可以自由进城打工。但是要注意的是，我们放松了对劳动力流动的管制，却没有彻底的废除户籍制度。劳动力可以自由进入工厂，可是劳动者作为一个人的完整需求，城市却不打算承担。这样一个“制度设计”维持了 30 年，到今天农民工已经进入第二代，却仍然看不到转化为城市工人的希望，我不得不说这是一个高度具有中国特色的现象。

我们会问，农民工这样一种制度设计既然这么不合理，这么荒谬，为什么会一直存在？仅仅是认识不到位吗？要回答这一回答，最简单的思路就是问：这样一个制度符合谁的利益？我们认为农民工的存在符合国家追求经济增长与资本追求最大化利润这两个方面的利益。首先，符合国家追求经济增长的利益，这个在前面我们已经讲了，中国在 30 年时间里维持了持续高速的经济增长，国家财政收入也以每年以百分之几十的速度往上增长。其次，符合资本追求最大化利润的利益。过去 30 年里，中国的经济增长以最快的速度制造了最多的富豪。今天中国已经超过日本了成为世界第二大奢侈品消费国，据说明年有望超过美国成为世界第一。

我想以下面这个表格为例，将农民工的存在和资本利润最大化之间的关系说得透彻一点。

农民工微薄的收入：深圳市历年最低工资标准		
年份	最低工资	平均工资
1992	245 元	（494）
1993	286 元	（679）
1994	300 元	（881）
1995	300 元	（1023）
1996	310 元	（1209）
1997	320 元	（1378）
1998	330 元	（1532）

1999	419 元	（1726）
2000	419 元	（1920）
2001	440 元	（2162）
2002	460 元	（2352）
2003	460 元	（2551）
2004	480 元	（2661）
2005	580 元	（2706）
2006	700 元	（2926）
2007	750 元	（3233）
2008	900 元	
2009	900 元	
2010	1100 元	

上表是深圳市 1992 年以来最低工资的变化情况。深圳市从 1992 年开始制定最低工资标准，当年是 245 元，括号内数字是深圳市当年职工的月平均工资。1992-2010 将近 20 年时间里，最低工资从 245 元增长到 1100 元，增长了 3 倍多，而同期深圳市 GDP 增长了几十倍，我们看到最低工资的增长幅度相对经济增长的速度而言是非常缓慢的。最低工资增长慢不去说它了，那么最低工资的水准如何呢？最低工资到是多少才合理，很难有一个绝对的标准，但一般认为最低工资相当于平均工资的 40%-60%是一个比较合理的水平，欧洲一些发达国家甚至高出 60%。我们看 1992 年最初制定最低工资的时候，大约相当于职工平均工资的 50%，这还在一个比较合理的范围内。但是再往后看，绝对数是在缓慢增加，但是相对于平均工资的比率却不断下降，2007 年已降到 30%以下，可见最低工资的水准已经低到一个很不合理的水平。我甚至想说，这么多年，最低工资的绝对购买力都是在下降，这个我没有做物价指数的研究，我只是给大家提供一个参考。1992 年一个农民工到深圳市去打工，如果企业执行最低工资的话是 245 元，我是 1993 年参加工作，在北京大学硕士留校任助教，工资具体多少我记不清楚了，但绝对没有 200 元。什么意思呢？今天一个北大的助教或者讲师工资仍然是比较低，整体上来讲都不合理，但是肯定比 1100 元高。农民工的工资购买力的绝对水准下降，这一点农民工自己一定有比较明确的体会。农民工 90 年代初到深圳打工，感觉到有钱赚，他的工资可能比很多在内地的公务员、事业单位的人员工资都要高，更不要说他作为一个农民的收入，工作虽累，但是有钱赚。但是今天的农民工进入深圳打工，他只能是为生存苦苦挣扎。你想想 2009 年的 900 元怎么维持生活？该年深圳市人均食物支出将近 700 元，一个农民工如果只拿最低工资，他的恩格尔系数就接近 80%，这绝对是超级贫困的水平。

大家也许会批评我，为什么拿最低工资说事？农民工是千差万别的，农民工有分化，有收入高一些的。但在现实中，一线制造业工人，或者普通服务员，8 小时工作拿到的基本上就是最低工资。这是一个不正常的现象，因为最低工资本来只适用于那些处于经营困难阶段的企业，或者其他一些特殊情况。可是今天我们会发现，中国的企业不管其盈利能力如何，不管是外资内资还是其他性质的资本，不管什么行业、什么地域，基本上都对一线普通员工执行最低工资。去年发生罢工的南海本田盈利水平高不高？即便这样一个高赢利的企业，对其普通员工执行的也只是比当地最低工资略高一点点的工资。富士康也是一样，去年发生连环跳悲剧的时候，富士康普工工资就是 900 多一点（比 2009 年最低工资 900 元略高）。最低工资成了一线农民工的最高工资（8 小时工作），这一极不正常的现象就是我们今天普遍面对的现实。当然多数农民工的实际收入会高出这点工资，他们“自愿”加班，为的是多挣一点加班费，以维持在城市的基本生存。

我刚才提到农民工的制度设计符合资本利润最大化的利益，这个表格揭示了全部奥秘。资本总是通过压低劳动力价格（工资）来获取最大利润，农民工的存在，使得资本可以以一种突破底线的方式压低劳动力价格，从而获取超额利润。这是什么意思呢？在所有的地方，资本的本性都是追逐利润最大化，但总会碰到一个绝对的底线，那就是劳动力再生产的基本费用。工人需要养活自己，需要组建家庭，养育后代，雇主支付的工资必须包含这些基本费用。

在中国，农民工这个制度设计的奥秘是什么？是突破了底线。为什么能突破呢？是因为资本不需要支付一个城市工人的工资，只需要支付一个农民工的工资，就是比他回去在农村干稍微工资高一点，但是没有办法养活他在城市生活这样一个工资。通过这样一种制度设计，通过把农民工的劳动力再生产很大一部分甩到农村去（一旦你生病了你得回农村，一旦你想要结婚就得在农村安家，想要生孩子还得在农村里养），资本对劳动力价格的压低成功地突破了城市工人的底线。这就是农民工制度设计背后的奥秘，它满足了资本追逐最大化利润的需要。大家以前看西方的电影，比如看卓别林的电影《摩登时代》，工厂一倒闭，经济一萧条，工人就会面临着生存的危机。电影中卓别林扮演的男主角找到一个女朋友，他必须去工厂挣回面包来养活自己和女朋友，一旦失业，生活就非常困难。大量的失业一定会造成城市的危机，最后造成这个国家的危机。但是我们似乎不怎么考虑农民工的失业问题，好象根本不存在这个问题一样。其实是不是存在呢？当然是存在的。比如 2008 年受美国金融危机的影响，珠三角很多工厂的农民工失去工作，可是我们根本不将他们当作失业工人来处理，而是说你们“回乡创业”吧。

农民工的制度设计满足了资本利润最大化的需要，但却给农民工带来巨大的伤害，整个农民工群体陷入难以摆脱的困境中。大家都知道，这样一个微薄收入勉强能维持他一个人在城市里面的生活，根本谈不上结婚生子，谈不上长久在城市里面居留的问题。农民工的处境，我讲得稍微夸张一点，是“有工作没有生活”。今天农民工在城市里找份工作不难，但这份工作只能让他在城市勉强生存，他没有生活，或者是只有非常有限的生活----这一点大家只要看看工厂宿舍和城中村的状况就明白了。在南方制造业发达的地区，工人住在哪里？我们经常说中国的城市没有贫民窟，咋一听有道理，可是我们有什么？我们有工厂宿舍！大量的农民工是在宿舍里面住的。深圳市一千二三百万人口，两百万户籍人口，剩下的一千万多数是农民工，他们居住在光鲜整洁的城市之外的工厂区。你一出关到宝安区，看到的是另外一个深圳，那里没有整洁的街道，没有繁华的商业大厦，没有绿荫匝地的公园；那是一个彻头彻尾的生产空间，到处是工厂，在每一个工厂围墙里面，兴建有为生产服务的宿舍，工人密集的住在宿舍里。可是宿舍并不是一个完整的生活空间，它仅仅是一个劳动力最简单再生产的场所，不要说不具备为农民工提供家庭生活的条件，即便是满足一个人完整的生活需求都有困难，说白了，宿舍就是一个睡觉的地方。

潘毅和任焰两位学者提出了“宿舍劳动体制”概念，在她们的文章里，宿舍不仅仅是一种特殊的建筑，而且是使得农民工进入工厂却不进入城市的一种制度安排。宿舍只是一个睡觉恢复体力的地方，作为一个人的完整的生活需求则被抑制和忽略。我们国家的城市化用宿舍替代了贫民窟，在维持城市建成区光鲜整洁的同时，却将数千万农民工置于“有工作没有生活”的处境中。

在北京、上海这样的城市，制造业不如商业服务业发达，农民工大多不住在工厂宿舍，而是住在城中村（或城乡接合部）。这些地方本是大城市的农村地区，它们之所以成为农民工集聚地，并不是城市政府的有意安排，而是当地农民出租房屋的市场需求与农民工在城市中的居住需求自然结合的产物。与工厂宿舍相比，城中村能够为农民工的生活需求提供更多满足，譬如很多城中村里的农民工可以维持家庭生活，但是他们仍然过的是一种简化、压缩的生活：在离北京大学很近的六郎庄村，十平方米左右的房间里往往挤居着一家数口，房间陈设简而又简，仿佛随时要搬家的样子。城中村不是农民工居留城市的合法化空间，不过是“寄住”之地罢了。一旦他们所在的城中村进入城市规划视野，就意味着他们“寄住”之地行将消亡。很多在北京居留的农民工都有频繁迁徙的历史，从二环到三环，从三环到四环，从四环到五环……

对于农民工来说，“有工作没有生活”的处境存在了 30 年，但是为什么到了最近这些年，农民工问题变得这么突出呢？一个最大的变化是，农民工这样一个“制度设计”遭遇了新生代农民工。过去的农民工制度设计也给第一代农民工带来了很大的伤害。但是新生代农民工的出现，以及他们的一些新特点，使得这样的制度设计在新生代农民工中难以维系。

第一代农民工进城打工，很多是抱着挣钱，回去建设美好的农村生活这样一个目的。打工是一种工具，是为了回家盖房子、结婚、养育子女。因此，他多少还能接受回去的安排，哪怕他有一种内在的想要留在城市的欲望，可是他还能接受回乡的命运。新生代农民工则不同，他们出生在上世纪 80 年代、90 年代，那是一个物质生活水平相对丰裕的年代，又是一个受教育水平普遍提高的年代。他们属于“无土”一代，在他们的名下，大多数人都没有分到土地，很少人由农业的生产技能和经验。在他们成长过程中，城市早就通过电视等大众传媒展现在他们的眼前，并成为他们的生活目标和梦想。对于新生代农民工中的很多人来说，自他们走出家门的那一刻起，就没有像其父母辈那样想过再回家做农民，就此而言，他们是踏上了一条进城打工的不归之路。但是以我们上面讨论过的微薄收入，打工根本没有可能通向城市生活。新生代农民工在城市里居留的时间越长，就越发看不到在城市长久生活的可能性。在这样的情况下，打工的意义忽然坍塌，打工就成了一种“漂在当下”“活在当下”的一种方式，而不能通向任何一个长远的生活目标。

前进之路已经堵死，后退之路早已关闭，身陷这种处境中的新生代农民工在身份认同方面出现了严重危机，由此带来一系列的心理和情绪乃至行为问题----这正是我们从富士康员工走上“不归路”背后看到的深层的社会和结构性原因。今天我们看到的是没有希望、进退两难的新生代农民工，身陷这一困境中的新生代农民工遇到了严重的身份认同危机。新生代农民工在走上打工之旅后面临着一个建构新的身份认同的历程，而这种历程的第一步是从自我否定开始的。在新生代农民工这里，“成为城市人”浮现为强烈的欲望，甚至明晰为长远的生活目标。他们在饮食起居、穿衣戴帽、交友婚恋、甚至文化消费等各个方面都不遗余力地划清与农村人的界限、尝试城市人的生活方式，然而，横亘在他们眼前的却是有着巨大反差的社会现实，生活在“宿舍劳动体制”之下或者城乡结合部的农民工，在物质和精神层面都遭遇着城市的排斥，由于收入微薄，加上缺乏住房、教育、医疗、社会保障等各种制度性的支持，他们越努力地追求城市生活，越会发现这个目标的遥不可及，通过打工这一手段似乎永远没有办法接近这一目标，打工的意义轰然坍塌。他们用行动和选择表明自己“不是农民”，却无法在现有的社会结构中确定自己的新的位置，自我否定的打工之旅通向的是一种漂泊的生存状态和主体体验，却没有办法形成新的身份认同。“我是谁”的问题实际上困扰着并影响新生代农民工的打工行为，我们常听到工厂老板抱怨这一代人不好管，情绪化，动辄辞工，没有人生规划等等，其实这些问题都和我刚才讲的认同危机联系在一起。在这样一种生存困境和认同危机之下，我们发现，在新生代农民工中间，“不爽”正成为一种弥散性的情绪，侵入骨髓，挥之不去。

我们分析了农民工问题的实质、症结以及由来。现在我再回过头来直接回应一些针对农民工问题的认识误区。可能有人认为农民工的问题是由于农民工的教育和技能等造成的，通过培训就可以解决。农民工受教育水平不高，技能不高，这是不是一个问题？当然是一个问题。今天农民工大多接受的初中和高中教育，教育水准确实有待于提高，农民工的职业技能培训普遍欠缺，难以胜任高技术的岗位。可是这是不是问题的症结？为农民工提供培训，提高他们的文化水平和职业技能，一定会有帮助，对特定的人群意义更大。可是，在现有的结构下，培训无法整体上解决问题。大家想一想，如果我们把今天的初中生都培养成高中生，或者大专生，他们不过变成高中的一线制造业员工，大专的一线制造员工，根本的问题仍然难以解决。通过培训提升职业技能很重要，可是培训如果不能连同回应结构性的问题是不能根本解决农民工问题的。还有人认为农民工的问题是城市根本不能容纳这么多农民工，我觉得这是很荒谬的认识。当然，城市的容纳能力不是无限的，但是用这种方式来取消我们对农民工问题更深一步的思考和取消农民工方向的政策倡导，我觉得完全是一个障眼法。为什么这样说？首先我们看今天的农民工，他们不是在城外，他们事实上已经是进城的农民工了。大家看一下北京的城市运转，环卫、商场、餐馆、物流、保安，我们这座城市运转最基础性的工作都是由农民工在承担，工厂的运转是由农民工在支撑，一旦这些人不在了，工厂马上就要停转，整个城市也要瘫痪。这哪里是城市容纳的问题呢？我们的城市政府只不过是用另外一种方式来安排这些已经进入城市和工厂的人，就像我前面提到的工厂宿舍和城中村。

新生代农民工希望在城市生活，这是一种非常基本的诉求，也是一种非常合情合理的诉求，一个人要求在自己工作的地点生活下来，这不是一个基本的诉求吗？我们认为，新生代农民工问题的解决就一个方向———“消灭农民工”。什么意思？他是农民就是农民，他是工人就是工人，让广大在城市有稳定生计的人在城市长久生活下来。具体而言则涉及两方面的责任，首先是企业的责任，应还给劳动者一份有尊严的工资，为劳动者过上正常的、有尊严的生活创造基础的物质条件，让农民工成为真正的“企业公民”。第二是政府的责任。农民工在城市中安家生活，碰到的最大障碍是住房、子女教育和医疗等问题。城市政府应拿出切实的举措，为农民工融入、扎根城市创造条件，让他们成为真正的“社区公民”，分享他们亲手创造的经济发展的成果。我们当然知道解决农民工问题会碰到种种困难和障碍，企业不会自动给农民工涨工资，城市政府也经常囿于短期利益而拒绝承担本应承担的责任。但是，我们可以确定的是，当新生代农民工进入历史舞台遭遇农民工这一“制度设计”时，紧张和冲突就注定不可避免。早日解决农民工问题，对于国家的长治久安和可持续发展都有重要的意义。

最后我愿意以我们的校友海子的诗句结束今天的演讲，也许将其中的“尘世”改为“城市”更符合今天的讲题：

愿你有一个灿烂的前程
愿你有情人终成眷属
愿你在尘世获得幸福

Kathleen Wittek

Interkulturelles Lernen im Schulaustausch[1]

Der vorliegende Aufsatz fasst die Ergebnisse einer empirischen Studie zu Möglichkeiten zur Förderung interkulturellen Lernens im Rahmen des Schulaustausches zwischen einer deutschen und einer chinesischen Schule zusammen. Über dieses Thema nachzudenken ist nicht nur deshalb notwendig, weil es bedingt durch die verhältnismäßig kurze Zeit, die das Fach Chinesisch an deutschen Sekundarschulen unterrichtet wird, kaum Untersuchungen zur Rolle des Schulaustausches beim interkulturellen Kompetenzerwerb gibt, sondern auch, weil gerade bei der Vermittlung distanter Fremdsprachen Lernangebote einbezogen werden sollten, die über den Rahmen des eigentlichen Schulunterrichts hinausgehen, um die Intensität der Beschäftigung mit der Sprache und dem distanten Kulturkreis zu erhöhen. Es soll untersucht werden, inwieweit ein Schulaustausch neben dem Erwerb landeskundlichen Hintergrundwissens und der Erhöhung der kommunikativen Kompetenz in der Zielsprache auch das interkulturelle kommunikative Lernen befördert. Erkenntnisse hierzu können bei der weiteren Vermittlung interkultureller kommunikativer Kompetenz und bei der Vorbereitung weiterer Schulaustauschfahrten genutzt werden.

Im ersten Teil des Aufsatzes werden für die Anwendung auf die Schulsituation relevante Theoriemodelle der interkulturellen Kommunikation sowie mögliche Problemfelder der Lerner bei der Beschäftigung mit der distanten Fremdsprache Chinesisch und der chinesischen Kultur dargestellt. Auf dieser Grundlage wird im zweiten Teil des Aufsatzes die Schulaustauschfahrt an die 22. Mittelschule in Beijing vom 12. bis 24. Mai 2010 als interkulturelles Lernangebot für Chinesischlerner der Bettina-von-Arnim-Oberschule in Berlin analysiert. Für die Untersuchung interkultureller Lernprozesse während und nach der Schulaustauschreise haben die Schüler unmittelbar zu Beginn und zum Abschluss der Reise, d.h. jeweils auf dem Hin- und dem Rückflug, Fragebögen ausgefüllt, die von der Verfasserin ausgewertet wurden.[2] Mit Hilfe dieser Fragebögen wurden einige Vorstellungen der Schüler von China, einschließlich möglicher Stereotype und der Schülersicht auf die deutsche Kultur, erfragt. Mit dem zweiten Fragebogen unmittelbar nach Abflug wurde versucht, Veränderungen in den Vorstellungen der Schüler zu China und Deutschland und mögliche Vergleiche der Kulturen zu erfassen. Die Fragebögen wurden von der Verfasserin zuerst quantitativ und im zweiten Schritt qualitativ ausgewertet.[3]

---

1 Bei dem vorliegenden Beitrag handelt es sich um eine gekürzte und überarbeitete Fassung der schriftlichen Prüfungsarbeit der Verfasserin zum 2. Staatsexamen für das Amt der Studienrätin (Chinesisch) im Land Berlin vom 24. August 2011.

2 Die Verfasserin ist sich bewusst, dass die Auswertung der Fragebögen aufgrund der niedrigen Teilnehmerzahl statistisch nicht signifikant ist. Dennoch besitzt sie Erkenntnispotenzial, auf das nicht verzichtet werden sollte. Eine umfassende Untersuchung, die verallgemeinernde Schlüsse für die Umsetzung interkulturellen Lernens während deutsch-chinesischer Schulaustauschprogramme ziehen könnte, steht noch aus.

3 An der Schulaustauschfahrt an die 22. Mittelschule in Beijing nahmen 11 Schüler der achten und sechs Schüler der neunten Klassenstufe teil. Von ihnen haben auf dem Hinflug 14 Schüler den Fragebogen ausgefüllt, auf dem Rückflug 13. Die Befragung erfolgte anonym. Um bei der Auswertung neben Gruppenvergleichen auch Einzelvergleiche ziehen zu können, hat die Verfasserin die Schüler gebeten, beide Fragebögen mit einem nur ihnen bekannten Zeichen zu markieren. Elf Schüler sind dieser Bitte nachgekommen. Auf den Fragebögen überwogen geschlossene Fragen mit vorgegebenen Kategorien. Auf beiden Fragebögen befanden sich auch offene Fragen, um Anreize zu spontanen Antworten zu

Berliner China-Hefte/Chinese History and Society 41 (2012), pp. 100-118

Zur Verifizierung und Ergänzung der in der Fragebogenauswertung gewonnenen Ergebnisse, werden die Beobachtungen der Verfasserin, Schülertexte, die während der Reise als Tagebucheinträge und im Anschluss als freie Aufsätze entstanden, Schülerinterviews sowie Gespräche und Befragungen der mitreisenden deutschen und der chinesischen Lehrer herangezogen, um im dritten Schritt interkulturelles kommunikatives Lernen während und unmittelbar nach der Schulaustauschfahrt zu beschreiben.

Interkulturelles Lernen zur Erweiterung der interkulturellen kommunikativen Kompetenz

Der Ansatz der interkulturellen Kommunikation und die damit verbundenen pädagogischen Konzepte hatten in ihren Ursprüngen rein operativen Stellenwert zur Unterstützung und Durchsetzung nationaler politischer Interessen.[4] In ihrer Weiterentwicklung wurden sie für ökonomische Ziele eingesetzt und werden erst seit ca. zwanzig Jahren als Beitrag zur Erlangung individueller Schlüsselkompetenzen, die auch in der Schule entwickelt werden können, verstanden. Aufgrund der Beteiligung vieler verschiedener Forschungsrichtungen an der Debatte und der sich daraus ergebenden fundamentalen Definitionsunterschiede des Konzepts interkultureller Kommunikation hat sich bislang kein Modell als übergreifend akzeptiertes durchsetzen können. Um interkulturelle kommunikative Kompetenz nicht nur zu thematisieren, sondern auch deren Erwerb zu initiieren, ist es erforderlich, vorhandene Ansätze miteinander zu verbinden und auf Transfer- und Anwendungsmöglichkeiten im Schulalltag zu überprüfen.

Es ist zunächst festzustellen, dass der Erwerb interkultureller kommunikativer Kompetenz als gesteuertes oder ungesteuertes interkulturelles Lernen verlaufen kann. Ungesteuertes interkulturelles Lernen vollzieht sich in erster Linie als kulturspezifischer Akkulturationsprozess (Berry 1996), der zu besserer Orientierung und Kommunikation in der fremden Kultur führt. Es gibt jedoch auch kulturübergreifende Komponenten, wie den Umgang mit Stress oder Ambiguitätssituationen, die auf zukünftige Kontakte mit anderen Kulturen universell transferiert werden können. Damit das ungesteuerte interkulturelle Lernen zu einem echten Kompetenzzuwachs führt, und nicht einfach durch Verfestigung vorhandener Stereotypen in interkulturelle Konflikte und Missverständnisse mündet, sind nach Kammhuber ein „hohes Maß an Stressresistenz und Ambiguitätstoleranz“, eine bewusste Auseinandersetzung mit den „fremden Elementen einer Kultur“, das selbständige Bemühen um „kulturrelevante Informationen“, die in adäquater Form von der sozialen Umwelt erhältlich sind, sowie die anschließende Integration in das eigene Orientierungssystem notwendig (Kammhuber 2000: 8).

---

geben. Mehrfachantworten und Hinzufügungen wurden ausdrücklich zugelassen, um die Befragten nicht zu sehr einzuschränken und das Informationspotenzial auszuweiten.

4 Erste Konzepte zur interkulturellen Kommunikation entstanden in den USA in den 1950er Jahren, als es mit der Übernahme der neuen Führungsrolle der USA in der Welt notwendig wurde, viele von den USA ins Ausland entsandte Spezialisten, Soldaten, Wissenschaftler oder Aufbauhelfer auf ihre Auslandseinsätze vorzubereiten. Der vom Foreign Service Institute mit geeigneten Schulungsmaßnahmen beauftragte Kulturanthropologe Edward T. Hall stellte nach kurzer Zeit fest, dass die reine Vermittlung ethnologischen Wissens über fremde Kulturen nicht ausreichte, die ins Ausland gesandten Personen bei ihren Aufgaben zu unterstützen. Er schätzte ein, dass unreflektierte kulturelle Vorurteile die Schulungsteilnehmer an einer adäquaten Verarbeitung ihres Wissens über andere Kulturen hinderten. Seine in Zusammenarbeit mit Psychoanalytikern und Linguisten entwickelten Theorien und Methoden zur Verringerung bzw. Auflösung kultureller Vorurteile und zur praxisnahen Vermittlung ethnologischen Wissens fasste er unter dem Begriff „Intercultural Communication“ zusammen. Seither gilt Hall als Begründer der „Interkulturellen Kommunikation“ (u.a. Rogers/Hart 2002: 1-18).

Angesichts der begrenzten Aufenthaltsdauer im Ausland, der unterschiedlich stark ausgeprägten Stressresistenz und Ambiguitätstoleranz, des eingeschränkten Zugangs zu kulturrelevanten Informationen und der positiven Erfahrung mit gesteuertem Lernen in der Schülerbiografie, ist die Ergänzung durch gesteuertes interkulturelles Lernen sinnvoll und dringend geboten. Gesteuertes interkulturelles Lernen soll Hilfestellungen geben, die eigenkulturellen Kategorien, durch die die fremde Kultur beim Erstkontakt gefiltert wahrgenommen wird, aufzuzeigen. Die Schüler sollen befähigt werden, den unter der Oberfläche liegenden Teil des Eisbergs (Hofstede 1993), in dem sich die für Interpretation und das Verständnis kommunikativer und non-kommunikativer Handlungsakte der anderen Kultur notwendigen Werte, Einstellungen etc. verbergen, zu erkunden.

Gesteuertes interkulturelles Lernen kann sich kulturübergreifend oder kulturspezifisch gestalten und kognitiv und bzw. oder erfahrungsorientiert ausgerichtet sein.

Beim kulturübergreifend kognitiven Lernen geht es um allgemeine Kenntnisse über kulturelle Bedingtheit menschlichen Wahrnehmens, Denkens, Handelns und Verhaltens sowie um die Kenntnis von Dimensionen zur Unterscheidung von Kulturen. Grundlage hierfür bieten die Unterscheidung von Kulturen nach starkem oder schwachem Kontextbezug (Hall/Hall 1990), Hofstedes Kulturdimensionen und die „Kulturthemen" (Cushner/Brislin 1996). Diese Theorien sind besonders für integrative oder interdisziplinäre kulturkontrastive Ansätze geeignet, da diese an mehreren Kulturen ausgerichtet werden.

Das Eisbergmodell oder auch das Zwiebelschalenmodell (Trompenaars/Hampden-Turner 1994) sind für den Fremdsprachenunterricht nutzbar, da sie die Aufmerksamkeit der Fremdsprachenlerner auf die verborgenen Teile der Kultur lenken. Sie können verdeutlichen, dass Ähnlichkeiten, die bei interkulturellen Begegnungen möglicherweise festgestellt werden, auf unterschiedlichen Konzeptionen der Realität beruhen. Unter jungen Menschen, die über (fast) alle Grenzen hinweg Popmusik hören, Jeans tragen und die Freizeit mit Computerspielen verbringen, sind kulturelle Unterschiede nicht immer so offensichtlich. Beim interkulturellen Lernen geht es daher darum, sich zuerst des unter der Oberfläche liegenden Teils des eigenen Eisbergs bewusst zu werden und die Fähigkeit zu erlangen, mit anderen darüber zu sprechen. Mit diesem Wissen wird es möglich, einander besser zu verstehen und Gemeinsamkeiten zu finden.

Der kulturspezifisch kognitive Ansatz ist im Moment am meisten anzutreffen. Im Schulunterricht ist das klassische Beispiel die Landeskunde in der Fremdsprachenausbildung. Landeskundliche Informationen zu Geografie, Geschichte, Politik, Wirtschaft und Lebensbedingungen des Zielsprachenlandes werden im Lehrbuch oder vom Lehrer in der Landes- oder Fremdsprache präsentiert und es wird auf kulturelle Unterschiede zwischen dem eigenen Lebensumfeld und der entsprechenden Situation im Zielsprachenland eingegangen. Geeignete theoretische Ansätze bieten Byrams „fünf savoirs" (Byram 1997) und die Kulturstandards von Thomas (1996) als zentrale Merkmale eines kulturspezifischen Orientierungssystems, anhand dessen eigenes und fremdes Verhalten beurteilt werden kann. Die Akzente haben sich damit längst vom reinen „landeskundlichen Wissen" hin zu individueller Fremdheitserfahrung, Sensibilisierung für kulturelle Unterschiede und damit zur Deutung kulturspezifischer Phänomene und Handlungsweisen verschoben (Maletzke 1996; Byram 1997).

Bei allem notwendigen Wissen um kulturelle Differenzen sollten diese nicht überbetont, sondern als Medium genutzt werden, Wahrnehmungs-, Interaktions- und Interpretationsfallen sichtbar zu machen. Kulturelle Differenzen dürfen weder geleugnet, noch überbetont werden. Die eingenommene Perspektive kann sowohl Gemeinsamkeiten als auch

Unterschiede in den Mittelpunkt stellen und liegt im Ermessen des Betrachters (Götz 2003:10-12). Für jüngere Lernergruppen bietet sich anfangs eine Beschäftigung mit den kulturellen Gemeinsamkeiten an, weil die Reflexion darüber zum einen die Angst vor dem Fremden und Unbekannten mildert und zum anderen das Neue mit dem Alten und Vertrauten verbindet. Die Beschäftigung mit den Gemeinsamkeiten beim deutsch-chinesischen Kulturvergleich kann den Schritt von der Selbstreflexion zur Fremdreflexion erleichtern.

Im weiteren Sinne unterstützt interkulturelles Lernen durch die Förderung von Empathie mit anderen Identitäten und Distanz zu den jeweils übernommenen eigenen Rollen sowie Toleranz gegenüber den Ambiguitäten die Ausbildung von Offenheit und einer vielschichtigen und stabilen Identität des Individuums, das „Spannungen aushält, für wechselnde Situationen offen bleibt und darum Verschiedenartigkeit, Infragestellung, Widerspruch in der sozialen Umwelt nicht als Bedrohung und Quelle lähmender Angst, als Verweigerung seiner Anerkennung empfinden muss"(Meyer 2002: 42) .

Interkulturelle kommunikative Kompetenz

Die Diversität der Konzepte und Diskurse zur interkulturellen Kommunikation spiegelt sich auch in den Konzepten zum interkulturellen kommunikativen Kompetenzerwerb. Doch bei aller Unterschiedlichkeit der Ansätze sind die Positionen nicht klar abzugrenzen. Sie differieren graduell mit variierender Schwerpunktsetzung hinsichtlich der Prämissen, Zielsetzungen und entsprechenden Methoden. Interkulturelles Lernen wird als sozialer Lernprozess verstanden und soll den Umgang mit kultureller Differenz bzw. mit Differenzen allgemein fördern. Durch multiperspektivische Allgemeinbildung sowie mehrsprachige und antirassistische Erziehung wird darauf hingearbeitet, Menschen in der Entwicklung ihrer interkulturellen Dialogfähigkeit und sozialen Kompetenz zu unterstützen (Steindl 2008: 8-10). Forderungen, „interkulturelle Kommunikation" und „interkulturelle Interaktion" (Maletzke 1996; Losche 1995) in den Bildungsprozess zu bringen, werden mit Vorschlägen vereint, eine „Deutschlandkunde" zu implizieren (Kalpaka 1998), da interkulturelle Kommunikation ebenso das Studium fremder Kulturen umfasst wie das der eigenen. Die Schüler werden somit idealerweise zu Reflexionen über die eigenen kulturellen Geformtheiten bzw. Limitationen befähigt (u.a.: Condon und Yousef 1975, Trompenaars/Hampden-Turner 1994). Eine solche auf die eigene wie die andere Kultur ausgerichtete Sensibilisierung kann das interkulturelle Verstehen und Verständnis fördern und somit die bilaterale oder multilaterale Kommunikation tatsächlich verbessern. Zur Vermeidung von Stilisierung, Zuschreibung, Verweisung, Verbreitung und Verfestigung von Stereotypen kann der hier implizierte Kulturbegriff nur prozesshaft verstanden werden (u. a. Schiffauer 1997; Kalpaka 1998), „als eine Arena, in der Werte, Normen, Denkmuster von kulturellen Akteuren ständig neu ‚verhandelt' werden" (Schiffauer 1997: 148). Wenn Kultur als dynamischer Prozess verstanden wird, der in der Interaktion entsteht, bedeutet dies für den interkulturellen kommunikativen Kompetenzerwerb, dass die Schüler befähigt werden, Kultur nicht als geschlossenen und abgegrenzten Verweisungszusammenhang innerhalb der territorialen Grenzen des Zielsprachenlandes zu verstehen. Für die Bildung im Sekundarstufenbereich eignet sich hier eine Fragmentierung durch das „Konzept der Subkulturen" der Kulturanthropologie, nach dem

> ...die Teilgruppen einer großen Gesellschaft eine je eigene Kultur aufweisen, eben eine Subkultur. Jede Subkultur hebt sich durch eigene subkulturspezifische Merkmale von anderen Subkulturen ab, fügt sich aber zugleich der übergreifenden Gesamtkultur ein. Dabei beschränkt sich dieses Konzept heute nicht auf ethnisch definierte Teilgruppen,

> sondern es erstreckt sich auch auf zahlreiche sonstige Untergruppen einer Großstadtgesellschaft. (Maletzke 1996: 17)

Für die Fremdsprachenvermittlung im Sekundarstufenbereich bedeutet dies einerseits die Problematisierung des Kulturbegriffs und andererseits für den interkulturellen Vergleich die Auswahl geeigneter Kategorien für Subkulturen wie beispielsweise Alter, Bildungsstand, urbane Herkunft zur Erzeugung oder Simulierung echter interkultureller Auseinandersetzung und zur Vermeidung intrakultureller Zuschreibungen.

Der Erwerb interkultureller kommunikativer Kompetenz hilft den Schülern auf Grund des angeeigneten Wissens, kulturelle Distanzen, Differenzen und Barrieren sowie bisherige emotionale Prägungen unvoreingenommen wahrzunehmen, zu reflektieren und gegebenenfalls zu reduzieren, und sich in interkulturellen Überschneidungssituationen, d.h. in Situationen, in denen Individuen verschiedener (Sub-)Kulturen aufeinander treffen, adäquat orientieren und verhalten zu können. Dabei ist es unerheblich, ob es sich um die multikulturelle Gesellschaft des Heimatlandes oder um einen Aufenthalt im Ausland handelt: Interkulturelle kommunikative Kompetenz bedeutet hier, dass keine Stereotype bedient werden, d.h. bestehende Klischees werden problematisiert und das Unbekannte wird vorurteilsfrei als etwas Neues wahrgenommen, hinterfragt und mit bereits bekannten Phänomenen aus verschiedenen (Sub-)Kulturen verglichen aber nicht gewertet.

Wichtige Teilkompetenzen für den Erwerb interkultureller Kompetenz sind Empathiefähigkeit, die Fähigkeit zur Selbstbeobachtung und die Bereitschaft zum Hinterfragen eigener Positionen, da die Frage der interkulturellen Kompetenz mit der eigenen Selbstwahrnehmung und kulturellen Identität verbunden ist. Der Mensch ist nur als Wesen in Gemeinschaft denkbar. Doch auch in den Schulklassen zeigt sich, wie schwierig es ist, harmonisch zu interagieren, wenn ehemals gemeinsame Bezugspunkte sich stets weiter durch den nicht nur medialen Import anderer Kulturen diversifizieren. Beim Thema des Umgangs mit dem Fremden geht es immer auch um den Umgang mit sich selbst; daher ist dies eine persönlichkeitsbestimmende Kernkompetenz des Individuums.

Um den interkulturellen kommunikativen Kompetenzerwerb im Kontext des Fremdsprachenerwerbs darstellen zu können, beschränkt die Verfasserin diesen in der vorliegenden Arbeit in Anlehnung an Annelie Knapp-Potthoffs (1997) Konzeption von Kulturen als Kommunikationsgemeinschaft auf Situationen, in denen Kontakte zwischen verschiedenen Sprachgemeinschaften bestehen, wobei „Sprache" hier auf der Ebene von Standardvarietäten verstanden wird.

Interkulturelles Lehren und Lernen bedeutet auch, über die Vermittlung von interkulturellen Lerninhalten im Unterricht hinaus Möglichkeiten zum Sammeln interkultureller Erfahrungen anzubieten. Zur produktiven Verarbeitung von kulturellen Unterschieden, Fremdheitssituationen und interkulturellen Aushandlungsprozessen sollten diese am besten selbst erfahren werden. Durch die Partnerschaft mit einer Schule im Zielsprachenland können solche Erfahrungen sehr intensiv gewonnen werden.

Potenzielle Problemfelder deutscher Schüler beim Austausch mit chinesischen Schülern

Zur Herausarbeitung möglicher Problemfelder bei der Beschäftigung deutscher Schüler mit chinesischer Kultur und Sprache bieten die Kulturmodelle von Hofstede und Hall/ Hall, Trompenaars und Hampden-Turner, Byram, Bennett u. a. Ansätze zu Strukturierung und Kategorisierung. Nach Hofstede und Hall/Hall kann die deutsche Kultur als überwiegend monochron, das Konzept der langsamen Kommunikation favorisierend, low-context-orientiert, individualistisch, maskulin, eher unsicherheitsvermeidend und mit geringer Machtdistanz dargestellt werden.[5] Die chinesische Kultur wird nach diesen Kategorien als polychron, das Konzept der langsamen Kommunikation favorisierend, high-context-orientiert, kollektivistisch, maskulin, unsicherheitsvermeidend und mit hoher Machtdistanz dargestellt. Ähnliche Unterschiede können mit den Kulturstandards von Thomas herausgearbeitet werden (Thomas/Schenk 2005). Starke Abweichungen zwischen chinesischer und deutscher Kultur gibt es nach den genannten Ansätzen im Bereich der sozialen Beziehungen in der unterschiedlichen Wertigkeit von Individuum und Gruppe, mit den daraus resultierenden unterschiedlichen Höflichkeitsstandards, Konfliktlösungs- oder Konfliktvermeidungsstrategien, Hierarchiestrukturen sowie einem verschieden hohen Akzeptanzgrad von flexiblem Zeitmanagement.

Mit dem sprachliche Verhaltensweisen analysierenden Ansatz der Ethnografie der Kommunikation lassen sich die folgenden, möglicherweise zu Problemen führenden Unterschiede beschreiben: Der direkten Ausdrucksweise im Deutschen steht die indirekte im Chinesischen gegenüber. Die vor allem bei der älteren Generation verbreitete verbale Bescheidenheit im Chinesischen, die es auch erfordert, die eigene Leistung den anderen gegenüber schlecht zu reden, stößt im deutschen Kulturkreis bestenfalls auf Unverständnis. Im schlechteren Fall wird sie als unehrlich und von der Gegenseite Lob erheischend verstanden. Auch das rätselhafte Lachen kann zu Irritationen führen, ebenso die im chinesischen Kulturkreis offen gezeigte Neugier, die sich beispielsweise am Beginn eines Gesprächs mit neuen Bekanntschaften in Fragen nach Alter, Familienstand, Einkommen, monatlichen Ausgaben u.v.a.m. ausdrückt (u.a. Jin 1994).

Mit den Ansätzen der kontrastiven Pragmatik können Sprechakte kulturvermittelnd erfolgreich ablaufen. Im Gegensatz zu sprachlich fehlerhaften Beschreibungen oder Darstellungen von Erlebnissen kann eine der Zielsprachenkultur nicht angemessene Realisierung dieser Sprachhandlungen das Verhältnis zwischen Sender und Empfänger gefährden (Hunfeld 1989: 71). Dies erfordert eine kontrastive Vermittlung, gerade in sensiblen Bereichen der sozialen Interaktion wie Bitten, Aufforderungen und Entschuldigungen. So formulieren beispielsweise deutsche Schüler Sprechakte wie Beschuldigungen, Beschwerden, Aufforderungen und Bitten direkter als chinesische. Diese größere Indirektheit in Sprechakten der Zielsprache korreliert auch mit einer stärkeren Beziehungsorientierung der chinesischen Partner, die sich u.a. in beziehungsorientierten Routineformeln bei Gesprächseröffnungen ausdrückt, während deutsche Schüler eher sachorientierte Eröffnungsformulierungen benutzen.

Für die immersionsartige Erfahrung des Schulaustausches treffen alle in den vorangegangenen Abschnitten beschriebenen Problemfelder zu, da die Schüler beim Austausch in den Familien, in der Schule und unterwegs ihre Fremdsprachenkenntnisse anwenden und mit hoher Sicherheit einige kulturell geprägte Eigenheiten auf die Situation im Ausland übertragen, was zu Missverständnissen führen muss. Da solche Missverständnisse zu einem nachhaltigeren Erkenntniserwerb führen können, sollten sie als Lernangebot während und nach der Reise produktiv genutzt werden. Es versteht sich von selbst, dass fundamentale Fehlannahmen, die zu einer gravierenden Störung der Kommunikation zwischen den deutschen Partnern und ihren Gastfamilien oder der Partnerschule führen können, im Vorfeld analysiert werden. Hierzu gehört die Sensibilisierung im Sprachunterricht für höflichere Formulierungen von Bitten, Aufforderungen und Entschuldigungen, für den höheren Anteil an indirekter Wortwahl und für eine größere Vagheit in chinesischen

5 Diese bereits von Hall/Hall und Hofstede in den genannten Untersuchungen vorgenommenen Zuschreibungen wurden von späteren Untersuchungen bestätigt (bspw. Kartari 1995).

Antworten. Diese Sensibilisierung impliziert auch, dass den Schülern das höhere Maß an Direktheit und Eindeutigkeit bei deutschen Formulierungen bewusst wird, und dass sie dies im Kontext unterschiedlicher kultureller Konventionen erklären können, ohne es zu bewerten.

Eine weitere mögliche Quelle interkultureller Missverständnisse, auf die im Vorfeld hingewiesen werden muss, ergibt sich aus den unterschiedlichen Konzeptionen von Zeit als monochron oder polychron. So führte beispielsweise die kurzfristige Planung und flexible Anpassung von Plänen der chinesischen Seite bei den deutschen Eltern mehr als einmal zu Irritationen darüber, ob ihre Kinder in China überhaupt willkommen seien. Diese Unsicherheiten, die einige Eltern auf ihre Kinder übertrugen, wurden trotz mehrfacher Erklärungen durch Austauschorganisatoren und Schulleitung erst nach Ankunft in China endgültig ausgeräumt.

Die unterschiedliche Stellung von Individuum und Gruppe ist zwar auch ein großer Unterschied, spielt aber in der Jugendkultur nicht so eine große Rolle wie in anderen gesellschaftlichen Subkulturen. Hier ist es ausreichend, die Schüler darauf vorzubereiten, dass sie während des Aufenthalts in China eine Reihe von Mitgliedern der Großfamilie kennenlernen werden, damit sie das beim Kauf von Geschenken wie Berlinsouvenirs einplanen können. Über die auch heute noch existierenden großen Unterschiede bei der Machtdistanz sollten die Schüler im Vorfeld informiert werden, damit sie für solche Beobachtungen sensibilisiert sind.

Bei allen möglichen kulturell bedingten Unterschieden sollte immer gesehen werden, dass die chinesischen Partner mindestens genauso intensiv auf die Eigenheiten der deutschen Partner vorbereitet werden, so dass die Begegnungssituation keine „ursprüngliche" interkulturelle mehr ist, sondern bereits von Interpretationen überlagert wird.

Interkulturelles Lernen durch den Schulaustausch

Eine Schulaustauschfahrt in das Zielsprachenland stellt zweifellos ein intensives interkulturelles Lernerlebnis dar, da es hierbei nicht einfach wie bei einer normalen Sprach- oder Urlaubsreise um die Anwendung und Erweiterung von Sprachkenntnissen geht, sondern vielmehr um eine immersionsähnliche Erfahrung, die sich aus dem Leben in der ausländischen Gastfamilie, der Interaktion mit Gleichaltrigen aus dem Zielsprachenland, dem Schulalltag, der gemeinsamen Freizeitgestaltung mit den Gastgeschwistern und Freunden, natürlich auch dem touristischen Programm sowie vielem anderen mehr zusammensetzt. Bereits zu Beginn des 7. Jahrgangs wird den Schülern und ihren Eltern das Austauschprogramm der Schule vorgestellt. Die Chinareise im 8. oder 9. Schuljahr sowie die Aufnahme der chinesischen Partner während ihres Gegenbesuches in Berlin sind Teil des Konzeptes, Chinesisch als Sprach- und Kulturfach zu unterrichten. Im ersten Jahr des Austausches – 2009 – sind 13 Schüler nach China gefahren, im zweiten – 2010 – nahmen 17 Schüler teil. Im Oktober 2010 fuhr bereits die dritte Schülergruppe nach China. 2012 geht der Schulaustausch mit der Hangzhouer Partnerschule in die dritte Runde und mit der Beijinger Partnerschule in die zweite Runde. Auch die Aufnahme eines Gastkindes in der deutschen Familie sowie das gemeinsame Schul- und Besichtigungsprogramm sind wichtige Aspekte interkulturellen Lernens und wären es wert, in einer weiteren Arbeit untersucht zu werden.

Die Reise nach China im Rahmen des Schulaustauschprogrammes hat vordringlich drei Ziele: die Anwendung und Verbesserung der erworbenen Fremdsprachenkenntnisse, die Ausbildung interkultureller Kompetenz und die Vertiefung und Erweiterung der Kenntnisse über einen anderen Kulturkreis. Das kann in knapp zwei Wochen nur an der Oberfläche bleiben. Deshalb setzen sich die Schüler bereits im Vorfeld der Reise mit ihrem Reiseziel auseinander.

Kultursensibilisierung vor dem Schulaustausch

Alle Teilnehmer an der Chinareise gaben ein Interesse an China und seiner Sprache an. Dreizehn von vierzehn Schülern begründeten ihre Entscheidung, Chinesisch zu wählen, mit intrinsischer Motivation. Für ungefähr ein Drittel war das eigene Interesse an chinesischer Kultur ausschlaggebend. Ein weiteres Drittel begründete diese Fächerwahl mit späteren Berufsmöglichkeiten und ein letztes Drittel mit dem Interesse an einer ungewöhnlichen Sprache. Lediglich ein Schüler gab an, überredet worden zu sein, in die Chinesischstammgruppe zu gehen. Aber auch dieser Schüler gab bei der Frage nach seinem Grund für die Teilnahme am Schüleraustausch ein starkes Interesse an China und Beijing und Neugier auf die chinesische Kultur an.

Auch wenn davon ausgegangen werden kann, dass eine vorhandene starke intrinsische Motivation die Sensibilisierung für die andere Kultur erleichtert, sollte diese nicht dem Selbstlauf überlassen werden. Die Schüler beschäftigten sich im Vorfeld der Reise mit verschiedenen Aspekten des chinesischen Alltagslebens wie den Auswirkungen der Ein-Kind-Politik auf die Familienstrukturen, dem Schulsystem, der Entwicklung von Megastädten oder der Bedeutung von Traditionen wie Festen und dem chinesischen Kalender für die moderne Familie. In den Monaten unmittelbar vor der Reise befassten sich die Schüler mit ihrem Reiseziel, der Stadt Beijing. Sie sammelten in Gruppenarbeit Informationen zu ausgewählten Sehenswürdigkeiten und zur Geschichte der Stadt und überlegten sich, was sie gern sehen wollten. Für alle Schüler war es wichtig, zur „Großen Mauer“ zu fahren und den Palast des Kaisers in der „Verbotenen Stadt“ zu sehen. Die Vorbereitung sollte die Schüler auf die Reise einstimmen und sie für Entdeckungen sensibilisieren.

Im Vorfeld der Reise haben die Schüler auch Steckbriefe über sich verfasst und nach China geschickt. Im Chinesischunterricht wurde ein Mailaustausch mit einer chinesischen Klasse in der Provinz Hebei initiiert, um den Schülern die Möglichkeit zu geben, mit gleichaltrigen Sprechern der Zielsprache in Kontakt zu kommen.[6] Damit sich die Schüler auch in Berlin mit gleichaltrigen chinesischen Jugendlichen treffen konnten, fanden Begegnungen mit Schülern der Huade-Schule[7] statt. Diese Kontakte trugen dazu bei, dass sich die Schüler mit dem Alltag in ausgewählten Subkulturen des Zielsprachenlandes auseinandersetzten. Manche Informationen aus den Mails hinterfragten sie im Unterricht; sie lernten einige neue Wörter oder ließen sich bei ihnen unverständlichen Wendungen oder Situationsbeschreibungen helfen.

Im Laufe der Reise erkannten die meisten Schüler, dass sie auf die Schulaustauschfahrt vorbereitet worden waren: Während sich zu Beginn der Reise nur ein Schüler von 14 ausreichend auf die Reise vorbereitet fühlte, nannten nach der Reise 6 von 13 Schülern die Vorbereitung „ausreichend“. Es gab nach der Reise auch keinen Schüler mehr, der sich

6 Leider war es trotz mehrfacher Bitten der Bettina-von-Arnim-OS nicht möglich, mit den chinesischen Austauschpartnern im Vorfeld des Austausches Mailkontakt aufzunehmen. Die Gründe hierfür mögen einerseits in der polychronen Organisationsarbeit und andererseits der Zurückhaltung aufgrund einer „high-context-Orientierung" des chinesischen Partners liegen. Nach dieser für beide Seiten positiv verlaufenen Austauschbegegnung ist zu hoffen, dass solche Mailkontakte bei der nächsten Schulaustauschreise bereits im Vorfeld organisiert werden können, damit jeder Schüler seine Gastfamilie von Deutschland aus kennenlernen kann. Das könnte den interkulturellen kommunikativen Erkenntnisgewinn maximieren.

7 Freie Schule, die sonnabends chinesischen Kindern Unterricht in chinesischer Sprache anbietet.

unzureichend vorbereitet fühlte. Vor der Reise gaben immerhin sechs Schüler an, dass die Reise aufgrund mangelhafter Vorbereitung „abenteuerlich" werden würde. Diese Fragebogenergebnisse bestätigen einerseits, dass die Vorbereitung im Vorfeld der Reise den Schülern erfolgreiche Strategien für ihr Leben in den Partnerfamilien und im chinesischen Schulalltag zu vermitteln vermochte, dass diese aber erst durch die Anwendung während der Reise zu anwendungsbereiten Kompetenzen entwickelt werden konnten. Dies sollte bei der Vorbereitung des nächsten Schulaustausches stärker berücksichtigt werden.

Bei der Reisevorbereitung wurden bei vielen Schülern sowohl diffuse als auch konkrete Stereotype von China, den Chinesen und der chinesischen Kultur genannt, z.B. die Angst, dort Hund oder Schlange essen zu müssen, in einem rückständigen Land nicht zurechtzukommen, immer Reis bzw. chinesische Gerichte essen zu müssen, keine aus „westlichen" Ländern gewohnte Unterhaltungsindustrie vorzufinden etc. Im Sprach- und im Projektunterricht wurden solche Klischees in Diskussionen, aber auch in Rollenspielen und Simulationen thematisiert und anschließend diskutiert. Dennoch hielten einige dieser Stereotype bis zur Reise an; bspw. wurde die Situation, beim Essen Hundefleisch angeboten zu bekommen, gern szenisch dargestellt. Hier hielt sich das Stereotyp hartnäckig, trotz vielfältiger Beschäftigung mit chinesischer Esskultur und vielen Gesprächen mit der chinesischen Gastlektorin und auch anderen chinesischen Besuchern an der Bettina-von-Arnim-Oberschule. Es lassen sich nicht alle Stereotype in Gesprächen ausräumen. Dennoch wurden einige Schüler durch die Vorbereitung dafür sensibilisiert, dass sie falsche oder überholte Vorstellungen von China haben könnten. So schrieb ein Schüler im Fragebogen vor der Reise, dass die Informationen durch Medien, Freunde und Familie ihm Sichten vermitteln, „die wahrscheinlich stimmen, aber das war so vor ca. 10-20 Jahren und stimmt bestimmt heute nicht mehr" (Auswertung Fragebogen 1, Frage 5).

Der Schulaustauschreise kommt hier die Rolle der Praxiserfahrung zu. Sie kann die Gelegenheit bieten, die Kenntnisse über China in Erkenntnisse umzuwandeln und einige falsche Vorstellungen zu revidieren. Damit wird die Schulaustauschfahrt zu einer sinnvollen Ergänzung des Wissenserwerbs im Unterricht, dessen Simulationen sich der Realität nur annähern können, diese aber wohl nie ersetzen werden.

Interkulturelles Lernen während der Schulaustauschfahrt vom 12. bis 24. Mai 2010

Da die Schüler während ihres Aufenthalts in Beijing an der 22. Mittelschule Unterricht hatten und ihre Freizeit sowohl im Rahmen von organisierten Stadtbesichtigungen als auch im Erleben des chinesischen Alltags mit ihren Gastgeschwistern verbrachten, haben sie in der Beobachtung des Alltags der Familie und des Schulalltags gleichaltriger Chinesen viele Informationen aufgenommen. Diese wurden teils als interessante Begebenheit unreflektiert weitererzählt, teils mit ähnlichen Situationen aus eigenem Erleben in Deutschland verglichen und teils kritisch hinterfragt.

Die 22. Beijinger Mittelschule hatte für die Partnerschüler aus Berlin ein umfangreiches Programm zusammengestellt. An Schultagen kamen die deutschen Schüler gemeinsam mit ihren Gastgeschwistern um 7.30 Uhr in der Schule an und hatten ab 8.00 Uhr Unterricht. Am ersten Tag nach der Ankunft, am Freitag, den 14. Mai, begleiteten die deutschen Schüler ihre Partner in deren Unterricht und erhielten so einen recht authentischen Einblick in chinesische Unterrichtsabläufe.

Vom 17. bis zum 21. Mai erhielten die deutschen Schüler je einen halben Tag lang Unterricht in Sport, Kunst, Musik, Chinesisch und traditioneller Kultur. Für die andere Tageshälfte hatte die Beijinger Partnerschule Ausflüge organisiert. Nur am Mittwoch, den 19.

Mai, hatten die deutschen Schüler wie ihre chinesischen Partner den ganzen Tag lang Unterricht. Die Unterrichtsinhalte spiegelten China überwiegend als traditionelles und geschichtsbewusstes Land. Dies schien zwar auf den ersten Blick ein absoluter Kontrast zu dem hypermodernen Leben zu sein, das die Schüler außerhalb der Schule beobachteten, half ihnen aber, die chinesische Gesellschaft als eine sich im Umbruch befindliche wahrzunehmen. Mit dem Unterrichtsangebot kamen die chinesischen Partner den deutschen Austauschschülern vermeintlich entgegen, da es vor allem Inhalte waren, die von ausländischen Chinesischlernern häufig nachgefragt werden wie der Daoismus oder die chinesischen Kampfsportarten, die den Schülern durch Kung-Fu-Filme bekannt sind, und die in China bei der jüngeren Generation erst als Re-Import eine Renaissance erleben. Durch die Akzeptanz der Fremdwahrnehmung werden Stereotype perpetuiert.

Die Schüler wohnten in ihren Gastfamilien. An Wochentagen hatten ihre chinesischen Partner sehr wenig Freizeit, da sie von 7.30 Uhr bis 16.30 Uhr in der Schule sein mussten und die meisten über eine Stunde zur Schule unterwegs waren. Alle Schüler erzählten, dass sie früher aufstehen mussten als in Berlin. Da ihre chinesischen Partner bis Mitternacht an ihren Hausaufgaben saßen, und die deutschen Partner mit ihnen gemeinsam aufblieben, hatten alle Schüler ein Schlafdefizit, was sich u.a. im von den Schülern formulierten Tipp an die nächsten Chinareisenden, dass sie vor der Reise viel schlafen sollten, zeigte (Auswertung Fragebogen 2, Frage 15). Andererseits unterscheidet sich diese Situation nicht von anderen Klassenfahrten, nach denen viele Schüler auch erst einmal das Bedürfnis verspüren auszuschlafen.

Da die deutschen Schüler nur ungefähr halb so viel Unterricht hatten, wie ihre chinesischen Partner, organisierte die 22. Mittelschule Besichtigungen für die Austauschschüler. Dabei lag der Schwerpunkt eindeutig auf historischen Kulturdenkmälern, wie dem „Platz des Himmlischen Friedens“, der „Verbotenen Stadt“, dem Konfuzius-Tempel, der „Großen Mauer“ u.ä. Der hohe Anteil historischer Kulturdenkmäler am Besichtigungsprogramm spiegelt einerseits das Selbstverständnis der mittleren und älteren Generationen wider, die China zuerst als ein Land mit traditionellen Werten und langer Geschichte sehen, steht andererseits jedoch in deutlichem Kontrast zum heutigen hypermodernen Straßenbild Beijings und der Freizeitkultur der jungen Generation in der Großstadt. So wurden nur zweimal moderne Teile Beijings besichtigt: der Olympiapark und die Wangfujin-Straße. Im Olympiapark wurde auf die Symbiose verschiedener traditioneller chinesischer Architekturprinzipien verwiesen und somit am Beispiel von „Vogelnest“ und „Wasserwürfel“ wieder der Bogen zurück zum chinesischen Geschichtsbewusstsein gespannt.

In der nicht von der Partnerschule organisierten Freizeit beschäftigten sich die Schüler ähnlich wie zu Hause auch. Sie gingen mit ihren chinesischen Partnern shoppen, trieben Sport, spielten in Spielhallen oder zu Hause am Computer, trafen sich mit gleichaltrigen Freunden ihrer Gastgeschwister, sahen Filme oder „chillten“ (Tagesprotokoll vom 20. Mai 2010).

Ein wichtiger Teil der Freizeitgestaltung war auch das Essen, dem in China bei der zwischenmenschlichen Kommunikation traditionell eine größere Bedeutung zugemessen wird als in Deutschland. Die Sorge, ob das Essen schmeckt, hatte fast alle deutschen Schüler vor ihrer Abfahrt beschäftigt. Andererseits wurden auch die chinesischen Gastfamilien vor Ankunft der deutschen Schüler über die „Gewohnheiten der Deutschen“ auf einer Schulversammlung aufgeklärt, so dass vielen Austauschschülern „westliches Essen“ serviert wurde. So begann für eine Reihe von Schülern der Tag mit einem Frühstück bei

McDonald's (Tagesprotokolle vom 19. und 20.5.2010; Gespräche mit der Verfasserin am 17. und 19. Mai 2010). Anderen wurden Hamburger u.ä. für die Schule mitgegeben. Dennoch wurde den Schülern schnell klar, dass sie nicht das Essen bekamen, das in ihrer Familie sonst üblich war:

> ... am Abend gingen wir, wie nun schon üblich, Fastfood essen. Ich denke, sie glauben, ich mag kein chinesisches Essen. Denn am nächsten Morgen, also Tag fünf in China gab es Chicken von der Fastfood-Kette KFC." (Schüleraufsatz „Die Reise nach China": 2)

Andererseits wollten die deutschen Schüler ihre chinesischen Gastgeber auch nicht beleidigen und erzählten ihnen daher nicht, dass sie in Deutschland nicht so häufig in Fastfood-Restaurants gehen.[8]

Schülerreflexionen zum Schulaustausch

Alle Teilnehmer des Austausches waren am Ende begeistert. Auch die Schüler, die mit einiger Skepsis nach China flogen und in den ersten Tagen starkes Heimweh verspürten, waren am Ende traurig, nach so kurzer Zeit wieder heimzukehren. Die meisten wären gern länger geblieben und drückten der Verfasserin gegenüber am letzten Tag mehrfach ihr Bedauern darüber aus, dass sie nun, da sie sich eingelebt und in Beijing gute Freunde gefunden hätten, schon wieder zurückfahren müssten. Alle freuten sich darauf, ihre Gastgeschwister und einige chinesische Begleitlehrer im Januar in Berlin wiederzusehen.

Die Schüler haben nach eigenen Aussagen viel über China während der Reise dazugelernt: Vor der Reise schätzten elf von vierzehn Schülern ihre eigenen Kenntnisse über chinesische Kultur, Geschichte und Politik als gering ein. Neun gaben an, gern noch mehr darüber erfahren zu wollen. Nach der Reise gaben elf von dreizehn Schülern an, viel über China gelernt zu haben.

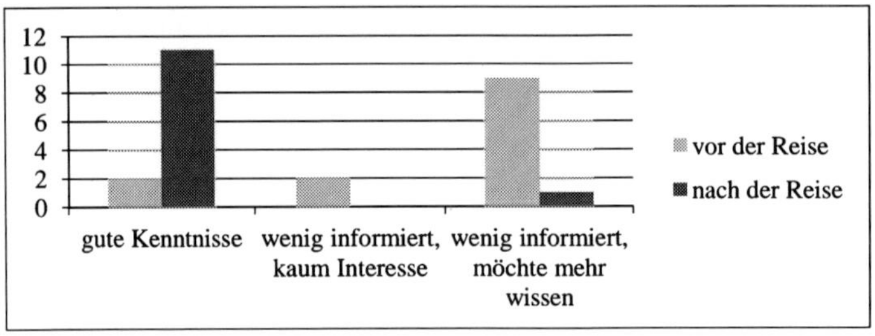

Selbsteinschätzung der Kenntnisse über die chinesische Kultur[9]

Auf den Fragebögen erwähnten die Schüler häufig, dass sie von den Tempeln, Palästen und der „Großen Mauer" beeindruckt waren. Allerdings fiel es den meisten schwer, Unterschiede zwischen den verschiedenen Tempeln zu erkennen, so dass A- und B-Schüler[10]

8 Dass sie gar nicht so gern immer nur Burger essen, wie von den Chinesen angenommen, geht auch aus folgendem Tagebucheintrag hervor: „Frühstück gab es wie jeden Morgen bei McDonald's und es schmeckte diesen Tag genauso schlecht wie an jedem anderen Morgen." (Tagesprotokoll vom 19. Mai 2010)

9 Auswertung Fragebogen 1, Frage 4 und Fragebogen 2, Frage 3.

10 In der vorliegenden Arbeit wird die in der englischen Fremdsprachendidaktik übliche Differenzierung nach A-, B- und C-Schülern übernommen, wobei die Gruppe der C-Schüler die leistungsstärkste ist und die der A-Schüler die leistungsschwächste. Diese Gruppen können nicht statisch aufgefasst werden, da

nach diversen Tempel- und Palastbesichtigungen kein Interesse an traditioneller Architektur mehr hatten. Das zeigte sich deutlich, als an einem Tag keine Besichtigung auf dem Programm stand und mehrere A-Schüler der Verfasserin gegenüber äußerten, dass Schule besser sei als die vielen Tempel. Am Vortag hatten die Schüler mit dem Lama-Kloster und dem Konfuzius-Tempel zwei in den Augen der Lerner gleich aussehende Anlagen besichtigt. Bei A-Schülern festigten diese Besichtigungen das Stereotyp eines traditionellen Landes mit vielen Tempeln (Schülergespräche und Auswertung Fragebogen 2, Fragen 6 und 13). B-Schüler mit Interesse für Geschichte fühlten sich bei der Besichtigung des Konfuzius-Tempels in die Kaiserzeit zurückversetzt und erkannten anhand der starken Verwitterung, dass die in Stein gehauenen Zeichen mehrere hundert Jahre alt waren (Tagesprotokoll vom 18. Mai 2010). C-Schüler stellten bei den Besichtigungen Fragen zum Unterschied zwischen dem Lamaismus und dem Konfuzianismus.

Durch den Lernzuwachs während der Reise wuchs das allgemeine Interesse an chinesischer Kultur bei den Schülern. In den Unterrichtsstunden unmittelbar nach der Chinareise tauschten sich die Schüler über ihre Erlebnisse in der Familie, in der Schule und bei Besichtigungen aus, ergänzten die Berichte der anderen und erweiterten so ihre Perspektive. In der zweiten Phase der Nachbereitung setzen sich die Schüler im Rahmen von Präsentationen mit ausgewählten Aspekten der chinesischen Kultur, Geschichte, Geographie oder des Alltags vertiefend auseinander. Beispielsweise zeigten einige C-Schüler in der Nachbereitungsphase ein verstärktes Interesse an einer eingehenderen Beschäftigung mit chinesischen philosophischen und religiösen Schulen. So entschieden sich im folgenden Schuljahr zwei Schülerinnen für eine Präsentation zu den Unterschieden buddhistischer Richtungen in China.

Besonders interessant fanden die deutschen Jugendlichen den Schulalltag ihrer chinesischen Partner. So waren viele Schüler erstaunt darüber, dass die Chinesen in Schuluniform zum Unterricht gingen, dass sie sich nicht schminken durften und dass ihnen Frisuren für die Schule vorgeschrieben waren. Erwähnenswert fanden viele Schüler, dass chinesische Schüler im Unterricht manchmal ihren Kopf auf den Tisch legten und schliefen, was zumindest im Beisein deutscher Gäste nicht von den unterrichtenden Lehrern kritisiert wurde.

Die konfuzianische Tradition des Lernens durch Nachahmen war während unseres Aufenthaltes häufig zu beobachten:

> Im vierten und letzten Block lernten wir ein chinesisches Gedicht bei einer Lehrerin, die nur Chinesisch sprechen konnte. Die Lehrerin wollte, dass wir das Gedicht gleich auswendig können, was einigen auch gelungen ist. Fast alle fanden das langweilig. (Tagesprotokoll vom 20. Mai 2010)

Der Chinesischunterricht war noch am stärksten von dieser beobachteten traditionellen Lernmethode des Zuhörens, Nachsprechens, Mitschreibens und Memorierens geprägt. Die deutschen Schüler verglichen den Unterricht, den sie aus Deutschland kannten, mit dem an der chinesischen Schule und äußerten der Verfasserin gegenüber mehrheitlich, dass sie den deutschen Unterricht abwechslungsreicher fanden. Andererseits bewunderten sie ihre chinesischen Partner dafür, dass sie bei einem hohen Unterrichtspensum zwischen täglich 9 und 12 Stunden, in Klassen, in denen 45 Schüler überwiegend frontal unterrichtet werden, gute Lernleistungen erzielten.

---

sich deren Zusammensetzungen je nach Lerninhalt ändert. Weitere für die Entwicklung interkultureller kommunikativer Kompetenz wichtige Differenzierungen wie die nach Alter, sozialer Herkunft, Interessen etc. müssen an dieser Stelle vernachlässigt werden.

C-Schüler stellten dann auch fest, dass diese Lehr- und Lerntradition in allen Bereichen, d.h. auch außerhalb der Schule anzutreffen war. Eine Schülerin schilderte ihre Erfahrung beim Spielen des ihr unbekannten „Fünf-Steine-Schachs“ (*wuziqi* 五子棋) mit dem Onkel ihrer Gastschwester wie folgt:

> Ich konnte aber nicht und sollte gleich losspielen. Ich dachte, es wäre wie Schach und habe einfach einen Stein gesetzt. Da hat er mit dem Kopf geschüttelt. Dann habe ich begriffen, dass fünf Steine nebeneinander gesetzt werden müssen. Ich habe mit dem Onkel gespielt und er hat mich gnadenlos verlieren lassen. Die ganze Familie saß drum herum und stöhnte, wenn ich den Stein setzte. Ich dachte: Warum sagt ihr mir nichts; ich kann es ja nicht. Der Onkel sagte nur: Setz den Stein woanders hin. Dann habe ich ihn woanders hingesetzt und dann war es wieder nicht richtig. (Gesprächsprotokoll vom 7. Juni 2010)

Der Schülerin waren die Parallelen zu den erlebten Sport- und Chinesischstunden in Beijing aufgefallen. Sie stellte fest, dass in China das Lernen durch Nachahmung und durch Fehlerreflexion ohne direkte Unterstützung durch Lehrpersonen überwiegt. Damit hat sie ein wichtiges konfuzianisches Bildungsprinzip erkannt.

Das Gebäude der Partnerschule wurde als „ärmlich“, „dreckig“ und „groß“ beschrieben (Auswertung Fragebogen 2, Frage 3; Placemat[11]-Auswertung „Schule“). Die technische Ausstattung der Unterrichtsräume wurde dagegen als besser als die der eigenen Schule eingeschätzt. Eine besondere Erwähnung erhielten die „Lochtoiletten“, die für die nächsten Chinareisenden als „nicht ganz so schlimm“ beschrieben wurden. Da bereits am Ankunftstag darüber informiert wurde, dass ein Teil der Schule im neuen Schuljahr abgerissen und neu gebaut werden würde, fügte sich besonders für die reiferen Schüler die Partnerschule in das Bild eines sich im Umbruch befindenden Landes ein.[12]

Das chinesische Essen war oft Gesprächsthema und nahm auch in den Auswertungen breiten Raum ein. Die deutschen Schüler lobten das sehr abwechslungsreiche Essen und die Restaurantkultur in China, äußerten sich aber auch häufig negativ über das vergleichsweise einfache Schulessen. Auf dem im Rahmen der Nachbereitung gestalteten Placemat zum Thema Essen fanden sich als Nahrungsmittel, die die Schüler mit der Reise spontan in Verbindung brachten, „Peking-Ente“, „Hund“, „exotische Früchte“, „Reis“ und „Eis“ mit je drei Nennungen gleich häufig, gefolgt von den Restaurantketten „McDonald's“ und „KFC“ mit je zwei Nennungen (Auswertung Fragebogen 2, Frage 3; Placemat-Auswertung „Essen“). Wie bereits beschrieben, fanden einige Schüler schon während der Reise heraus, dass das Servieren von Fastfood in der chinesischen Gastfamilie der „interkulturellen Aufklärung“ seitens der Partnerschule bzw. dem in China verbreiteten Vorurteil, dass die Menschen in Westeuropa und in den USA sich vorwiegend von Fastfood ernährten, geschuldet ist. Andererseits beobachteten die Gastfamilien auch die starke Zurückhaltung einiger Schüler beim Probieren unbekannter Gerichte und wollten ihrer Fürsorgepflicht dann mit „westlichem Essen“ nachkommen. Im Laufe der Reise war zu beobachten, wie die anfängliche Zurückhaltung unbekanntem Essen gegenüber allmählich einer zaghaften Offenheit wich (Auswertung Fragebogen 2, Frage 14). Die Schüler beschrieben in den morgendlichen Gesprächen ihnen bislang unbekannte Gerichte als

---

11 Methode des kooperativen Lernens, bei der Lernende zu einer Fragestellung eigene Gedanken entwickeln und anschließend in schriftlichen Austausch miteinander treten.

12 Als weitere sichtbare Zeichen der Veränderung werteten die Schüler die vielen Baustellen und die krassen Gegensätze von großen modernen Gebäuden, achtspurigen Autobahnen, riesenhaften Einkaufspalästen neben kleinen alten Hütten, engen Gassen und Verkaufsangeboten aus der eigenen Wohnung.

merkwürdig aussehend und dennoch äußerst schmackhaft. Selbstverständlich gab es weiterhin Gerichte, die die Schüler nicht essen wollten. Ein wichtiges Thema war den Schülern der Unterschied in der Esskultur. Ihnen fiel auf, dass das Essen, wenn Zeit war, in einem größeren Kreis eingenommen wurde. Die meisten Schüler wurden jeden Abend ins Restaurant eingeladen. Am Wochenende trafen sie beim Essen oft Mitglieder der weiteren Familie. Die Schüler schätzten die als Gäste erlebte größere Geselligkeit in der durch eine „high-context"-Orientierung geprägten chinesischen Kultur, besonders die älteren unter ihnen reflektierten aber auch, dass die sich daraus ergebenden Pflichten anstrengend werden könnten und dass sie für diesen Lebensstil neben Geld auch viel Zeit aufwenden müssten (Schüleräußerungen in der Unterrichtsstunde „Essen & Restaurantkultur" am 24. Juni 2010).

Die wichtigste während der Schulaustauschfahrt gewonnene Erkenntnis war für die deutschen Schüler, dass die chinesischen Jugendlichen ihnen in ihren Interessen und ihrer Freizeitgestaltung sehr ähnlich sind. Die Schüler erzählten, dass sie sich mit ihren Gastgeschwistern über Musik austauschten, gemeinsam am Computer spielten, Sport trieben oder einfach in die Shopping-Malls oder in Spielhallen gingen.

Es gab keinen Schüler, der mit seinem Austauschpartner unzufrieden war. Die meisten Schüler waren von den Partnerfamilien begeistert, weil sie „wie Könige behandelt wurden" (Auswertung Fragebogen 2, Frage 6), und zählten die chinesischen Partner sofort zum Freundeskreis:

> Ich habe mich mit Anni sehr gut verstanden, denn sie ist auch sehr ruhig und so freundlich wie ihre Mutter. Und daher wurden wir gute Freunde. Anni hat für mich ein Armband machen lassen. [···] Dieses Armband trägt ihre beste Freundin, Anni und ich. (Tagesprotokoll vom 15. Mai 2010)

Die deutschen Schüler verglichen häufig ihren Alltag mit dem ihrer Partner und stellten fest, dass das Leben chinesischer Jugendlicher anstrengender ist. So schrieb ein Schüler über seinen Partner: „Er dachte, wir tragen Schuluniform, haben länger Schule, haben mehr Hausaufgaben. Ja, wir haben doch ein einfacheres Leben als die Chinesen." (Auswertung Fragebogen 2, Frage 8).

Als weitere auf der Schulaustauschfahrt gewonnene Erkenntnis wurde von deutschen Schülern formuliert, dass „Chinesische Jugendliche versuchen, solange es geht, Kind zu sein" (Auswertung Fragebogen 2, Frage 3). Damit ist gemeint, dass Eltern und Schule in China viele Entscheidungen für die chinesischen Schüler treffen und dass sie dadurch im Alltag weniger selbständig agieren konnten als ihre deutschen Austauschpartner. Am häufigsten wurde auf die Frage nach dem Erkenntnisgewinn der Reise das Erleben des chinesischen Alltags genannt und „die positive Lebenseinstellung, dieses Fröhlichsein" (zu diesem Abschnitt: Auswertung Fragebogen 2, Frage 3).

Bei der Reflexion zum Leben chinesischer Jugendlicher fiel es den Schülern am leichtesten, die Perspektive der gleichaltrigen chinesischen Freunde einzunehmen, da aufgrund der Zugehörigkeit zur gleichen Altersgruppe die Gemeinsamkeiten schnell gesehen und verstanden werden konnten.

Kultursensibilisierung

Während des Aufenthaltes veränderte sich das Chinabild unserer Schüler. Sie revidierten einige Stereotype, verfestigten andere und nahmen evtl. neue auf. Es war deutlich zu erkennen, dass die Schüler durch ihre Reiseerfahrungen ihre Akzeptanz für China und seine Kultur erhöhten und allgemein ihr Wissen über ihr Zielsprachenland vertiefen konnten. Sie waren aber auch gezwungen, sich mit ihrer eigenen Kultur auseinanderzusetzen. Zum einen, weil sie als „authentische Deutsche" in den Deutschunterricht eingeladen wurden und dort mit Stereotypen bzw. Symbolen über ihre eigene Kultur konfrontiert wurden, wie dem Weihnachtsbaum als ganzjähriger Dekoration des Deutschraumes, oder den Vorstellungen von deutscher Esskultur. Zum anderen, weil sie in der Gastfamilie über ihre Heimat ausgefragt wurden oder von allein erzählten. Die Reflexion über die eigene Kultur setzte aber schon im Vorfeld ein – spätestens bei der Auswahl der Geschenke, der Berlin-Souvenirs. Diese Auseinandersetzung mit der eigenen und der fremden Kultur führte dann auch zu Vergleichen der beiden und durch Vergleich zu einem gewissen Verständnis bis hin zur Akzeptanz der unterschiedlichen Positionen. Die Schüler, die aus unterschiedlichen Gründen vor der Reise viele Ängste hatten, kamen alle begeistert zurück, fühlten sich in Bezug auf China sicherer und genossen es, ihre Reiseerlebnisse und auch veränderte Sichtweisen im Freundeskreis zu erzählen.

Ein eindeutiges Ergebnis des Schulaustausches war, dass China als weniger distantes, exotisches Land wahrgenommen wurde. Vor allem die junge Generation wurde in ihrem Lebensumfeld als den deutschen Schülern ähnlich empfunden. Vor der Reise stimmten 13 Schüler zu, dass die Chinesen sehr anders seien in ihrem Verhalten, sowohl in der Schule als auch in der Familie und in anderen Alltagsbereichen. Nach der Reise hatte sich die Zustimmung zu diesem Satz fast halbiert. Es gab nach der Reise auch keine Zustimmung mehr zu einer pauschalen Gleichsetzung aller Menschen und der Vernachlässigbarkeit der Rolle von Kultur. Die Schüler sahen jetzt die Rolle der Kultur differenzierter. Sie nahmen die Unterschiede zwar wahr, hielten sie aber nur noch für interessante, kulturunterscheidende Merkmale. Es gab viel weniger konkrete oder diffuse Ängste.

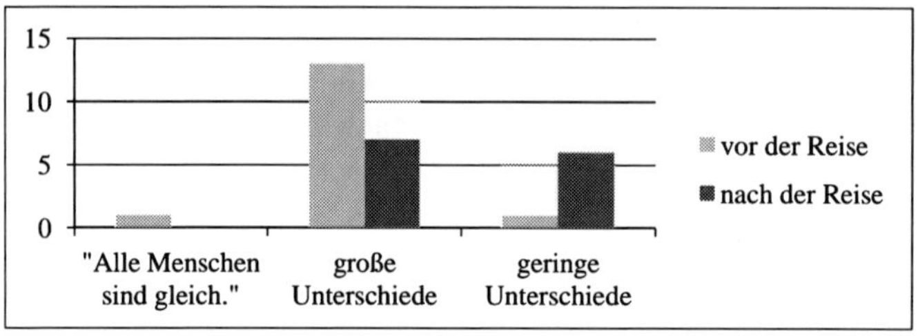

Verhaltensunterschiede bei Chinesen und Deutschen[13]

Im Einzelnen lässt sich konstatieren, dass die Schüler während der Reise ein viel differenzierteres Bild von China entwickelt haben. Charakterisierten die Schüler vor der Reise China in erster Linie als ein traditionsreiches Land mit einer großen Bevölkerung, freundlichen Menschen, Umweltproblemen, guten sportlichen Leistungen, dem Fahrrad als wichtigem Verkehrsmittel und Reis als Hauptnahrungsmittel, so beschrieben sie unmittelbar nach der Reise China als modernes Land mit vielen Autos. Sport, Fahrräder und Reis wurden nicht mehr genannt. Die Tradition spielte nach Einschätzung der Schüler weiterhin eine wichtige Rolle, konnte nun aber nicht mehr losgelöst von der modernen Entwicklung gesehen werden. Zwar war die Häufigkeit bei der Nennung der abstrakten Begriffe wie „Tradition" und „modern" gleich geblieben, wenn aber bei der Auswertung repräsentative Symbole für diese Kategorien berücksichtigt werden, wie „Drachen", „Konfuzius" bzw. „Auto", „Handy", so hatten sich die Nennungen im Bereich der „Moderne" von 7

[13] Auswertung Fragebogen 1, Frage 3 und Fragebogen 2, Frage 2.

auf 13 fast verdoppelt, während die Nennungen im Bereich der „Tradition" von 15 auf 11, d.h. um fast ein Drittel und damit auf einen niedrigeren Wert als bei den Kategorien der „Moderne" gesunken waren. Der Bevölkerungsreichtum wurde nach der Reise nur noch zwei Mal zur Charakterisierung Chinas herangezogen. Vor der Reise war dieses Merkmal fünf Mal so häufig genannt worden:

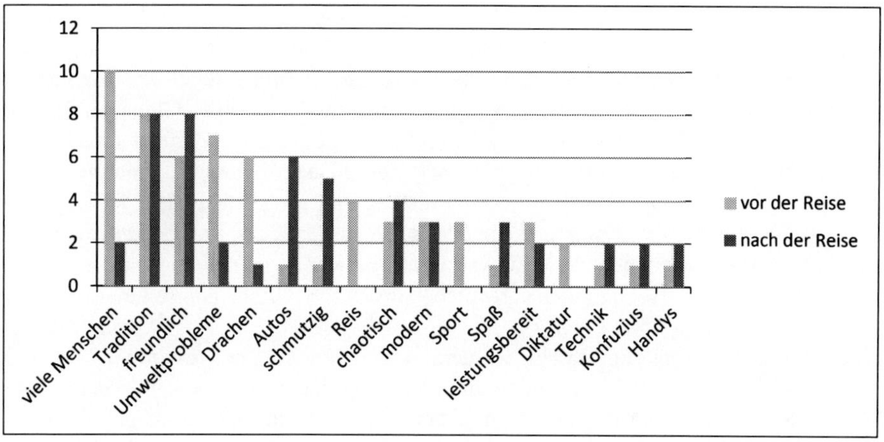

Wörter, die China am besten beschreiben[14]

Erwähnenswert ist auch die veränderte Einschätzung chinesischer Gleichaltriger. Wurden sie vor der Reise als eher leistungsbereit charakterisiert mit wenig Zeit für Spaß, so wurde die Leistungsbereitschaft nach der Reise bei chinesischen Jugendlichen zwar weiterhin konstatiert, aber weniger häufig genannt. Dafür wurde „Spaß" zur Beschreibung drei Mal so oft wie vor der Reise genannt.

China wurde nach der Reise als etwas chaotischer als vorher wahrgenommen, was auch auf die Beobachtungen unserer Schüler im Beijinger Großstadtverkehr mit „äußerst abenteuerlustigen" Autofahrten (Tagesprotokoll vom 22. Mai 2010) und der Nichteinhaltung von Vorschriften wie der Anschnallpflicht zurückgeht: „Als ich eingestiegen war, schnallte ich mich an und die Chinesen begannen zu lachen, denn es war (wie ich im Laufe der Zeit merkte) nicht üblich, sich im Auto anzuschnallen." (Schüleraufsatz „Die Reise nach China": 1).

Zusammenfassend kann festgestellt werden, dass die Schüler China während der Reise als modernes Land wahrgenommen haben, und dass ihnen nach der Reise das Leben der gleichaltrigen Jugendlichen in der Familie dem eigenen Leben recht ähnlich erschien. Politische Themen, die vor der Reise durchaus mit China in Verbindung gebracht wurden, spielten nach der Reise eine untergeordnete Rolle, da sie in den Gesprächen mit den Austauschpartnern und deren Familien nicht vorkamen.[15] Die Schüler hatten sich ihr eigenes Chinabild erarbeitet, in dem bisherige Vorstellungen integriert oder revidiert waren. Die Schüler waren nach der Reise eher in der Lage, Stereotype, Vorurteile oder veraltete Vorstellungen zu erkennen und zu benennen. Im Großen und Ganzen sahen sie aber ihre

[14] Auswertung Fragebogen 1, Frage 12 und Fragebogen 2, Frage 11.

[15] Waren vor der Reise noch zwei von 14 Schülern der Meinung, dass die Chinesen ihr Land sehr kritisch sehen würden, da es keine Demokratie sei, vertrat nach der Reise keiner der Befragten mehr diese Auffassung (Auswertung Fragebogen 1, Frage 2 und Fragebogen 2, Frage 1).

bisherigen Vorstellungen von China, die sie im Unterricht, aus Medieninformationen oder in privaten Gesprächen gewonnen hatten, bestätigt.[16]

Obwohl nur ein Schüler von 13 nach der Reise der Meinung war, dass sich seine Vorstellungen von Deutschland und den Deutschen während der Reise geändert hätte (Auswertung Fragebogen 2, Frage 7), belegt die Auswertung der Fragebögen eine deutliche Veränderung bei der Sicht auf das eigene Land. So beschrieben die Schüler vor der Reise Deutschland eher als „demokratisches Land“ oder nannten zur Charakterisierung Schlagwörter wie „Fußball“, „gutes Essen, vor allem Fleisch“ und „viel Stadt aber dazwischen grüne Flecken“. Nach der Reise nutzten sie ihre Chinaerfahrungen bei der Beschreibung Deutschlands und charakterisierten es viel konkreter im Vergleich zu China als Land mit „weniger Menschen“, „kleineren Straßen“, und „weniger Autos“. Darüber hinaus wurde Deutschland als „bunt“, „sauber“ und als Land mit „blauem Himmel“, „anderem Essen“ und „lockerem Schulleben“ dargestellt (Auswertung Fragebogen 1, Frage 11; Fragebogen 2, Frage 10). Deutschland wurde nach der Reise als „reiches Land“ beschrieben mit freundlichen und rücksichtsvollen Einwohnern (Auswertung Fragebogen 2, Frage 10). Dinge, die als selbstverständlich erachtet wurden, erfuhren nun eine Aufwertung (Auswertung Fragebogen 2, Frage 14).

Zusammenfassend kann konstatiert werden, dass obgleich die Auslandserfahrung im Mittelpunkt der Reise stand, der Kontakt mit den chinesischen Partnerschülern, die Erlebnisse in den Familien, in der Schule und bei gemeinsamen Unternehmungen zu einer eigenen, differenzierteren und facettenreicheren Sicht auf Deutschland geführt hat.

Gesamtreflexion

Die Reise an die 22. Mittelschule in Beijing hat gezeigt, dass die immersionsartige Erfahrung eines Auslandsaufenthalts im Vergleich mit Mitschülern, die nicht mitfuhren, deutlich zu interkulturellem kommunikativem Kompetenzerwerb geführt hat. Die Auswertung der Fragebögen ergab, dass die Schüler durch die Reise in unterschiedlichem Maße zu Fremd- und Selbstbeobachtung angeregt wurden. Alle Schüler bemühten sich, ihr Verhalten dem ihrer chinesischen Partner im Alltag anzupassen. A-Schülern fiel es dabei schwerer, sich auf die fremde Umgebung einzulassen. C-Schüler und ältere B-Schüler zeigten eher Neugier und Offenheit für das Leben in China und wollten es so authentisch wie möglich erleben.[17] Am deutlichsten zeigte sich der interkulturelle Kompetenzzuwachs bei allen Schülern beim Vergleich ihrer Lebens- und Alltagssituation mit der gleichaltriger Chinesen. Hier war ein Perspektivwechsel für alle Schüler erreichbar. Die Fragebogenauswertungen und die begleitenden und nachbereitenden Gespräche mit den Schülern ergaben, dass es C-Schülern und B-Schülern des älteren Jahrgangs besser gelang, sich in Alltagssituationen kulturspezifisch angemessen zu verhalten und abweichende Wertvorstellungen vorurteilsfrei zu hinterfragen und zu tolerieren. Zweifelsohne initiierte die Schulaustauschreise bei allen Schülern eine Bewusstwerdung über kulturelle Differenzen.

---

16 Auswertung Fragebogen 1, Frage 5 und Fragebogen 2, Frage 4. Als Beispiel für überholte Informationen zur chinesischen Kultur wurde hier zwei Mal das Essen von Hunden genannt. Die Schüler hatten in mehreren Familien erlebt, dass Hunde als Haustiere zur Familie gehörten und dass keiner der (jüngeren) chinesischen Partner die Vorstellung, Hund zu essen, gutheißen würde.

17 Ein Schüler, dessen Gastfamilie nicht mit ihm am Wochenende die von der Partnerschule vorgegebenen Sehenswürdigkeiten besichtigte, lehnte eine diesbezügliche Nachfrage bei seinen Gasteltern ab, da er sie einerseits nicht brüskieren wollte und andererseits das Alltagsleben seines Gastbruders miterleben wollte. Er hatte bereits einen hohen Grad an Empathie, Offenheit und Sensibilität für die interkulturelle soziale Interaktion entwickelt.

Darüber hinaus initiierte die Reise bei den meisten Schülern ein differenzierteres Nachdenken über die eigene Kultur. Sich selbst zu reflektieren, lernt man erst wirklich durch den Abstand vom Heimatland. Zusammenfassend lässt sich konstatieren, dass die Schulaustauschreise zu einem interkulturellen kommunikativen Kompetenzerwerb in heterogener Qualität geführt hat. Da bei C-Schülern und älteren B-Schülern neben dem Zuwachs an interkultureller kommunikativer Kompetenz auch die Erweiterung der Fremdsprachenkompetenz nachweisbar am größten war, was durch die Interrelation der beiden Kompetenzen noch potenziert wurde, haben sie aus schulischer Sicht am stärksten von der Reise profitiert.

Literatur

Berry, John W. (1996) „Acculturation and psychological adoption“ in: Klaus J. Bade (Hrsg.) (1996) *Migration - Ethnizität - Konflikt: Systemfragen und Fallstudien,* Osnabrück: Rasch, S. 171-186.

Byram, Michael (1997) *Teaching and assessing intercultural communicative competence*, Clevedon: Multilingual Matters.

Condon, John C. und Fathi S. Yousef (1975) *An Introduction to Intercultural Communication,* Indianapolis & New York: Intercultural Press.

Cushner, Kenneth und Richard W. Brislin (1996) *Intercultural interactions: A practical guide*, Thousand Oaks: Sage Publications.

Götz, Klaus (2003) *Interkulturelles Lernen / Interkulturelles Training*, München & Mering: Rainer Hampp.

Hall, Edward T. und Mildred R. Hall (1990) *Understanding Cultural Differences*, Yarmouth, Me: Intercultural Press.

Hofstede, Geert (1993) *Interkulturelle Zusammenarbeit. Kulturen – Organisationen – Management,* Wiesbaden: Gabler.

Holenstein, Elmar (2009) *China ist nicht ganz anders: Vier Essays in global vergleichender Kulturgeschichte,* Zürich: Ammann.

Hunfeld, Hans (1989) *Sprichwörtlich*, München: Klett Edition Deutsch.

Jin, Xiufang (1994) *Kontakte, Konflikte und Kompromisse: Interkulturelle Kommunikation zwischen Deutschen und Chinesen in einem Joint Venture*, Saarbrücken: Verlag für Entwicklungspolitik.

Kalpaka, Anita (1998) „Interkulturelle Kompetenz: Kompetentes (sozial-)pädagisches Handeln in der Einwanderungsgesellschaft“ in: ISS Frankfurt/M. (Hrsg.) *Zeitschrift für Migration und Soziale Arbeit,* Heft 3-4. Frankfurt/M., S. 77-79.

Kammhuber, Stefan (2000) *Interkulturelles Lernen und Lehren,* Wiesbaden: Deutscher Universitäts-Verlag.

Kartari, Asker (1997) *Deutsch-türkische Kommunikation am Arbeitsplatz: Zur interkulturellen Kommunikation zwischen türkischen Mitarbeitern und deutschen Vorgesetzten in einem deutschen Industriebetrieb*, Münster: Waxmann.

Knapp-Potthoff, Annelie (1997) „Interkulturelle Kommunikationsfähigkeit als Lernziel“ in: Knapp-Potthoff, Annelie/Liedke, Martina (Hrsg.) (1997) *Aspekte interkultureller Kommunikationsfähigkeit*, München: iudicium, S. 181-205.

Losche, Helga (1995) *Interkulturelle Kommunikation: Sammlung praktischer Spiele und Übungen*, Alling: Sandmann.

Maletzke, Gerhard (1996) *Interkulturelle Kommunikation: Zur Interaktion zwischen Menschen verschiedener Kulturen*, Opladen: Westdeutscher Verlag.

Meyer, Thomas (2002) *Identitätspolitik: Vom Missbrauch kultureller Unterschiede*, Frankfurt/M.: Suhrkamp.

Rogers, Everett M./Hart William B. (2001) „The Histories of Intercultural, International and Development Communication" in: Gudykunst, William B./Mody, Bella (Hrsg.): *Handbook of International and Intercultural Communication.* 3. Aufl. Thousand Oaks: Sage, S. 1-18.

Schiffauer, Werner (1997) „Kulturalismus vs. Universalismus" in: Ders. (1997) *Fremde in der Stadt: Zehn Essays über Kultur und Differenz*, Frankfurt/M.: Suhrkamp, S. 144-156.

Steindl, Maria (2008) *Interkultureller Dialog, interkulturelles Lernen: Texte, Unterrichtsbeispiele, Projekte.* Wien: Zentrum Polis - Politik Lernen in der Schule.

„Tagesprotokolle" in: Stammgruppe 108-7 (2010) *Schulpartnerschaft 22. Middle School Beijing Bettina-von-Arnim-Oberschule: Reisebericht der Stammgruppe 7 Großgruppe 108 Reisezeitraum 12.5.2010 – 24.5.2010*, Berlin: Bettina-von-Arnim-Oberschule.

Thomas, Alexander (1996) *Psychologie interkulturellen Handelns*, Göttingen: Hogrefe.

Thomas, Alexander und Eberhard Schenk (2005) *Beruflich in China: Trainingsprogramm für Manager, Fach- und Führungskräfte,* Göttingen: Vandenhoeck & Ruprecht.

Trompenaars, Fons and Hampden-Turner, Charles (1994) *The seven cultures of capitalism – Value systems for creating wealth in the United States, Britain, Japan, Germany, France, Sweden and the Netherlands,* London: Piatkus.

Mechthild Leutner

Opiumhandel – Opiumkriege – „Opiumfalle“: Chinas gewaltsame Einbindung in die globale Ökonomie und ihre gravierenden Auswirkungen

Opiumhandel und Opiumkriege (1840-42 und 1856-60) gelten als wichtige Themen der neueren chinesischen Geschichte, als bedeutende historische Zäsuren und vielen Chinesen als schmachvolle Ereignisse nationaler Erniedrigung. Sie sind im vergangenen Jahrzehnt aus globaler Perspektive verstärkt untersucht worden. Auch die politisch-gesellschaftlichen Auswirkungen des Drogenhandels und der Opiumsucht im nachfolgenden Jahrhundert wurden auf breiterer empirischer Basis aufgearbeitet. In der Zusammenführung dieser neuen Forschungsergebnisse, wobei auch Quellen zur Position des deutschen Reiches einbezogen werden, ist eine Betrachtung des gesamten Opium-Komplexes im Kontext der neueren Geschichte Chinas erforderlich.

Meine These ist: Nicht nur wurde China durch den die Wirtschaft, Gesellschaft und Gesundheit der chinesischen Bevölkerung schädigenden Opiumkonsum und -handel mit brutaler militärischer Gewalt in die globale Wirtschaft eingebunden. Vielmehr führten die außen- und innenpolitischen Auswirkungen die Qing-Regierung und sukzessive die republikanischen Regierungen direkt in eine „Opiumfalle“[1] hinein. Opium wurde ein Faktor systemischen Charakters, der alle Lebensbereiche durchdrang. Sowohl die finanzielle Ausblutung des Landes, die durch vielfältige Faktoren der halbkolonialen Herrschaft im „Jahrhundert der nationalen Schande“ bedingt war,[2] als auch die wachsende ökonomische Abhängigkeit des Staates von Opiumsteuern und -einkünften einerseits und der zugleich

1 Bereits in einem Memorandum von 1877 hatte Guo Songtao, der erste chinesische Gesandte in London, Opium zum entscheidenden Faktor für die Stabilität bzw. Zerrüttung des Staates erklärt (zitiert bei Bello 2005: 304). Guo sprach davon, dass die „Mohncultur sich wie ein rankendes Schlinggewächs nach allen Richtungen hin verbreitet“ (PA AA Peking II 2 Bl. 241, übersetzt von Carl Arendt). Bello stellte den Zusammenhang von ausländischem Handel und einheimischer Produktion her, als er von einem „cycle of opium in the Qing empire” sprach: “The activities of foreign elements were prerequisite for the establishment and development of both the regional and the empirewide Chinese opium market systems” (Bello 2005:301). Lin Man-Houng adressierte die Problematik auf der Diskursebene: die chinesischen Denker hätten sich immer mehr in einem Dilemma verfangen (Lin Man-Houng 2004: 119). Selbst die japanischen Besatzer waren in den 1940er Jahren in dieser „Falle“ gefangen; Brook führt aus: „Japan also was trapped in this bargain and had to sustain the traffic to feed its hungry puppets“ (2000: 338).

2 Als Faktoren sind insbesondere zu nennen: wachsende Verteidigungslasten der Zentralregierung gegen die zunehmende territoriale Bedrohung des Landes, Intensivierung der Anleihepolitik, die wiederum durch die Seezolleinnahmen finanziert wurde, niedrige Zölle auf ausländische Waren und damit negative Konsequenzen für die einheimische Warenproduktion und Verarmung betroffener Bevölkerungsschichten sowie ein Rückgang der Staatseinnahmen. Dies führte zur Entwicklung von Räumen begrenzter Staatlichkeit, in welchen es wiederum zur sozialen Destabilisierung und in der Folge zu Aufständen größeren Ausmaßes und zum Anwachsen von Kriminalität kam. Dies ließ die Militärausgaben ansteigen und belastete den Staatshaushalt. Hinzu kamen horrende Entschädigungszahlungen an die Regierungen zur Entschärfung vielfach auch provozierter sogenannter Zwischenfälle, die oftmals Widerstandsaktionen der chinesischen Bevölkerung und Beamter waren. Sie waren aber auch Kompensation für die Ausgaben der militärischen Aggressionen der ausländischen Mächte, die als von China verursacht dargestellt wurden.

Berliner China-Hefte/Chinese History and Society 41 (2012), pp. 119-145

gegebenen ökonomischen, politischen, gesundheitlichen und moralischen Notwendigkeit der Unterdrückung des Opiums andererseits konstituierten eine Situation, aus der das Land sich erst Anfang der 1950er Jahre durch radikale gesellschaftspolitische Transformation und Kampagnen zur Ausrottung des Opiums befreien konnte.[3] Der insbesondere seit der Einbindung Chinas in die globale Marktwirtschaft ab den 1990er Jahren in der VR China wieder zu beobachtende Drogenkonsum und -handel unterscheidet sich grundlegend von dem früheren, hier behandelten, er ist Teil des Kriminalitäts-Spektrums und hat nicht mehr systemischen Charakter.[4]

Die Opiumkriege 1840/42 und 1858/60 werden in der westlichsprachigen Literatur bis heute vielfach als „Öffnung" Chinas bezeichnet, ein Begriff, der zunächst positive Assoziationen hervorruft. Dem zugrunde liegt die Annahme von einer „Isolation" Chinas zu dieser Zeit. Die These von der „Öffnung" des „geschlossenen" Landes bestimmt bis zur Gegenwart wissenschaftliche und populäre Diskurse zur Geschichte Chinas im 19. Jahrhundert. Sie wird auch kaum durch die Einzelforschungen der vergangenen beiden Jahrzehnte in Frage gestellt, die die These von einer ökonomischen Isolation Chinas vor den Opiumkriegen als längst überholt dargelegt haben. Hier wird nicht nur der erste Opiumkrieg, der die gewaltsame Einbindung Chinas in die globale Ökonomie einleitete – mit Betonung auf „gewaltsam" – und den ersten Höhepunkt des Prozesses der Umformung Chinas zu einem kolonialen Objekt bedeutete, sondern auch die Rolle des Opiumhandels neu gewertet. Opium in China insgesamt wird zunehmend über den Kontext westlicher Diplomatiegeschichte hinaus ins Zentrum sozio-politischer Analysen der chinesischen Entwicklung gestellt (Madancy 2003: 7f).[5] Insbesondere wird auch seine Bedeutung in der globalen Ökonomie als eine zentrale Komponente des britischen Imperialismus in Asien behandelt (Trocki 1999: 7). Als wesentliche Ursache der Opiumkriege, sowohl des Ersten als auch des Zweiten Opiumkrieges wurde die Zugänglichmachung Chinas für den illegalen Opiumhandel herausgearbeitet. Der China aufgezwungene Opiumhandel war nicht das Ergebnis eines geschwächten (und „verschlossenen") Qing-Staates, wie die erste umfangreiche und bis heute einflussreiche englischsprachige Monographie zu dieser Thematik von Chang 1970 argumentierte, sondern legte seinerseits erst die Grundlagen für dessen ökonomischen und politischen Niedergang. Thesen vom „Zusammenstoß der Kulturen", der kulturalistisch konfuzianisch chinesischen mit der nationalen europäischen, wie sie bereits in den 1930er Jahren von Otto Franke und seit den 1960er Jahren paradigmatisch auch von John King Fairbank und der nach wie vor stark von seinem Ansatz geprägten Historiographie zur Geschichte Chinas im 19. Jahrhundert vertreten

3 Ich danke den Studierenden meiner Lehrveranstaltung zu Opium in China (Sommersemester 2012) für die anregenden Diskussionen, in denen ich die hier entwickelten Thesen vorstellen und weiter schärfen konnte, und Laura Stangl für die Unterstützung bei Recherchen. Die Beschäftigung mit diesem Thema geht auf einen Vortrag zurück, den ich im Sommer 2009 auf Einladung von Lutz Leisering am Institut für Weltgesellschaft der Universität Bielefeld gehalten habe. Auch ihm gilt mein herzlicher Dank.

4 Ausführlich dazu insbesondere Zhou Yongming 1999: 115-167.

5 Auch die Forschung auf Taiwan und in der VR China hat neben der generellen Einordnung der Opiumkriege als Beginn von Chinas halbkolonialer Phase und der Kennzeichnung der verheerenden Wirkungen des britischen Opiumhandels erst in den letzten Jahrzehnten mit Einzelstudien zur umfassenden Rolle des Opiums in der neueren Geschichte Chinas begonnen (Madancy 2003: 17ff). Die chinesischen Studien gehen in der Regel erst verzögert in den westlichen Diskurs ein und werden in diesem Beitrag nur punktuell einbezogen.

wird,[6] erweisen sich angesichts der vorliegenden empirischen Daten ebenso als späte Legitimationsversuche europäisch-amerikanisch kolonialer Expansion, wie die von Chang gegenüber Fairbank modifizierte These, dass es primär um einen „Handelskrieg", um handelspolitische Ziele und die Absicht gegangen sei, China überhaupt, egal für welche Produkte, zu „öffnen" (Chang 1970: X, 15).

In modifizierter Form findet sich die These auch in der 2012 publizierten „Geschichte Chinas" von Kai Vogelsang. Auch Vogelsang, der ohne jegliche Beschönigung den ersten Opiumkrieg als „das erste moderne Verbrechen, das der Westen an China verübte" (2012: 453), bezeichnet und klar die Ursachen des Zweiten Opiumkrieges auf die Notwendigkeit der Steigerung des Opiumverkaufs zur Finanzierung der kostspieligen britischen Kolonien zurückführt, sieht insgesamt die Kriege als schonungslose Konfrontation der chinesischen Gesellschaft mit den „Konsequenzen der Moderne", mit „der Durchschlagskraft ihrer Waffen, aber auch mit der kühlen Logik ihrer Ökonomie und der moralfreien Ideologie des Nationalismus" (2012: 453). Vor allem aber – und das suggerierten bereits Fairbank und neuerdings Bickers[7] – spricht Vogelsang China einen entsprechenden Eigenanteil an der gesamten Entwicklung rund um die Kriege und die spätere Entwicklung zu. Die Frage der Ausgangsbedingungen für den illegalen Schmuggel und der chinesischen Kollaboration hinsichtlich der Ausbreitung der Droge, die in fast allen Werken latent oder offen berührt wird,[8] wird auch bei Vogelsang thematisiert: „Die Qing standen am Rande des Bankrotts", als der illegale Handel forciert wurde; das Opium „fand in China reißenden Absatz"; die „Qing bemühten sich" – nach dem ersten Krieg – „keineswegs darum, die Barbaren ... zu ‚kontrollieren' oder gar ‚anzugreifen'". Daher musste China die Barbaren, so Vogelsang, „auch das macht das spezifisch Moderne an dieser Erfahrung aus – in ihrem Eigenwert" anerkennen. „China musste sich mit ihnen (d.h. den Barbaren, d.V.) arrangieren, und zwar indem es sich selbst änderte" (Vogelsang 2012: 446-457). Kurz: Die europäische Moderne hielt laut Vogelsang durch die zwar verbrecherischen, aber immerhin „modern" verbrecherischen Kriege Einzug in China.

Die These von der „Öffnung" Chinas durch die Opiumkriege hat den Charakter eines Mythos angenommen, der als solcher – auch von chinesischer Seite – sogar aufgegriffen und übertragen wird auf eher jüngste Entwicklungen im Gefolge der kulturrevolutionären Entwicklungen der 1950er bis 1970er Jahre. Es ist neben der Charakterisierung als „Reformpolitik" auch wieder die Rede von einer „Öffnungspolitik", welche die Phase der „Isolation" des Landes beendet habe. Die Interdependenz von Isolation und Öffnung ist – deutlich wird eine essentialistische Perspektive gegenüber der historischen präferiert – gekoppelt mit der Rede von einer „Abwehrhaltung Chinas gegenüber Außen".[9] Die Pro-

6 Die Tradierungslinien sind zum Teil nicht so einfach nachvollziehbar. Tatsächlich beziehen sich Brook/Wakabayashi 2001: 35 auf Tan Chung „China and the Brave New World" der sich wiederum auf Chang Hsin-Pao (1970) als denjenigen bezieht, der den Begriff „Clash of Cultures" zuerst hervorgehoben und damit Fairbanks Thesen weiter geführt habe (Tan 1978: 12), Fairbank sieht das Versagen des konfuzianischen China, sich an kommerzielle, industrielle und nationalistische Reformen anzupassen, als einen Grund für den Ausbruch des Opiumkriegs und die Ausdehnung des Handels über die Grenzen des alten Kanton-Systems hinaus als einen zweiten Grund (Fairbank 1964: 22, 65).

7 Bickers argumentiert, dass der Handel mit Opium zwar in den 1830er Jahren enorm zugenommen habe, doch sei Opium schon seit langem Teil der Freizeitkultur der chinesischen Elite gewesen und die Briten hätten nur noch den für sie gewinnträchtigen Markt zu schaffen gehabt (Bickers 2011:29).

8 Ein deutliches Beispiel für die Kollaborationsthese ist Madancy 2003.

9 Ein prägnantes Beispiel ist die Rezension zu Sabine Dabringhaus (2009) „Geschichte China`s im 20.

klamation einer solchen, geradezu als anthropologische Konstante erscheinenden Abwehrhaltung „der Chinesen" gehört zur Mythologisierung der „Öffnungs"-Rhetorik ebenso wie die langlebige und bis zur Gegenwart vertretene These, dass das chinesische Volk in besonderer Weise dem Opiums zugeneigt gewesen sei, wegen des aus konfuzianischer Tradition herrührenden ritualistischen Aktes des Opiumrauchens (Slack 2001: 34).
Dieser Teil des Mythos verweist auf ein zweites Charakteristikum der Mehrzahl der Werke, nämlich auf die Verharmlosung des Aktes der Süchtigmachung signifikanter Bevölkerungsschichten zur Erzielung großer wirtschaftlicher Profite und immenser politischer Macht, nicht durch einzelne Kriminelle, sondern durch gezieltes Agieren ganzer Staaten und Regierungen. Ein Akt mit außerordentlich gravierenden Konsequenzen für China. Durchgängig werden zu diesem Zweck Euphemismen bei der Behandlung der Thematik benutzt. Selten ist die Rede von Opium als Droge, kaum jemals werden die großen Handelshäuser als Drogensyndikate oder die Händler als Kriminelle und Dealer bezeichnet und damit die Begriffe „richtiggestellt".
De-Mythologisierung und Richtigstellung der Begriffe – das versucht dieser Beitrag. Ich zeige zunächst auf, wie Chinas Einbindung in die Weltgesellschaft vor den Opiumkriegen aussah, bevor ich auf die ökonomischen und politischen Faktoren eingehe, die den Opiumhandel zur Ursache der Kriege machten. Schließlich werde ich die gravierenden, vielfältigen und langfristigen Auswirkungen dieser gewaltsamen Einbindung Chinas in die globale Ökonomie skizzieren.

Chinas Einbindung in die globale Ökonomie vor den Opiumkriegen

China war im 16. Jahrhundert die dominante Wirtschaft der Welt und spielte im globalen Handel eine wesentliche Rolle. Spätestens mit dem Jahre 1571, der Gründung Manilas als spanisch-kolonialem Handelsplatz[10], kann – entgegen der These Immanuel Wallersteins von zwei unabhängigen Systemen – von einer hoch integrierten Weltwirtschaft und einem entwickelten globalen Handelsnetz für Silber, Gold, Kupfer, Muscheln, Porzellan und Seide gesprochen werden (Flynn/Giráldez 2010: IX).[11] Nicht nur Europa wurde mit Asiens Luxusgütern versorgt, auch europäische Waffen, Edelmetalle und Manufakturwaren gelangten nach Asien. Zu beobachten ist erstmalig eine „weltumfassende" Ausdehnung des Silberhandels von Acapulco über Manila, Nagasaki, Macao, Goa und Ormuz, der in Lissabon begann und endete (Feldbauer 2003: 118). China exportierte vor allem Seide, Tee und Keramik, aber auch Gewürze, Lacke und feines Baumwolltuch. Allein die Ostindische Kompanie erwarb in China jährlich etwa 630.000 Stück Keramik und zahlte mit hunderten Millionen Silberpesos, vor allem aus Mexiko. Silber, das in den mexikanischen Minen gefördert wurde, war besonders rein und damit stabil im Silbergehalt. Bis zum Anfang des 19. Jahrhunderts war China direkt oder indirekt das Hauptziel und die Endstation dieses Silbers, Schecks wurden in China nur in Ausnahmefällen als Zahlungs-

Jahrhundert", München: C.H. Beck von Thomas Speckmann mit der markanten Überschrift „Abwehrhaltung gegen Außen", in: Der Tagesspiegel, 12.10.2009.

10 Manila, im 16. Jh. eine unabhängige Handelsstation, wurde 1571 von Spanien, später zeitweilig auch jeweils von China, den Niederlanden und Großbritannien besetzt. Spanische Händler kontrollierten den Silberhandel; sie brachten das Silber von Südamerika nach Ostasien bzw. China (Walsh 2007).

11 S. ausführlich die wirtschaftshistorischen Argumente zu dieser These und zur dominanten Rolle Chinas im globalen Handel in : Flynn/Giráldez 2010. Die Autoren unterscheiden drei globale Zyklen: zwei Silberzyklen: 1540 bis 1640 und 1700 bis 1750 und einen dritten Silber-Tee-Zyklus nach 1750 (Flynn/Giráldez 2002: 101f, auch in: Flynn/Giráldez 2010), sie sprechen neben dem Opium dem Tee als globalem Handelsgut ab dieser Zeit eine große Rolle zu.

mittel akzeptiert. Bereits im 16. Jahrhundert hatte das Land seine Währung auf Silber umgestellt.[12] Im 17. Jahrhundert wurden jährlich Silberpesos im Wert von 2 Mio., das waren mehr als 50 Tonnen, nach China eingeführt. Im Zeitraum von 1719 bis 1833 sollten insgesamt 256 Mio. Silberpesos, etwa 6.243 Tonnen pures Silber, als Gegenwert für chinesische Waren nach China gebracht werden (Irigoin 2009: 210).

Im globalen Handel gab es zwei Handelsrouten nach China: einmal der Weg über Europa, d.h. chinesische Produkte, in erster Linie Tee, Seide und Porzellan wurden nach Europa transportiert, europäische Waren nach Nord- und Südamerika, mexikanisches Silber dann wiederum nach China. Europäische Händler waren wichtige Mittler dieser Handelsströme und Handelsrouten. Zum zweiten lief der Handel und damit der Transport des Silbers direkt über Manila. Chinesische Dschunken liefen mit Porzellan, Baumwoll- und Seidenwaren Manila an – im Austausch für Silber. Zugleich existierte ein intensiver Handel mit Südostasien: Keramik, Textilien, Medizin und Kupferkäsch wurden als Kompensation für Weihrauch, Elfenbein, Pfeffer und Reis gehandelt (Naquin/Rawski 1988: 102).[13] Insbesondere nach 1683, der Integration Taiwans in das Mandschu-Reich, entfaltete sich der Außenhandel in den südchinesischen Hafenstädten Kanton, Amoy, Quanzhou, Fuzhou und Ningbo, da Handelsbeschränkungen von chinesischer Seite zunächst aufgehoben wurden (Gernet 2008: 409). Erst 1757 wurde dann auf Intervention der Kantoner Kaufleute der Auslandshandel auf Kanton beschränkt, ab 1770 wurde hier ein permanenter Handelsplatz für die ausländischen Händler etabliert. Zwischen 1719 und 1833 stieg der auf Kanton konzentrierte Handel kontinuierlich um das dreizehnfache. Beziffert man die Tonnage der ausländischen Schiffe in Kanton in den Jahren von 1719 bis 1726 auf 2.803 Mio. Tonnen, so war sie hundert Jahre später, in den Jahren 1828 bis 1833, auf 37.507 Mio. Tonnen gestiegen (Naquin/Rawski 1988: 103).

Neben Silber wurde auch bereits im 18. Jahrhundert Reis aus Südostasien, den Philippinen und Siam in die Küstenprovinzen des Landes importiert. Hier ist nicht zuletzt auf Grund der hohen Nachfrage nach Exportgütern bereits eine hohe Kommerzialisierung zu beobachten. Denn die große weltweite Nachfrage nach chinesischen Produkten führte auch zu einer Umstrukturierung der chinesischen Ökonomie. Verschiedene Regionen spezialisierten sich: das Gebiet südlich des Yangzi etwa auf Seidenproduktion. Statt Reis wurden Maulbeerbäume gepflanzt, so dass nun – neben dem Import von Reis – auch aus der innerchinesischen Provinz Hunan Reis dorthin geliefert wurde. Hunan selbst wurde zu einem wichtigen Reisanbaugebiet. Als Folge der weltweiten Handelsnetze waren auch neue Getreidesorten aus Nord- und Südamerika nach China gebracht worden. Im 17. Jahrhundert kamen Maispflanzen nach China, später Süßkartoffeln, die in Fujian und Guangdong angebaut wurden, während in der Region von Shanghai Erdnüsse kultiviert wurden. Der Anbau dieser neuen Nutzpflanzen trug nicht unerheblich zur Veränderung der Grundstruktur der Wirtschaft bei. Das kultivierte Land in China insgesamt verdoppelte sich und die Bevölkerung wuchs stark. Während sie um 1600 auf etwa 100–200 Mio. geschätzt

---

[12] Ab der Song-Zeit war verstärkt Silber als Zahlungsmittel in Gebrauch. Versuche, Anfang des 15. Jahrhunderts und erneut zu Beginn der Qing-Zeit, Banknoten einzuführen, erwiesen sich als nicht durchsetzbar, so dass sich faktisch ab dem 15. Jahrhundert der Umlauf von Silber im ganzen Land stetig erhöhte und der Silberbarren seit den Steuerreformen von 1530-1581 de facto allgemein als Zahlungsmittel verbreitet war (Gernet 2008: 353).

[13] Chinas Außenhandel lief im 15. und 16. Jahrhundert über die drei konzessionierten Ämter für Handelsschiffe in Ningbo (für Japan, große Handelsgesandtschaften, Verbot 1530), Fuzhou (für die Philippinen) und Kanton (vor allem für Indochina).

werden kann, so verdreifachte sie sich bis 1850 auf etwa 410 Mio. Eine verstärkte Binnenmigration fand statt, da nun auch die Gebiete besiedelt wurden, in denen bisher kein Getreide angebaut werden konnte, beispielsweise Berggebiete in Zentral- und Westchina wie Jiangxi und Hunan, wo Mais angebaut werden konnte, aber auch die sog. Grenzgebiete Chinas, die Mandschurei und Taiwan. Der Anbau von Mais und Kartoffeln laugte allerdings im Unterschied zu den traditionellen Produkten wie etwa Tee den Boden stärker aus, daher wurden immer wieder Wälder für neue Anbaugebiete gerodet. Das bedeutete nicht allein erhebliche ökologische Folgen, sondern führte auch zur Entstehung einer mobilen Landbevölkerung mit spezifischen Charakteristika, so dass manche Autoren, ähnlich wie für die USA, von der Herausbildung einer „frontier society" im 18. Jahrhundert sprechen (Naquin/Rawski 1988).

Die überwiegende Mehrheit der Wissenschaftler geht davon aus, dass der starke Silberzufluss im Austausch mit den heiß begehrten chinesischen Exportgütern das Land bereichert habe (Osterhammel 2009: 1040). Seit einigen Jahren wird im Unterschied dazu allerdings argumentiert, dass für China die faktische Umstellung der Währung auf Silber im 16. Jahrhundert statt auf Papier große Werte absorbiert und damit für die innere Entwicklung benötigte Ressourcen gebunden habe (Flynn/Giráldez 2002).[14] Welche These auch zutreffend sein mag, fest steht jedenfalls, dass das oben skizzierte globale Handelsgeflecht, in dem mit Silber für chinesische Produkte gezahlt wurde, die in dieser Qualität und zu diesem Zeitpunkt allein in China produziert werden konnten, bis ins frühe 19. Jahrhundert so bestehen blieb. Allerdings vergrößerte sich mit zunehmender Nachfrage nach chinesischen Waren in Europa und Amerika auch das Handelsdefizit insbesondere für die britischen Händler. Die Menge der europäischen oder amerikanischen Güter – vor allem Zinn, Kupfer, Wollwaren, Baumwolle und Blei – die in China abgesetzt werden konnten, reichte immer weniger aus, um die chinesischen Waren zu kompensieren. Neun Zehntel der in Kanton einlaufenden Handelsschiffe zur Ladung chinesischer Waren – und das waren ab etwa 1750 jährlich etwa 190 bis 210 Schiffe – führten Ballast.

Das Silber, das als Ware und als Zahlungsmittel zugleich fungierte, hatte allerdings für die ausländischen Händler große Nachteile. Es war teuer in der Gewinnung und im Transport und stand auch nicht unbegrenzt zur Verfügung. Daher wurde einerseits begonnen, durch die Einfuhr chinesischer Technologien die stark nachgefragten Waren in Europa selbst oder in den Kolonien herzustellen. Beispielsweise wurden Maulbeerbäume gepflanzt in Spanien und Frankreich, selbst im deutschen Brandenburg,[15] um mit der Zucht von Seidenraupen eine Basis für die Seidenherstellung zu schaffen – meist ohne oder nur mit geringem Erfolg, besonders hinsichtlich der Qualität der Seide.

Andererseits begannen die Händler nach Handelsgütern zu suchen, die die in Europa und Amerika stetig wachsende Nachfrage nach chinesischen Gütern, vor allem nach Tee, kompensieren konnte. Tee wurde zum Genussmittel breiter Bevölkerungskreise besonders in Großbritannien und sollte für die sich herausbildende Industriearbeiterschaft – in Verbindung mit Zucker – ein wichtiges Aufputschmittel zur Steigerung der Produktivität werden. Allein 1761 transportierte die Britisch-Ostindische Kompanie 2.626 Mio. Pfund Tee im Wert von 831.000 engl. Pfund, im Jahr 1800 waren es bereits 3.665 Mio. Pfund

[14] Bereits ab 1575 hatte der Wert des Silbers im Verhältnis zu Gold stetig abgenommen. Betrug 1575 das Verhältnis Silber zu Gold 1 zu 4, so 1635 bereits 1 zu 10 (Gernet 2008: 454). Mitte des 19. Jahrhunderts sollte im Zuge kolonialer Expansion in China der Goldstandard übernommen werden.

[15] Eine kurzlebige systematische staatliche Förderung der Seidenproduktion in Brandenburg erreichte im 18. Jahrhundert ihren Höhepunkt.

Tee. Und mit dem Handelsdefizit und der steigenden Nachfrage nach chinesischen Produkten beginnt de facto die Geschichte des Opiumhandels in China und damit auch die Vorgeschichte der beiden Opiumkriege.

Vorgeschichte der Opiumkriege

Ende des 18. Jahrhunderts wurde die Suche nach einer Kompensationsware für die in Europa und Amerika nachgefragten chinesischen Produkte verstärkt. Beispielsweise war die Suche nach einem solchen Produkt, das in China vermarktet werden konnte, ein wesentlicher Motor, pazifische Ressourcen zu erschließen. So wurden Sandelholzwälder auf den Fidschi-Inseln und Hawaii gerodet und nach China verschifft. Die chinesische Nachfrage nach Holz erwies sich allerdings als zu gering, die Transportkosten waren überdies zu hoch und die Gewinnmargen zu niedrig. Nun geriet Opium in den Fokus der Händler. Opium hatte einen großen Nachteil: Es war Schmuggelware, da die Einfuhr nach China verboten war. Gleichzeitig hatte es drei große Vorteile für die Händler: Erstens es war leicht abzusetzen, der Bedarf konnte nahezu unbegrenzt erzeugt werden und zwar für Kunden jedes Alters und jeder Schicht. Zweitens nahm es als Handelsgut wenig Frachtplatz ein und drittens konnte es daher jederzeit jegliche andere Ware kompensieren und damit Handelsdefizite ausgleichen. Es war also das ideale Produkt, das Silber ersetzen konnte und sich hervorragend zur Zirkulation in der globalen Welt eignete (Trocki 1999: 61).

Opium als medizinische Droge war bereits im 8. Jahrhundert in China bekannt. Es war vor allem durch muslimische Händler auf dem Landweg, u.a. aus den Gebieten des heutigen Afghanistan, nach China gebracht worden. Dass Opium als Droge konsumiert wurde, begann erst allmählich im 17. Jahrhundert, als portugiesische und englische Händler aus Goa und holländische Händler aus Bengalen Opium mit Tabak versetzten und diesen in China verkauften. Der Kaiserhof hatte auf Grund der Zunahme des illegalen Handels und des Opiumkonsums erneut 1729 in einem Edikt den Verkauf von Opium verboten. Opium sei eine Ware, die „gerissene Barbaren an Chinesen verkauften, um sie um ihr Geld zu betrügen" (zitiert in: Brook/Wakabayashi 2000: 6). Doch trotz dieser Verbote stieg der Verkauf und Konsum von illegal importiertem Opium im Laufe des 18. Jahrhunderts allmählich an.

Im Jahre 1729 wurden etwa 200 Kisten, je Kiste 63,5 kg, im Jahr 1773 bereits etwa 1.000 Kisten illegal nach China eingeführt. Nach den Siegen britischer Truppen 1757 und 1764 über die holländischen Kolonialtruppen in Indien begann die Britisch-Ostindische Kompanie ab 1773 auf der Basis ihres Monopols über Bengalen mit dem Export des bengalischen Opiums ganz gezielt den Chinahandel auszubauen und den Verkauf des bengalischen Opiums als Mittel zum Ausgleich ihrer Finanzen zu nutzen. Siebzehn Jahre später, im Jahre 1790, hatte sie den illegalen Handel bereits vervierfachen können: mehr als 4.000 Kisten wurden nach China verbracht. Allerdings sollte die Kompanie ab 1784 nach einer britischen Parlamentsentscheidung, die sich gegen eine staatliche illegale Einfuhr nach China aussprach, diesen Handel nicht mehr selbst durchführen, sondern an private Händler vergeben, die den Transport des Opiums an die chinesische Küste bzw. nach Kanton organisierten.

Mit der Etablierung eines Zwischenhändlernetzes in Südchina durch die chinesische Regierung, den sog. Hongs, die von chinesischer Seite das Monopol für den Außenhandel erhielten, wurden in China selbst überdies Strukturen geschaffen, die den Export insgesamt, wie auch die illegale Einfuhr von Opium im Besonderen, begünstigten (Brook/ Wakabayashi 2000: 6). Es waren nämlich diese chinesischen Kaufleute, die – teils durch

Anleihen finanziell an die britischen Händler gebunden – vielfach die Löschung der Opiumschiffe veranlassten. Für das Jahr 1782 ist beispielsweise in den Büchern der Ostindischen Kompanie festgehalten, dass die Händler ein Schiff mit einer Ladung Opium, welches ursprünglich für Südostasien bestimmt war, in Kanton illegal löschen ließen (Morse 1926 II: 76f).
Für die Lizenzen zum Handel zwischen Indien und China hatten die privaten Händler an die Britisch-Ostindische Kompanie hohe Gebühren zu zahlen, die sehr profitträchtig für diese waren. Allein aus diesem Handel konnte in den Jahren 1775 bis 1795 die Britisch-Ostindische Kompanie ein Drittel ihrer Einkünfte erzielen. Als der chinesische Kaiser im Jahre 1796 erneut den Konsum von Opium und 1800 auch den Handel mit Opium unter Strafe stellte, war Opium schon so wichtig und profitabel für die britischen Händler geworden, dass an eine freiwillige Beschränkung des lukrativen Handels nicht zu denken war. Hinzu kam, dass auf Grund der hohen Profitraten nun auch amerikanische Kaufleute in großen Mengen Opium aus Persien und der Türkei nach China schmuggelten.
Insgesamt führte der steigende Schmuggel mit Opium allmählich zu einer Verringerung insbesondere des britischen Handelsdefizits und zu einer Umkehrung des Silberflusses zu Gunsten nicht-chinesischer Händler. Das chinesische Reich hatte nun erstmals einen Silberabfluss zu verzeichnen: Für seine Exportwaren erhielt es zunehmend Opium statt Silber. Opium, welches nicht nur die Gesundheit und Moral breiter Bevölkerungskreise schädigte, sondern überhaupt keinen äquivalenten volkswirtschaftlichen Wert darstellte.

Chinesische Silberimporte und -exporte:

Handelsjahr	Import	Export	Handesdefizit
1828-29	$ 730.200	$ 4.703.202	$ 3.973.002
1829-30	1.158.644	6.755.372	5.596.728
1830-31	255.355	6.595.306	6.339.951
1831-32	683.252	4.023.003	3.339.751
1832-33	745.319	5.155.741	4.410.422
1833-34	703.019	6.731.615	6.028.596
1834-35	60.000	3.959.453	3.899.453
1835-36	71.211	4.468.411	4.397.200
	$ 4.307.000	$ 42.392.103	$ 37.985.103

Tabelle nach: Chang 1970: 42.

Erstmals konnte die Britisch-Ostindische Kompanie im Jahre 1807 in Umkehrung bisheriger Praxis von einer Verschiffung von 3,4 Mio. Silberpesos von Kanton nach Kalkutta berichten. Dieser Silberabfluss hielt in den folgenden Jahren an, wurde allerdings zu diesem Zeitpunkt noch durch die Verschiffung von 6,2 Mio. Silberpesos durch amerikanische Händler nach China, die Gewürze und Tee in die Neuenglandstaaten importierten,

teilweise ausgeglichen (Irigoin 2009: 211, 214).[16] Ab 1825/26 floss dann insgesamt mehr Silber aus China ab als eingeführt wurde (Irigoin 2009: 215).
Nachdem das Monopol der Britisch-Ostindischen Kompanie auf Opium im Jahre 1813 erlosch und eine wachsende Zahl konkurrierender Handelshäuser in den Opiumhandel einstiegen, ist erneut ein rapider Anstieg der Einfuhr von Opium zu beobachten.

Opiumhandel von 1729-1832

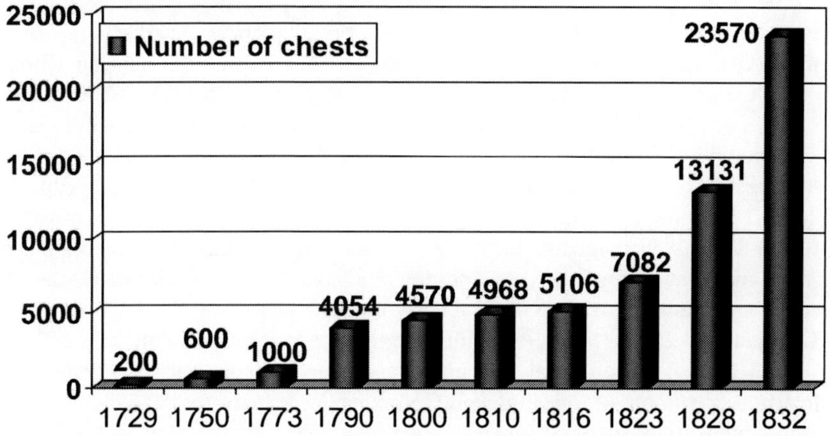

Tabelle nach Spence 1990: 129.

Im Jahr 1832 wurden 23.570 Kisten Opium, 1838 bereits über 30.000 Kisten à 63,5 kg illegal nach China verbracht, in der Regel zunächst in das zentrale Opiumlager vor Kanton. 1821 war dieses Großlager auf der Insel Lintin, an der Mündung des Perlflusses angelegt worden, also außerhalb der Reichweite des in Kanton residierenden Gouverneurs. Von diesem Lager ausgehend schufen sich die Drogenhändler entlang der Küste östlich und nördlich von Kanton bis hoch an die Yangzi-Mündung Stützpunkte vor den Hafenstädten Kanton, Fuzhou, Quanzhou und Ningbo. Von hier aus wurde das Opium meist bei Nacht und Nebel auf kleine Dschunken umgeladen und von chinesischen Händlern dann weiter ins Landesinnere verbracht. Etwa 25 britische Opiumschiffe gab es, auf chinesischer Seite übernahmen bewaffnete Schnellboote, etwa 100 bis 200 an der Zahl, nachts die Ladungen, um sie ins Inland zu transportieren. In diese Transport- und Handelsnetze in China waren auch Geheimgesellschaften eingebunden. Die zuständigen lokalen Beamten suchten teilweise gegen diesen Schmuggel vorzugehen, teilweise wurden sie durch Drohungen und Bestechungen zur Duldung des Schmuggels veranlasst (Chang 1970: 32ff). Androhung und Ausübung von Gewalt waren bei diesem Schmuggel ebenso an der Tagesordnung wie die Verteilung von Bibeln etwa durch Karl Gützlaff, der als Übersetzer und Chinaexperte die britischen Opiumschiffe begleitete und die Kapitäne für den Umgang mit chinesischen Beamten und Händlern beriet.

[16] Für das 18. Jahrhundert sehen wir trotz temporären Rückgangs insgesamt eine hohe Steigerungsrate, insbesondere wird deutlich, dass nun ein Großteil des Silbers direkt aus den USA nach China kam.

Mit Ausnahme eines einzigen amerikanischen Händlers waren bereits vor 1840 alle ausländischen Händler und Handelshäuser in Kanton am Opiumhandel beteiligt. Führend waren die Briten Jardine und Matheson, später das Handelshaus Dent, und Bostoner Kaufleute, u.a. Samuel Russell[17]. Sie alle gründeten ihren Reichtum auf das Opiumgeschäft – und dies war auch bekannt. Die führenden britischen und amerikanischen Auslandsmagazine, so etwa Hunt's Merchant Magazine in New York oder auch die Edinburgh Review oder das Quarterly Review berichteten über die großen Mengen Opium, die nach China geschmuggelt wurden (Chang 1970: 30f).

Die Einfuhr von Opium nach China bot aber nicht nur den Händlern und Schmugglern eine hohe Profitrate, sondern der dadurch bewirkte Silberabfluss stärkte wiederum das koloniale Projekt in Indien. Im Jahr 1800 erzielte die Britisch-Ostindische Kompanie einen Profit durch Opium von mehr als 2,3 Mio. Rupien, 1815 dann 8,2 Mio. und im Jahre 1838 fast 30 Mio. Rupien (Chang 1970: 48). Zum einen stiegen also die auf dem Opium basierenden Einnahmen kontinuierlich an, zum anderen hatten diese einen wachsenden Prozentanteil an den Einnahmen Indiens: 1821 lag der Anteil an den Einnahmen noch bei 6,7 Prozent, 1837 bereits bei mehr als 10 Prozent. Das nach Indien transferierte Silber beförderte darüber hinaus durch die Vergabe von Lizenzen der Kolonialmacht an die Bauern die Ausweitung und Konzentration auf Mohnanbau. Sie trieb damit die Monetarisierung und Eintreibung der Grundsteuer voran, die elementar für die Kolonialmacht war (Osterhammel 2009: 1041). Somit finanzierte die britische Kolonialmacht sich immer mehr durch Grundsteuereinannahmen und Handelssteuern, die auf den Transport von Opium erhoben wurden. Mohnanbau und Opiumhandel wurden für das koloniale Projekt in Indien – und wie wir später sehen werden, auch für die Kolonien in Südostasien – immer wichtiger. Nicht zuletzt sollte der Handel mit Opium aus Zentralindien nach China die zentrale Rolle bei der Integration dieses Gebietes in das Handelssystem des britischen Empire spielen und nicht primär einen indigenen Kapitalismus befördern (Markovits 2009: 89). Angesichts des großen Profits erschien es den Mitgliedern des britischen House of Commons, denen die Zahlen vorlagen, nicht ratsam, den Opiumanbau einzuschränken (Chang 1970: 48).

In China, vor allem im Süden des Landes, führte die gestiegene Einfuhr von Opium dazu, dass die Zahl der Süchtigen[18] in nahezu allen gesellschaftlichen Schichten stetig zunahm. Es gibt einzelne grobe Schätzungen: In Guangdong und Fujian sollen neun von zehn Personen süchtig gewesen sein, in der Stadt Suzhou wurde im Jahr 1820 die Zahl der Drogenabhängigen insgesamt auf mehr als 100.000 geschätzt. Ein britischer Opiumhändler vertrat Ende der 1830er Jahre die Meinung, dass die importierten 40.000 Kisten Opium der „Versorgung" von mehr als 2 Mio. Süchtigen dienten – Chinas Gesamtbevölkerung wird in dieser Zeit auf 350 Mio. geschätzt (Chang 1970: 35).[19] Besonders hoch soll die Zahl der süchtigen Soldaten und Beamten (hier insbesondere die Angestellten der Distriktverwaltungen, also der Steuereintreiber, Gerichtsdiener und Sekretäre des Magistrats) gewesen sein. Doch auch Eunuchen und Mitglieder des Kaiserhofes waren dem Opium verfallen. Die Folgen der Opiumsucht wurden in den Küstenprovinzen besonders sichtbar und Zeichen einer offensichtlichen politischen Destabilisierung traten zutage. Ein

---

17 Russel kam im Jahr 1819 als Supercargo nach China; er begann mit Opium zu handeln und gründete das von 1842 bis 1891 führende US-Handelshaus in Kanton.

18 Eine Schilderung der Sucht und eine Typologie von Opiumsüchtigen findet sich bei Slack 2001: 34ff.

19 Robert Hart schätzte 1879, dass die importierten 200.000 Kisten Opium jährlich etwa 2 Mio. Süchtige erreichten, d.h. auch die Menge des von den Süchtigen konsumierten Opiums stieg (Chang 1970: 35).

Feldzug gegen den Aufstand von Angehörigen der Yao-Ethnie in Nord-Guangdong im Jahre 1832 schlug fehl – wohl vor allem wegen der Abhängigkeit der Truppen vom Opium (Naquin/Rawski 1988: 234).

Die Folgen der illegalen Opiumeinfuhr bezogen sich inzwischen auf alle gesellschaftlichen Bereiche: Da die chinesische Wirtschaft auf einen kontinuierlichen Silberzufluss angewiesen war,[20] wurde als Folge des steigenden Silberabflusses insbesondere der Süden des Landes von einer Deflationskrise heimgesucht. Die Preise für Getreide sanken, während die Steuern, die in Silber zu entrichten waren, stiegen. Infolgedessen gingen die staatlichen Steuereinnahmen maßgeblich zurück (Osterhammel 2009: 1040).[21] Der Wert des Silbers stieg, der Wechselkurs zu Kupfer verschlechterte sich und ging damit zu Lasten der Mehrheit der Bevölkerung – Kupferkäsch war die Münze und das Zahlungsmittel des kleinen Mannes. Vor 1820 betrug der Wert von 1 Liang Silber 1.000 Kupfermünzen, im Jahre 1845 bereits 2.200 und mehr (Naquin/Rawski 1988: 234). In der wohlhabenden Provinz Jiangsu etwa ging der Handel enorm zurück. Die Kaufleute konnten im Jahre 1838 nur etwa die Hälfte der Waren absetzen, die sie 20 Jahre früher noch verkauft hatten. Die andere Hälfte war inzwischen durch das Opium ersetzt worden. Etwa 50 Prozent ihres Lohns gaben die ärmeren Schichten der Bevölkerung nun für den Kauf von Opium aus. Ein ranghoher chinesischer Beamter schätzte, dass zwischen 1823 und 1831 jedes Jahr etwa 17 Mio. Tael für den Drogenkonsum aufgewendet wurden. Einige Jahre später, im Zeitraum von 1834 bis 1838, war die Summe weiter angestiegen. Die für den Opiumkauf benötigte Summe betrug nun allein in Kanton etwa 30 Mio. Tael (Chang 1970: 40).

Arbeitslosigkeit, Landkonzentration und Abstieg der Kleinbauern zu Landarbeitern, das waren die gravierenden Folgen in den ländlichen Gebieten. Eine zunehmende Verarmung breiter Bevölkerungskreise ist zu beobachten. Diese schlug sich teilweise in sozialen Unruhen nieder, wie etwa 1794 bis 1804 in Nordwestchina und in den 1820er Jahren in Yunnan.

Die Opiumkriege

Ab Anfang der 1830er Jahre gerieten die wachsenden gesamtgesellschaftlichen Probleme in den Fokus der Zentralregierung in Peking (Bello 2003: 1113). In Dokumenten des Jahres 1836 stellte der chinesische Kaiserhof erstmals einen direkten Zusammenhang zwischen Silberabfluss und illegaler Opiumeinfuhr her (Naquin/Rawski 1988: 235). Nun wurden umfassende Gegenmaßnahmen ergriffen. Provinz- und Lokalbehörden im Südwesten des Landes gingen strikt und zum Teil auch recht erfolgreich gegen hier inzwischen florierenden Mohnanbau sowie gegen Konsum von und Handel mit Opium vor. Nach Kanton, dem Zentrum des Opiumschmuggels wurde der entschiedene Opium-Gegner und mit Sondervollmächten ausgestattete Kommissar Lin Zexu entsandt. Dieser veranlasste neben innenpolitischen, durchaus erste Erfolge zeitigenden Maßnahmen[22] im

[20] Im 19. Jahrhundert erfolgte ein Anstieg der Silberlasten für die Bevölkerung und eine Entwertung des Kupfergeldes im Verhältnis zum Silber (Gernet 2008: 448).

[21] Weitere Gründe für die Krise waren der Rückgang der Nachfrage nach Seide und Tee und die Verknappung der mexikanischen Silberproduktion (Osterhammel 2009: 1041).

[22] Lin hatte einen Sechs-Punkte-Plan folgenden Inhalts entwickelt: Zerstörung des Opiums und der Utensilien zum Opiumrauchen, Aufklärung über Gefahren und Auswirkungen des Opiumkonsums, Ausgabe von Übergangsdrogen an Abhängige, gegenseitige Kontrolle und Verantwortungsübernahme in kleinen, so genannten *Baojia*-Gruppen, rigorose Verfolgung der Händler und Schmuggler, bei Verurteilung Todesstrafe, Begnadigung für Einsichtige und Reuige. Verschärfend wurden im Juli 1839 weitere

März 1839 die Beschlagnahme von 20.000 Kisten, nämlich 1,4 Mio. Kilogramm, illegal von ausländischen Händlern in Kanton eingeführten Opiums, um den Schmuggel zu unterbinden. Lin Zexu ließ das Opium anzünden und ins Meer kippen – für die Drogenhändler ein großer finanzieller Verlust. Sie rüsteten zum militärischen Gegenschlag, um ihre Profite absichern zu können.

Es gelang den Drogenhändlern, den in Indien stationierten Militärs und den Politikern in England die Wichtigkeit der Ware Opium nicht nur für ihre eigenen Profite, sondern für das Empire insgesamt deutlich zu machen: Opium war *die* Substanz, die jede beliebige Ware zu Silber machen konnte (Brook/Wakabayashi 2000: 6).[23] Die Durchsetzung der britischen Interessen hinsichtlich der Aufrechterhaltung des illegalen Opiumhandels wurde somit nicht bloß zum Anlass für den Krieg, sondern war Ursache für den Krieg und die daraufhin erfolgende „Öffnung" des Landes. Dies wurde von der Mehrheit der Zeitgenossen auch so wahrgenommen. Die Argumente, China zu „öffnen", um freien Handel zu ermöglichen – dieser Handel lief seit Jahrhunderten über Kanton – sollten dies ebenso verschleiern wie die Thesen von Wissenschaftlern späterer Generationen, die die Opiumkriege als „Zusammenstoß der Kulturen" betrachteten (Chang 1970: 15). Den moralisch-ethischen Bedenken der Opium-Gegner, die sich durchaus schon früh artikulierten, wurde schon zu diesem Zeitpunkt, wie auch später immer wieder, entgegengehalten, dass Opium harmlos sei und als medizinisches Mittel zur Linderung von Schmerzen diene.[24] Für Chinesen sei Opium überdies wie Alkohol für Europäer, es stelle gar einen speziellen Zug ihrer Rasse dar (Gao 2010: 458ff). Erste Darstellungen von Opiumsüchtigen in westlichen Medien ähneln vielfach den Darstellungen zechender Europäer in Wirtshäusern.

Das fundamentale Interesse britischer Opiumhändler und des britischen Kolonialreiches insgesamt wurde in mehreren Feldzügen ab 1839 mit brutaler Waffengewalt durchgesetzt. Hatten sich die chinesischen Truppen noch 1834 beim ersten Vorstoß zur sog. Öffnung des Landes – der britische Kommandant, Lord Napier, widersetzte sich allen von China gesetzten Regeln, um die lokalen Beamten zur „Öffnung" Kantons zu zwingen – noch erfolgreich zur Wehr setzen können, so waren die britischen Kriegsschiffe und Waffen den Mandschu-Truppen jetzt militärtechnisch überlegen. Der Krieg, der heute als Erster Opiumkrieg bezeichnet wird, endete 1842 mit dem Ungleichen Vertrag von Nanjing. Das offiziöse britische Gemälde zur Vertragsunterzeichnung bringt die Ungleichheit der Unterzeichner deutlich zum Ausdruck: Während eine überwältigende Phalanx dutzender britischer Militärs stehend die Kulisse für die Unterzeichnung bildet, sitzen die vier Unterhändler bzw. Unterzeichner selbst an einem kleinen Tisch in der Mitte des Bildes. Die beiden chinesischen Unterhändler werden von der schieren Übermacht der Militärs nahezu erdrückt. Diese Übermacht ist nicht allein symbolisch zu sehen: Militärische Ge-

Gesetze zum Opiumverbot erlassen, u.a. mit der Androhung der Todesstrafe für Opiumgroßhändler und deren Komplizen, Berater, Käufer, Transporteure und bestochene Beamte. Mitwisser und Kleinhändler sollten mit Verbannung, Degradierung bzw. mit Schlägen durch den Bambusstock bestraft werden. Die Süchtigen sollten innerhalb von 18 Monaten einen Entzug durchführen, andernfalls drohte auch ihnen die Todesstrafe (Vetter 2009: 34ff).

23 Das britische Empire hätte nach verbreiteter zeitgenössischer Auffassung nicht überleben können, wenn ihm diese wichtige Kapitalquelle genommen worden wäre.

24 Trotz aller medizinischer Evidenz, dass Opium zwar als Schmerzmittel, besonders bei Malaria und Durchfall sowie als Sedativum diene, aber keinesfalls die Ursachen der Krankheiten heilen könne, wurde das medizinische Argument immer wieder bemüht (Gao 2010: 459f). Auch die britischen Mediziner betrachteten Opium nicht as Droge, sondern als Arznei (Lin Man-Houng 2004: 136).

walt und Kriege sollten das Vorgehen nicht nur der Briten in China in den nächsten Jahrzehnten bestimmen. Die im Ungleichen Vertrag von Nanjing 1842 durchgesetzten Bedingungen, insbesondere die Klassifizierung von fünf chinesischen Hafenstädten als sogenannte Vertragshäfen, ermöglichten nun in noch breiterem Maße den Schmuggel mit Opium, auch wenn dieser anfangs noch illegal blieb. Dass das System der chinesischen Vertragshändler zwangsweise aufgehoben wurde, trug zur weiteren Einschränkung der staatlichen Kontrolle des Schmuggels bei. Zudem hatte die chinesische Regierung 6 Mio. Dollar als Entschädigung für das zerstörte Opium sowie weitere 12 Mio. als Reparationszahlung für die Kriegskosten Großbritanniens zu zahlen und sie hatte niedrige Importzölle auf ausländische Waren, lediglich ca. 5 Prozent, zu akzeptieren. Überdies wurden die nun für die Vertragshäfen durchgesetzten ausländischen Konsuln der chinesischen Gerichtsbarkeit entzogen. Die Insel Hongkong, in der Nähe Kantons gelegen, wurde britisches Territorium. Mit diesem Ungleichen Vertrag, dem weitere folgten, waren dem chinesischen Reich erstmals entscheidende Souveränitätsrechte entzogen und der Prozess der formellen und informellen Kolonisierung eingeleitet worden.

Karl Friedrich Neumann, der erste deutsche Sinologe, der nach Kanton reiste und Feld- und Quellenstudien vor Ort unternahm, charakterisierte die Dimensionen und Auswirkungen des Krieges bereits 1846[25] in seiner „Geschichte des englisch-chinesischen Krieges" folgendermaßen:

> Der Krieg des Westens gegen den äußersten Osten Asiens ruht nun, soweit er mit Feuer und Schwert geführt wird, auf kurze Zeit; nicht so der nicht minder verderbliche Krieg vermittels des Schleichhandels mit Opium, vermittelst amtlicher Zumuthungen der verschiedenen fremden Regierungen; nicht so der Krieg der europäischen Civilisation und der christlichen Sendboten aller Bekenntnisse und Sekten. (Neumann 1855: 337)

Neumann war klar, dass dieser Krieg für China eine entscheidende Zäsur bedeutete. Er argumentierte im Einklang mit teleologischen Fortschrittsideen seiner Zeit und sprach vom „Krieg des unvermeidlichen Fortschritts und des neuerungssüchtigen Beispiels der Fremden gegen das verknöcherte Chinesenthum". Zugleich tradierte er den Topos von der „Abgeschlossenheit" des Landes – auch wenn er den Krieg des „gewinngierigen Kaufmanns" gegen eben diese Abgeschlossenheit durchaus kritisch sah (Neumann 1855: 358). Das Modernisierungs- und Öffnungsparadigma ist hier in seinen Grundzügen bereits angelegt.

Nach den Unterzeichnungen der Ungleichen Verträge 1843 kam mit den USA eine weitere Kolonialmacht hinzu, der illegale Opiumhandel wurde stetig fortgesetzt, ohne dass ihm von chinesischer Seite Einhalt geboten werden konnte. In den 1840er Jahren wurden jährlich allein aus Britisch-Indien etwa 30.000 Kisten Opium nach China geschmuggelt, Ende der 1840er Jahre stieg die Menge auf 40.000. Ein Jahrzehnt später waren es bereits etwa 60.000 Kisten (Blue 2000: 36). Trotz dieser immensen Steigerung wuchs das britische Defizit im Handel mit China weiter an, denn auch die Nachfrage – werbewirksam gefördert – nach chinesischen Produkten in Europa stieg. Die Einfuhr chinesischer Waren nach Großbritannien, vor allem von Tee, der zu diesem Zeitpunkt noch nicht in Indien angebaut wurde, machte beispielsweise im Jahre 1854 den neunfachen Wert der britischen Exporte nach China aus. Opium blieb weiterhin die ideale Kompensationsware chinesischer Waren. Es wurde – und bezüglich der 1840er und 1850er Jahre liegt hier die

---

25 Die im Folgenden zitierte zweite Auflage erschien 1855.

sehr informative Studie von Wong vor – zentral in der britischen Handelskette.[26] Großbritannien bezahlte die amerikanische Rohbaumwolle mit Schecks. Davon kauften die Vereinigten Staaten in Kanton Tee. Die aus dem Teeverkauf erzielten Gewinne wiederum wurden durch den Verkauf von Opium abgeschöpft. Diese Gewinne wurden teilweise nach England transferiert, um neue Baumwolle zu kaufen bzw. die Institutionen des Empires zu finanzieren, teilweise nach Indien transferiert, zum Kauf weiteren Opiums, zum Aufbau privater Vermögen in Indien und nicht zuletzt zur Finanzierung der Kolonialregierung. Die Einkünfte aus den Opium-Verkäufen machten insgesamt etwa 38 bis 48 Prozent der Kosten der US-Baumwolle aus, die letztlich die Textilfabriken Manchesters und die industrielle Revolution Englands überhaupt antrieb (Wong 1998: 409f).

Der Opiumhandel nach China war inzwischen für das Britische Empire zu einer ökonomischen Notwendigkeit geworden, damit das sich industrialisierende England schwarze Zahlen schreiben konnte. Das gesamte imperiale System war abhängig von den Mitteln, die direkt oder indirekt durch den Opiumhandel gewonnen werden konnten, ganz zu schweigen von der Finanzierung der teuren Kolonie Indien und dem Ausbau der neuen britischen Kolonien Hongkong und Singapur. Je mehr das Empire wuchs, umso größer wurde die Abhängigkeit vom Opium, umso weniger waren ethisch-moralische Argumente der Anti-Opium-Vertreter politisch durchsetzbar (Brook/Wakabayashi 2000: 7).

Unter diesen Bedingungen wurde 1856 ein sogenannter Zwischenfall um ein chinesisches, kurzzeitig unter britischer Flagge segelndes Schiff, die Arrow – lokale Behörden hatten chinesische Mannschaftsmitglieder unter Schmuggel- und Piraterie-Verdacht festnehmen lassen – als Vorwand genutzt, um die britische Handelsposition durch weitere Kriegszüge in China noch zu verbessern. Durch diese Kriege in den Jahren von 1856 bis 1860, die heute als Zweiter Opiumkrieg bezeichnet werden, wurde die chinesische Regierung zu weiteren Konzessionen und zur Abgabe weiterer Souveränitätsrechte an Großbritannien und Frankreich gezwungen. Alle anderen Großmächte, auch Deutschland, die in der Folge Verträge mit China durchsetzen konnten, profitierten davon durch die Einführung einer Meistbegünstigungsklausel. China wurde gezwungen, weitere sogenannte Vertragshäfen für den Import ausländischer Waren mit niedrigen Importzöllen von 5 Prozent zu deklarieren und die Transitsteuer für alle ausländischen Waren abzuschaffen. Es hatte diplomatische Vertretungen in Peking zu dulden, Missionaren den Zugang ins Innere des Landes zu erlauben und allen Ausländern Exterritorialitätsstatus zu gewähren, d.h. diese unterlagen nicht der chinesischen Gerichtsbarkeit. Und erneut waren große sogenannte Entschädigungssummen zu leisten: 21 Mio. mexikanische Silberdollar waren bereits nach dem Ersten Opiumkrieg zu zahlen gewesen, nun wurden weitere 8 Mio. fällig. Nicht zuletzt wurde der Opiumhandel legalisiert. Mit den neuen Verträgen war der optimale Zugang zu Chinas Waren und Ressourcen und zum Markt insgesamt erreicht. Die finanzielle Ausblutung des Landes, die in den nachfolgenden Jahrzehnten durch weitere Kriege direkt und indirekt durch hohe Verteidigungskosten und Anleihen sowie durch die Überschwemmung des chinesischen Marktes mit ausländischen Waren und entsprechend negativen Auswirkungen für die einheimische Produktion weiter verstärkt wurde, nahm solche Dimensionen an, dass nicht nur das Kaiserreich im Jahre 1911 zusammenbrechen sollte, sondern auch die nachfolgenden republikanischen Regierungen keine finanziellen

[26] Die internationalen Handelsrouten, in die der illegale Opiumhandel eingebunden war, werden von Benedict dafür verantwortlich gemacht, dass bereits im frühen 19. Jahrhundert von Yunnan aus die Beulenpest sich in ganz Asien und bis nach Europa und Amerika ausbreitete (Benedict 1996: 51-71).

Ressourcen besitzen würden, um der Aggression Japans oder den innenpolitischen Erosionsprozessen etwas entgegensetzen zu können. Und auch die japanischen Besatzer in den 1930er und 1940er Jahren machten sich das Opiumsystem für die Finanzierung ihrer Aggression zunutze – selbst wenn sie keine zielgerichtete Narkotisierung der chinesischen Bevölkerung betrieben haben sollten, wie es von einigen Autoren bestritten wird (Brook 2000: 323ff).

Gesamtgesellschaftliche und globale Auswirkungen des Opiumhandels

Die Jahrzehnte ab 1860 sind geprägt von einer weiteren massiven wirtschaftlichen und – man kann nun sagen – gesamtgesellschaftliche Durchdringung des Landes durch das Opium. Opium wurde, wie Hevia herausgearbeitet hat, zu einem entscheidenden Mechanismus der kolonialen „Deterritorialisierung" des Landes (Hevia 2003: 54). Zum nun legal eingeführten ausländischen Opium kam der inzwischen auch von staatlicher Seite als Konkurrenz forcierte, einheimische Anbau von Mohn und dessen Verarbeitung zu Opium hinzu. Die bereits seit den Anfängen bestehende Verbindung von Drogenhandel, Politik und organisierter Kriminalität wurde weiter gefestigt. Gleichzeitig – und dieser Widerspruch ist der Problematik inhärent – fanden politische Abwehrkämpfe nicht nur chinesischer und internationaler Anti-Opium-Gesellschaften, sondern auch chinesischer Regierungen statt, die darauf abzielten, Opiumkonsum und -handel zu kontrollieren und zu reduzieren.

Zunächst ist festzuhalten, dass die seit Anfang des 19. Jahrhunderts in Gang gesetzten Prozesse sich dramatisch fortsetzten und die im Umfeld der beiden Opiumkriege bereits sichtbaren Auswirkungen sich verschärften. Große Mengen an Opium wurden nach China verbracht oder dort produziert, die Zahl der Süchtigen stieg stark an. Der chinesische Staat – der Qing-Staat ebenso wie die nachfolgenden Lokal- und Zentralregierungen der Republik – hatte nur eingeschränkte Möglichkeiten zur Erhebung von Steuern und setzte diese auch zum Teil nur begrenzt ein, da sowohl die Bevölkerung als auch die zentrale wie die lokale Administration auf die aus Mohnanbau, Opiumherstellung und -konsum resultierenden Profite ebenso wie auf die später erhobenen regulären Steuern als wichtige Einnahmequelle angewiesen waren, ganz abgesehen von der Gewinngier einzelner korrupter Beamten. Die gesamte Gesellschaft und Wirtschaft war zu einer „narco-economy" (Slack 2001) geworden: Staat und Gesellschaft befanden sich in der „Opiumfalle".

Im Folgenden werden acht wichtige Charakteristika und Auswirkungen des Systems Opium in China skizziert, die ihren Ursprung im aufgezwungenen illegalen Drogenhandel und den Opiumkriegen haben:

1) Opiumimporte: Die Einfuhr von Opium stieg stetig an, gleiches gilt speziell für den Anteil britischen Opiums: Es machte die Hälfte der gesamten britischen Importe nach China aus. In den 1880er Jahren wurden allein aus Indien 80.000 Kisten jährlich nach China verschifft und fanden durch die Vertragshäfen, die ab 1876 durch die Yangzi-Häfen ergänzt worden waren, breiten Zugang im ganzen Land. Alle Versuche der Qing-Regierung, Vereinbarungen mit den ausländischen Mächten zur Reduktion der Importe zu führen, schlugen fehl. Auch die deutsche Regierung ließ die großangelegte Einfuhr der Drogen zu und stellte sich hinter deutsche Drogenhändler.[27] Gleichzeitig glaubte der

[27] Die Beschwerde des Drogenhändlers Schomburg in Kanton 1880 über aus seiner Sicht unrechtmäßig erhobene Binnenzölle verfolgte der Gesandte Brandt mehr als zwei Jahre lang als Vertragsbruch; der

deutsche Vertreter in China, der Gesandte Max von Brandt, die Opiumfrage zur Erlangung von Zugeständnissen in anderen profitablen Feldern ausspielen zu können. Er zeigte sich im Jahr 1875 bereit, die chinesische Regierung in ihren Bemühungen zur Eindämmung der Droge zu unterstützen, sofern China im Gegenzug Deutschland politische und wirtschaftliche Konzessionen wie z. B. die Öffnung weiterer Vertragshäfen machen würde. Dies stieß allerdings beim Auswärtigen Amt in Berlin auf Ablehnung.[28]
In der China von Großbritannien aufgezwungenen Zhifu-Konvention von 1876 war es der chinesischen Regierung nach zahlreichen diplomatischen Vorstößen erstmals gelungen, Sonderbestimmungen zur Opiumeinfuhr durchzusetzen, nämlich die Droge gesondert im Hafen zu lagern und auf deren Handel im Innern des Landes Binnenzölle zu erheben.[29] Diese wegen des entschiedenen Widerstandes der Opiumhändler lange nicht ratifizierte Konvention wurde dann noch zu Gunsten Chinas leicht verschärft und im Juli 1885 als britisch-chinesische Opium-Konvention beschlossen.[30] Die 1885 festgelegten Tarife, nämlich auf 100 Kisten Opium Einfuhrzoll und Binnenzoll gemeinsam zu erheben und zwar in Höhe von zusammen 110 Tael,[31] akzeptierte schließlich auch die deutsche Regierung, allerdings nur, nachdem der Gesandte von den chinesischen Ministern am 24. Januar 1886 die geheime Zusage einer bevorzugten Behandlung deutscher Banken und Firmen bei der Vergabe von Aufträgen zum Eisenbahnbau, bei der Beschaffung von Schiffen und Waffen sowie bei der Aufnahme von Staatsanleihen, einem äußerst lukrativen Geschäft, erpresst hatte.[32] Das deutsche Reich und sein Vertreter Max von Brandt hatten nun

---

Distriktbeamte hatte schließlich eine Entschädigung an Schomburg zu zahlen (PA AA Peking II 1120 Bl. 41ff, 186f).

28 Um in den Vertragsverhandlungen u.a. die „Öffnung" weiterer Häfen und Zulassung von Kaufleuten zum Handel im Inneren des Landes durchsetzen zu können, sah Brandt die einzig mögliche Konzession an die chinesische Seite beim Thema Opiumhandel: Deutschland könne sich anderen Mächten anschließen und Opium ganz verbieten oder höher besteuern oder auch die Opiumeinfuhr in den neu zu eröffnenden Häfen verbieten (PA AA Peking II 2 Bl. 33-37). Das AA ließ sich von Brandts Argumenten nicht beeinflussen und votierte, um die Beziehungen zu Großbritannien nicht zu belasten, gegen ein Entgegenkommen in der Opiumfrage (BA-B, R 1401 Reichskanzleramt Nr. 119 Bl. 11-16); vgl. dazu auch ausführlich das Memorandum des Zongli Yamen in: PA AA Peking II 2 Bl. 203ff.

29 Nachfolgend die ursprünglich formulierten Bestimmungen der Zhifu-Konvention: (iii) On opium: Sir Thomas Wade will move his Government to sanction an arrangement different from that affecting other imports. British merchants, when opium is brought into port, will be obliged to have it taken cognisance of by the Customs, and deposited in bond, either in a warehouse or a receiving hulk, until such time as there is a sale for it. The importer will then pay the tariff duty upon it, and the purchasers the *likin,* in order to the prevention of the evasion of the duty. The amount of *likin* to be collected will be decided by the different Provincial governments according to the circumstances of each. The date for giving effect to the stipulations affecting exemption of imports from *likin* taxation within the foreign settlements, and the collection of *likin* upon opium by the customs Inspectorate at the same time as the tariff duty upon it, will be fixed as soon as the British Government has arrived at an understanding on the subject with other foreign Governments. <http://www.chinaforeignrelations.net/node/147>, Zugriff am 13.5.2012.

30 So kam es zu öffentlichen Initiativen der Anglo-Oriental Society for the Suppression of the Opium Trade, die sich für die Ratifizierung einsetzten (PA AA Peking II 1120 Bl. 20ff). Sie votierten zugleich für die Freiheit der chinesischen Regierung, ein Opiumverbot auszusprechen.

31 So die Ausführungen in den deutschen Gesandtschaftsakten: PA AA Peking II1121 Bl. 51. In der Forschungsliteratur wurde dieser Konvention kaum Beachtung geschenkt.

32 Brandts Versuch allerdings, eine Erweiterung des Hafengebiets – und damit des zollfreien Raums –

die Opiumfrage zur Erlangung größerer Profite in anderen Bereichen genutzt. Ein Verbot des Opiumhandels für ihre Kaufleute, wie dies die US-Regierung im Jahre 1880 bereits verfügt hatte, erfolgte allerdings auf deutscher Seite nicht.
Erst ab Mitte der 1880er Jahre ist ein Rückgang der Opiumeinfuhr, allerdings bei gleichzeitiger Steigerung der Produktion, des Handels und des Konsums von einheimischem Opium, zu verzeichnen.[33] Im Jahre 1907 wurde unter starkem öffentlichem Druck und angesichts dessen, dass nun Opium auch durch andere Waren ersetzt werden konnte, ein britisch-chinesisches Abkommen unterzeichnet, welches die Opiumeinfuhr bis 1917 auf Null reduzieren sollte.[34] 1913 wurde wegen einer Überfüllung der Opiumspeicher – eine Anti-Opium-Kampagne der neuen republikanischen Regierung war erfolgreicher als ursprünglich angenommen – der Handel von indischem Opium kurzfristig gestoppt. In den 1920er Jahren jedoch nahm die Einfuhr nicht zertifizierten (und damit illegalen) Opiums wieder zu. Vielfach wurde indisches Opium zuerst nach Hongkong und Singapur – in den beiden Kolonien wurde nach wie vor die Hälfte der Steuern aus dem Opiummonopol erzielt – sowie nach Macao, Niederländisch-Indien, Japan oder Indochina gebracht und gelangte teilweise von dort nach China (Blue 2000: 42f). Erst ab 1926 wurde die lizenzierte Einfuhr von Opium aus Indien allmählich gestoppt.

2) Anstieg einheimischer Opiumproduktion: In China selbst stieg als Folge der mit der Droge zu erzielenden Gewinne, die gerade auch wegen der dem Land von Außen aufgezwungenen Silberabflüsse dringend notwendig waren, die Opiumproduktion dramatisch an, obwohl sie bis 1890 illegal war. Große Mengen eigen produziertes Opium kamen also zusätzlich zum importierten in Umlauf. In den inneren Provinzen Chinas ersetzte der Anbau von Mohn vielfach den Anbau von Getreide. Bohnen- und Weizenfelder waren bereits um 1840 in einigen Präfekturen Yunnans durch den Anbau von Mohn ersetzt worden. Neben Yunnan wurden Sichuan und Guizhou im Südwesten zu Zentren des Mohnanbaus. Seit 1801 ist Mohnanbau in Yunnan belegt[35] und in den 1830er Jahren sind Inland-Routen für den Vertrieb des Opiums ebenso wie Routen nach Vietnam und Siam bekannt. Gegen Ende des 19. Jahrhunderts wurde in diesen Gebieten weltweit die größte Menge an Opium produziert. Involviert in die Produktion waren auch nicht-Han: muslimische Händler und Händler der Ethnien der Yi, Dai und Miao (Bello 2003: 1111ff). Das ursprünglich fremde Opium wurde zu einem integralen Bestandteil des Steuersystems. Die lokale Administration, die eigentlich Anbau und Handel verhindern sollte, wurde von

---

auszuhandeln, scheiterte (PA AA Peking II 1121 Bl. 1ff). Doch Brandt konnte eine von Arendt und Ketteler als Zeugen unterzeichnete vertrauliche Erklärung dieser Zusagen des Prinzen Qing an das AA schicken (PA AA R 17972 Bl. 29-33).

33 S. Einschätzungen des deutschen Gesandten Max von Brandt in: PA AA Peking II 1121 Bl. 12f. Die Umsetzung der in der Opium-Konvention festgelegten Bestimmungen stieß auf großen Widerstand der Opiumhändler. Entgegen ursprünglichen Meldungen intensivierte sich auch der Schmuggel an den Küsten wieder (PA AA Peking II 1121 Bl. 158ff). Zugleich begannen die Gouverneure in den Provinzen intensiv den Anbau von Mohn und den Handel mit einheimischem Opium höher zu besteuern; die Steuern waren in Konkurrenz zum ausländischen Opium in den vergangenen Jahrzehnten niedrig gehalten worden (PA AA Peking II 1121 Bl. 176f, 202).

34 1909 in Shanghai (erste) Internationale Opium-Kommission eingesetzt, 1912 zweite Internationale Konferenz in Den Haag Einschränkung und Verbot.

35 Bereits 1736 wird in Lokalchroniken aus dem Südwesten Chinas Opium genannt, allerdings wurde es nicht geraucht, sondern lediglich für medizinische Zwecke genutzt (Bello 2003: 1118f).

den durch die Besteuerung des Opiums erzielten Mitteln abhängig und konnte daraus ihre Verpflichtungen gegenüber der Zentrale bezahlen. Die Bauern ihrerseits konnten, wie in Indien, mit dem Anbau von Mohn ihre hohen Steuerabgaben zahlen und erzielten zusätzlich Gewinn (Bello 2003: 1118, 1135).[36] Denn für die bis dahin armen Bauern bedeuteten Mohnanbau und Opiumproduktion die Möglichkeit, von einer Subsistenzwirtschaft weg einen Einstieg in die Warenwirtschaft zu finden. Es bedeutete für sie wie für die lokalen Landbesitzer, Händler und Beamten eine erhebliche Einkommenssteigerung.[37] Produktion und Verteilung von Opium erleichterte also auch in China wie in Indien die Kapitalakkumulation, weitete den Geldfluss aus, ermöglichte das Knüpfen von (Handels-)Netzwerken und war zudem ein Mittel der Umverteilung von Ressourcen weg von den Küstenstädten, gefolgt auch von einem steigenden politischen Einfluss der innerchinesischen Provinzen. Unter den Bedingungen der zunehmenden Integration des Opiums in die Volkswirtschaft – spätestens ab den 1830er Jahren dienten im Südwesten Chinas der Mohnanbau und die Opiumproduktion zur Finanzierung lokaler und zentraler Steuern und zwischen 1885 und 1905 machten die Opiumsteuern 6 bis 7 Prozent der gesamten Staatseinnahmen aus (Bello 2005: 294) – wurden auch in China selbst sowohl das Streben nach Subsistenz oder individuellen Profiten als auch die Notwendigkeit der Erzielung größerer staatlicher Einnahmen, u.a. zum Aufbau einer Landesverteidigung gegenüber ausländischer Aggression, zur wichtigen Triebkraft des kontinuierlichen Ausbaus der Opiumproduktion – trotz aller Versuche der Beschränkung, Kontrolle und Ausrottung der Sucht,[38] trotz aller moralisch-ethischen Bedenken. Selbst die Kommunistische Partei Chinas, der es Anfang der 1950er Jahre letztlich gelingen sollte, das Opium auszurotten, war in den Jahren ihrer „tödlichen Krise“ von 1941 bis 1943 gezwungen, den Opiumanbau als wichtigstes Handelsprodukt zu fördern (Chen Yung-fa 1995: 263f). China war in der „Opiumfalle“ gefangen. Die zunächst aus finanziellen, wie auch aus patriotisch-nationalen Gründen teilweise forcierte staatliche Förderung der einheimischen Opiumproduktion,[39] auch um die gedachten, noch verheerenderen Auswirkungen des eingeführten ausländischen Opiums zu konterkarieren, sollte dann, neben den ökonomischen Interessen, dazu führen, dass im Jahr 1906 nach offiziellen Zahlen neun Zehntel des in China konsumierten Opiums aus der Eigenproduktion stammte (Brook/Wakabayashi 2000: 13).

3) Ökologische Folgen: Die Entwicklung der einheimischen Opiumproduktion ging zum Teil mit gravierenden ökologischen Konsequenzen einher. Monokultur und speziell der Anbau von Mohn laugte den Ackerboden extrem aus. So ist die große Hungersnot in Nordchina in den Jahren von 1876 bis 1878 wesentlich auf die durch Mohnanbau ausgelaugten Böden in Zusammenhang mit einer großen Trockenheit zurückzuführen – so sah

---

36 Guo Songtao zeigte in seinem Bericht an den Kaiser 1877 diese umfassende Einbindung des Opiums in Politik und Wirtschaft Chinas auf (PA AA Peking II 2 Bl. 236-243, übersetzt von Carl Arendt).

37 Lin Man-Houng (2004: 125) verweist auf das Beispiel von Fuling in Sichuan, welches sich mit der Opiumproduktion rapide von einer einstmals armen zu einer wohlhabenden Region entwickelte.

38 Eine informative Darstellung der staatlichen Maßnahmen zur Reduzierung des Opiums findet sich in Lu/Miethe/Liang 2009, s. besonders Auflistung der Anti-Opium-Dekrete (S. 60); ausführlich dazu ebenfalls Baumler 2007.

39 Prominente Politiker wie Li Hongzhang, Wang Tao und auch später Sun Yatsen setzten sich aus ökonomischen und national-patriotischen Gründen für eine einheimische Opiumproduktion ein (Lin Man-Houng 2004: 142).

es auch die chinesische Regierung.[40] Zudem waren die öffentlichen Getreidespeicher auf Grund des Mohnanbaus für den lukrativeren Opiumhandel leer (Cumming 1888: 356ff, 484), so dass keine Nahrungsreserven vorhanden waren. Eine der von der Hungersnot am meisten betroffenen Provinzen war Shanxi. Sie war zu diesem Zeitpunkt zu einem der Hauptanbaugebiete von Mohn geworden, auch zu einem Zentrum von Opiumsüchtigen. 70 Prozent der Einwohner, Frauen wie Männer, sollen Berichten zufolge von der Droge abhängig gewesen sein, deren Produktion sie selbst verantworteten – ein Kreislauf von Abhängigkeiten. Bis auf die Beobachtungen in Zusammenhang mit der Großen Hungersnot wurden die längerfristigen ökologischen Folgen der Umwidmung des Ackerlandes für Mohnanbau in der Forschung bisher nicht systematisch thematisiert.

4) Destabilisierung der Gesellschaft: Der Opiumhandel war nicht nur Ursache der Opiumkriege, die das Kaiserreich auf den Status einer Halbkolonie reduzieren sollte, er hatte insgesamt einen großen direkten und indirekten Anteil an der stetig voranschreitenden sozialökonomischen Umstrukturierung des chinesischen Reiches, der Pauperisierung breiter Bevölkerungsschichten und nicht zuletzt der Demoralisierung einer signifikanten Zahl von Süchtigen. Die Umstrukturierung hatte bereits nach dem ersten Opiumkrieg zu großen sozialen Unruhen geführt. Der Aufstand der Taiping in den Jahren 1851 bis 1863, dessen Führer in Nanking eine eigene Dynastie begründeten, war der größte in der chinesischen Geschichte und betraf mehrere Provinzen des Landes. Er wurde blutig niedergeschlagen. Die mit dem Opiumhandel und den Vertragshäfen sowie der unkontrollierten Einfuhr von ausländischen Waren einsetzenden neuen Handelsströme und Transportwege in Südchina entlang der Vertragshäfen hatten zu einer Wirtschaftskrise in Südwestchina und zur Verarmung der Bevölkerung entlang der alten Handelsrouten geführt. Viele Transportarbeiter, Köhler und Bauern schlossen sich dem Aufstand der Taiping an (Wakeman 1966: 126f). Von der sozialen Trägerschaft und auch von seiner Ideologie her, einer Absorbierung christlicher Ideen in konfuzianisch-volksreligiösem Kontext, ist der Aufstand im Kontext kolonialer Durchdringung Chinas zu sehen.

5) Erzwungene Emigration: Die Verarmung breiter Teile der Bevölkerung – hier vor allem auch in den Küstenprovinzen Guangdong und Fujian – setzte nach dem ersten Opiumkrieg eine starke, weltweite Migration aus den südchinesischen Provinzen in Gang. In Form eines Kontraktarbeitersystems fand in den folgenden Jahrzehnten eine organisierte Anwerbung, Verschleppung und Verschiffung von Arbeitern statt, die letztlich die afrikanischen Sklavenarbeiter in den USA, Kuba und Peru ablösten. Verstärkt ab den 1860er Jahren suchte die chinesische Regierung immer wieder in Verhandlungen mit den imperialistischen Mächten diesen Menschenhandel zu regulieren, v.a. mit Blick auf die unmenschlichen Zustände während des Transports und auf den Plantagen. In den 1870er Jahren wurden erste Regulierungen getroffen und die Migrationsbedingungen, nicht zuletzt durch die Aufgabe des Kontraktarbeitersystems und Abkommen Chinas mit Peru und Spanien, leicht verbessert.[41] Auch in die britischen Kolonien Südostasiens fand eine massive Migration statt, sowohl von Arbeitern als auch von Kaufleuten. Sie betrieben

---

40 PA AA R 17627 Bl. 107.

41 S. zur Involvierung deutscher Akteure in den Kulihandel: Andreas Steen: Deutschland, China und die „Kulifrage". Transfer, Anwerbung, Widerstand, 1850-1914. Typoskript 2012 im Rahmen des DFG Projektes: (Preußen) Deutschland und China, 1848-1911: Interkulturelle Handlungsmuster und internationale Geschichte.

dort sog. Opiumfarmen, Produktionsstätten von Opium. Die dort wie auf den Plantagen und in den Minen der Kolonien beschäftigten chinesischen Arbeiter konnten die harten Arbeitsbedingungen im feuchtheißen Klima nur durch den Konsum des von ihnen produzierten Opiums ertragen – die Sterblichkeitsrate war außerordentlich hoch (Trocki 2002: 303).

6) Kolonien in Südostasien: Die Opiumproduktion, wie auch die Ausbeutung der Minen und die Plantagenproduktion in Südostasien geschah mittels kapitalkräftiger Gesellschaften, in die auch die chinesischen Geheimgesellschaften verwickelt waren. Sie erhielten von den Kolonialregierungen, etwa in Singapur und auf Java, Konzessionen zum Betrieb der Opiumunternehmen.[42] Diese stellten einmal für die Investoren der Gesellschaften mit ihrem Handelsmonopol gewinnträchtige Unternehmen dar; die Profite wurden auch in andere Unternehmen gesteckt und es wurden zum Teil große Imperien mit Schifffahrtslinien, Banken und Versicherungsgesellschaften aufgebaut. Zum anderen waren sie profitabel für die Kolonialregierungen, die einen Großteil ihrer Steuereinnahmen den Opiumbetrieben verdankten: Singapur etwa bezog ab 1819 etwa 40-50 Prozent seiner jährlichen Einnahmen aus dem Opium, Niederländisch-Indien verdankte zwischen 1886 und 1895 jährlich 18 Prozent seiner Steuereinnahmen dem Opium (Trocki 2002: 298). Opium wurde damit entscheidend für die Kapitalakkumulation in Südostasien. Es generierte hohen Kapitalfluss, die Betriebe finanzierten eine Warenproduktion und eine Infrastruktur für die Konsumindustrie mit Opium als eine der wichtigsten Waren. Die Opiumbetriebe finanzierten auch den Aufbau quasi-staatlicher Strukturen: Bürokratie und Polizei, letztlich das koloniale Projekt insgesamt, auch in Südostasien. Um 1880 begannen die so erstarkten Kolonialregierungen allmählich, die Opiumbetriebe in staatlichen Besitz zu übernehmen. Im Jahr 1907, nach dem Abschluss des chinesisch-britischen Vertrags zur Reduzierung der Opiumeinfuhr in China, wurde diese Übernahme abgeschlossen und das Netzwerk der Opiumbetriebe brach zusammen.

7) Opium als allgemeine Freizeitdroge: Zu Beginn des 19. Jahrhunderts wurde Opium als Importdroge hauptsächlich von Männern in den Küstenstädten Südchinas konsumiert: die Wohlhabenden konsumierten es zur Entspannung, die Armen zur Linderung von Erschöpfung und Hunger. Ab der zweiten Hälfte des Jahrhunderts änderte sich das: Opium war inzwischen in alle Bereiche der Gesellschaft eingedrungen, in den Geist, den Körper und das gesamte Leben chinesischer Bürger. Als kostspielige Droge zerstörte es die Familien wirtschaftlich und führte zur Degeneration gesellschaftlicher und familiärer Moral (Slack 2001: 34, 45ff). Es wurde vielfach zur „Freizeitdroge" in allen Schichten. In eleganten Geschäften der Küstenstädte wurde es ebenso verkauft wie in den kleinen Dorfläden, zur gemeinsamen Erholung von Männern ebenso wie von Frauen, individuell oder in Gesellschaft. Besonders deutlich wird dies an der Metropole Shanghai: Shanghai war ein Handelszentrum, ein faszinierendes Freizeitzentrum und zugleich ein Ort vielfältiger Gefahren. In all diesen Bereichen spielte Opium eine maßgebliche Rolle. Wie teilweise auch in anderen Gebieten Chinas, basierte die Wirtschaft Shanghais auf Opium – nicht allein als Ware, sondern auch als Währung. Opium stand für Freizeit, es repräsentierte die

[42] Zum Betrieb solcher komplexen Opiumfarmen waren nicht nur Opiumfelder anzulegen, auch Gebäude zur Produktion der Droge, Wohnhäuser und Läden – ein komplexes Arbeits- und Wohnsystem wurde geschaffen.

Stadt. Während Opium vorher nur ein Beiprodukt sozialer Aktivitäten gewesen war, wurde es nun ein zentraler Bestandteil dieser Aktivitäten (Des Forges 2000: 167ff).

8) Opium – Kriminalität – japanische Aggression: Es fand immer mehr eine Durchdringung der Gesellschaft mit kriminellen Geheimbünden, wie etwa der Green Gang in Shanghai mit ihrem Chef Du Yuesheng, statt. Diese organisierten Kriminellen bezogen ihren Reichtum aus dem Handel mit Opium sowie mit Morphium und Heroin und bestimmten durch ihre Verbindungen mit politischen Akteuren die gesamten politischen Strukturen Chinas mit. In den 1920er und 1930er Jahren wurden so das Opium und andere Drogen zur ökonomischen Basis des organisierten Verbrechens. Zugleich diente es der Versorgung des Guomindang (GMD)-Staates mit Steuereinkommen: Die bis 1938, zunächst gegen der Widerstand der Anti-Opium-Gesellschaft, relativ erfolgreich durchgesetzte Monopolisierung und Kontrolle von Mohnanbau und Opiumhandel durch den Staat sollte, so die politische Legitimierung, auf die schlussendliche Eindämmung der Sucht abzielen – war allerdings zweifellos auch ein Instrument der Abschöpfung lokaler Finanzressourcen und politischer Herrschaftsabsicherung gegenüber lokalen Gouverneuren und Warlords (Baumler 2000: 279ff). Tatsächlich belief sich die Opiumproduktion in der Zeit der GMD-Herrschaft bis 1937 auf jährlich schätzungsweise 12.000 bis 15.000 Tonnen (Lu/Miethe/Liang 2009: 75).

Opium wurde auf diese Weise auch die Basis der Verbindung von GMD-Staat und organisierter Kriminalität zur Bekämpfung politischer Gegner (Brook/Wakabayashi 2000: 13f). Und die Droge wurde ein wichtiges Instrument japanischer Aggression in China: In den 1890er Jahren hatten japanische Händler begonnen, über Tianjin Opium nach Korea und in die Mandschurei zu schmuggeln. Im Jahre 1922 sollen 7 Prozent der 5.000 in Tianjin lebenden Japaner, die nicht der chinesischen Gerichtsbarkeit unterlagen, mit Morphium und anderen Drogen gehandelt haben. Opium diente zur Akkumulation von Kapital allgemein, verstärkt nach dem Ersten Weltkrieg auch der Finanzierung von Undercover-Aktivitäten mit dem Ziel japanischer Expansion. Opiumgeld finanzierte rechtsextreme Kreise in Japan während seiner faschistischen Periode und teilweise über 1945 hinaus. Und nicht zuletzt wurden aus den Opiumgeldern die in China von Japan inthronisierten Marionettenregierungen, insbesondere das Kaiserreich Manzhuguo, finanziert. Pu Yi erhielt ein Sechstel, nämlich 300 Mio. Yuan, seiner gesamten Staatseinkünfte aus dem Opium. Doch nicht nur Japans Expansion, auch die politischen Regime der Warlords, der GMD und selbst der KPCh der Republikzeit bezogen einen Großteil ihrer Einnahmen aus den Opiumsteuern (Brook/Wakabayashi 2000: 15ff). Während des antijapanischen Krieges organisierten japanische Beamte, zuerst individuell, dann die Zaibatsu, die großen Syndikate, schließlich die Regierung, den systematischen Mohnanbau, kauften die Ernte auf, verarbeiteten den Saft zu Rohopium, raffinierten dieses zu Morphium und Heroin und exportierten die Drogen in andere Teile Chinas und nach Südostasien. Der Einsatz der Drogen diente neben der Kapitalakkumulation auch als „Kriegsmittel", sollte die Bevölkerung demoralisieren und die Widerstandskraft der chinesischen Bevölkerung, wie der Bevölkerung in Südostasien insgesamt, schwächen (Trocki 2000). Ähnlich wie im 19. Jahrhundert britische Händler und nachfolgend der britische Staat vom illegalen Opiumhandel profitierten, so setzte im 20. Jahrhundert der japanische Staat das profitable Geschäft mit dem Opium fort (Kobayashi 2000).

Anti-Opium-Aktivitäten

Im Kampf gegen das Opium vereinigten sich staatliche mit zivilgesellschaftlichen Aktivitäten, nationale mit internationalen Aktionen. Von Beginn an waren Anti-Imperialismus, Nationalismus und Patriotismus der bestimmende Faktor der Anti-Opium-Aktivitäten, auch wenn darüber hinaus ethische und gesundheitliche Gründe sowie das Ziel der Bekämpfung der Kriminalität angeführt wurden. Immer wieder gab es auch nach 1860 politisch-diplomatische Versuche von Seiten chinesischer Regierungsvertreter, die Opiumeinfuhr zu reduzieren und zu verbieten. In einem Memorandum im Jahr 1869 an den britischen Gesandten in Peking, Rutherford Alcock, suchte die chinesische Regierung unter Darlegung der schädlichen Auswirkungen dieses „tödlichen Gifts" und seines hemmenden Einflusses auf die Beziehungen die englische Regierung zur Aufnahme von Verhandlungen zwecks Regelung und letztlich Verbot des Handels zu bewegen. Sie argumentierte einmal moralisch:

> Hinzu kommt, dass es weder der Gerechtigkeit entsprechen, noch auch vor dem Gefühle zu verantworten sein dürfte, wenn englische Kaufleute das menschenverderbliche Gift des Opiums in China verbreiten während chinesische Kaufleute England mit Tee, Seide und anderen nützlichen Produkten beschenken.

Und sie drohte, nationale Interessen über das gesundheitliche Wohl des Volkes zu setzen, für den „äußersten Notfall" mit der Aufhebung des Opiumverbots im eigenen Land, welches die britischen Opiumgewinne ebenfalls reduzieren würde:

> Da man Einfuhr fremden Opiums nicht verhindern kann, so würde die Aufhebung des Verbots gegen den Anbau der Mohnpflanzen auch weiter nicht schaden, im Gegenteil würde man den fremden Kaufleuten dadurch die Haupthandhabe des Gewinnstes entziehen, und gleichzeitig die Steuereinnahmen vermehren. (...) so widerstrebt es uns doch, schon jetzt in voreiliger Weise zu der Aufhebung des Verbots zu schreiten, denn die Prinzipien einer gesunden Regierungskunst müssen sich im Einklang halten mit dem am Leben Freude findenden Willen der Vorsehung, welche verlangt, dass Alles, was dem Volke zum Verderben gereicht, weggeräumt werde.[43]

Erfolge zeitigte das Memorandum zu diesem Zeitpunkt nicht.

Mitte der 1870er Jahre wurde ein letztlich erfolgloser Vorstoß auch beim deutschen Gesandten Max von Brandt gemacht, die Unterstützung Deutschlands in der Opiumfrage zu gewinnen.[44] Auch Anti-Opium-Aktivisten und Anti-Opium-Gesellschaften in Großbritannien – im Jahre 1874 hatte William Pease in England die Gesellschaft zur Unterdrückung des Opiumhandels gegründet – wie auch einzelne ausländische Experten in China selbst, der Missionar und Arzt John Dudgeon[45] in Peking und seine Kollegen William Lockhart und Joseph Edkins, setzten sich, ebenso wie der Missionar und Sinologe James Legge, entschieden für ein Verbot ein. Erste Einschränkungen beim Opiumhandel konnte die Qing-Regierung auf dem Verhandlungsweg mit der Zhifu-Konvention 1876 erreichen, die aber gerade wegen dieser Paragrafen lange nicht ratifiziert werden sollte. 1877 wurde ein Bericht Guo Songtaos Auslöser für erneute Anstrengungen der chinesischen Regierung,

---

[43] PA AA Peking II 2 Bl.203, 205; das Memorandum von 1869 wurde 1877 der deutschen Gesandtschaft in Peking übergeben, vom Ersten Dolmetscher Carl Arendt übersetzt – dem folgt die obige Übersetzung – und dem Auswärtigen Amt zugestellt.

[44] BA-B, R 1401 Reichskanzleramt Nr. 119, Bl. 11-16.

[45] S. zu Dudgeon die Studie von Gao 2010.

zumindest unter Beamten und Soldaten den Drogenkonsum auszurotten[46]. Und nicht zuletzt ordnete ein kaiserliches Edikt 1878 unter dem Eindruck der auch dem Mohnanbau geschuldeten großen Hungersnot im Norden des Landes radikale Maßnahmen zur Ausrottung des Mohnanbaus, einschließlich von Ersatzbepflanzungen, seitens des Provinzgouverneurs von Shanxi an.[47] Doch erst die britisch-chinesische Opium-Konvention vom 18. Juli 1885, in Nachfolge der Bestimmungen der Zhifu-Konvention, legte die gemeinsame Erhebung von Einfuhrzoll und Binnenzoll auf Opium auf insgesamt 110 Tael fest,[48] eine erste Beschränkung der hohen Gewinnmargen.
Die chinesischen Politiker suchten immer wieder diplomatische Wege, auch auf Kosten von anderen Zugeständnissen an die ausländischen Mächte, Opiumhandel und -produktion einzuschränken oder in Denkschriften anzuprangern. In Shanxi und Gansu ließen die Provinzgouverneure 1878 bzw. Anfang der 1880er Jahre die Mohnkultur zerstören und Ersatzkulturen, andere Feldfrüchte, auch Baumwolle und Maulbeerbäume anpflanzen (Bello 2005: 291, PA AA Peking II 2 Bl. 96ff). Immer wieder, wie 1898 Zhang Zhidong, wiesen Politiker eindringlich auf die schädlichen Folgen des Opiumrauchens hin: Opiumrauchen wurde als „Symptom des moralischen Niedergangs Chinas" gewertet (Vetter 2009: 73f). In den südlichen Provinzen, in Fujian und Guangdong, hatten sich früh zivilgesellschaftliche, patriotisch und ethisch motivierte Anti-Opium-Gesellschaften, auch als Teil eines neuen nationalen Verständnisses, gegründet, die sich in öffentlichen Aktionen insbesondere der Unterstützung der Süchtigen annahmen und sich gegen die Verpachtung von Land zum Mohnanbau einsetzten (Madancy 2000: 228-247; Madancy 2003: 27). Im Jahr 1906 wurde ein großangelegter Zehnjahresplan gestartet, der auf die Ausrottung des Opiums abzielte, also politische mit wirtschaftlichen Maßnahmen verband – mit beträchtlichem Erfolg, letztlich jedoch zunichte gemacht durch den Sturz des Kaiserreiches und das nachfolgende politische Machtvakuum (Vetter 2009: 78ff, 87f). Neben zivilgesellschaftlichen Anti-Opium-Aktivitäten[49] suchten auch die späteren wechselnden republikanischen Regierungen, teils durch Monopolisierung des einheimischen Opiumanbaus und damit der Abschöpfung von Steuern, teils durch groß angelegte patriotische Kampagnen gegen Handel und Konsum von Opium überhaupt, die Verbreitung des Opiums einzuschränken. Neben wiederholten Regierungserlassen ist hier insbesondere der 1935 von der GMD-Regierung vorgelegte Sechs-Jahres-Plan zu nennen, der eine langfristige Abschaffung der Opiumsucht durch Monopolisierung und Kontrolle vorsah (Baumler 2007: 177ff). Selbst die Marionettenregierung Wang Jingweis in Nanjing suchte Anfang der 1940er Jahre, teils im Bündnis mit studentischen Bewegungen und im Kontext der Rhetorik von nationaler Entwicklung gegen das „soziale Übel" Opium, wie gegen Glücksspiel und Prostitution, vorzugehen (Eykholt 2001: 360ff). Da die Regierungen jedoch fast alle von eben den durch Mohnanbau und Opiumproduktion erzielten Steuern ebenso wie von den inzwischen starken organisierten Verbrechersyndikaten abhängig waren, waren diese

[46] PA AA Peking II 2 Bl. 153ff.

[47] PA AA Peking II 2 Bl. 96ff; PA AA R 17627 Bl. 107.

[48] Das erschien den meisten Händlern, auch der deutschen Firma Schomburg, nicht mehr profitabel genug. Hongkong hatte zwar den Einfuhrzoll nicht erhöht, er betrug 1887 statt 110 nur 27 mex. Silberdollar pro Kiste, doch der Landhandel von Hongkong aus nach China war teuer. Die Fa. Schomburg wollte sich demnach aus dem Opiumhandel zurückziehen. Brandt war der Auffassung, dass die Zhifu-Konvention und die Opium-Konvention von 1885 vor allem den Anbau einheimischen Opiums gefördert und sanktioniert habe (PA AA Peking II 1121 Bl. 12ff, 103ff).

[49] S. dazu u.a. Slack 2001: 54ff.

Versuche auch im 20. Jahrhundert letztlich nicht erfolgreich.[50] Noch im Jahre 1949 gab es in China 20 Mio. Süchtige (etwa 4 Prozent der Bevölkerung), 600.000 Drogenhändler und 10 Mio. Bauern, die ihre Existenz auf den Anbau von Mohn gründeten (Liu/Miethe/ Liang 2009: 67). Erst nach der radikalen Zerschlagung der politisch-wirtschaftlichen Strukturen der Republik und des halbkolonialen Systems, das China mit dem Opiumhandel aufgezwungen worden war, waren die landesweiten, nahezu geheim geführten großen Anti-Opiumkampagnen der KPCh 1952 erfolgreich darin, das Land quasi vom Opium – und somit aus der „Opiumfalle" – zu befreien (Zhou 2000: 380ff).

Zusammenfassung

Die Opiumkriege stellten jeweils Höhepunkte der gewaltsamen Einbindung Chinas in die Weltgesellschaft mittels Opium dar. Die „Öffnung" des Landes durch die Opiumkriege für die (westliche) Moderne, zunächst für den Handel, dann für die technischen Errungenschaften und die industrielle Produktion, zuletzt für die politischen Institutionen und Ideen des Westens, bedeutete faktisch, dass die bis zu diesem Zeitpunkt stattfindende Einbindung Chinas in weltweite Handels- und Kommunikationsströme eine völlig neue Qualität erhielt. Das Land wurde schrittweise unter Ausübung und Androhung militärischer Gewalt seiner gleichrangigen Position beraubt und ihm wurde in der neuen Hierarchie einer kolonial strukturierten Weltgesellschaft eine nachrangige Position zugewiesen. Im Unterschied zum chinesischen globalen Handel vom 16. bis zum frühen 19. Jahrhundert nämlich verlor nun der Kaiserhof seine Souveränität. Nicht er bestimmte mehr die Konditionen, zu denen Außenhandel betrieben wurde, und die Art der einzuführenden Produkte, sondern Art und Höhe der Importe und der zu entrichtenden Zölle wurden ihm von finanzstarken ausländischen Händlern und ihren politischen Vertretungen in einer Weise aufgezwungen, dass er im Unterschied zur Einbindung in globale Handelsnetze vor dem 19. Jahrhundert nun die binnenwirtschaftlichen und innergesellschaftlichen Konsequenzen der Integration in eine kolonial strukturierte Welt kaum noch steuern konnte.

Die Spezifik des Landes als Halbkolonie, als „informal empire", in der es nur in Teilen um territoriale Besetzung ging, kann nicht darüber hinwegtäuschen, dass das Land faktisch ökonomisch und finanziell „ausgeblutet" wurde. Das betrifft nicht nur das Kaiserreich. Auch die nachfolgenden republikanischen Regierungen ab 1911 hatten ein Jahrhundert lang allein durch die aufgezwungenen immensen Verteidigungsausgaben und die Reparationszahlungen an die kolonialen Mächte sowie durch die niedrigen Zolleinnahmen nur sehr eingeschränkte Möglichkeiten der Gestaltung von Politik, so dass Politiker und Intellektuelle sich über Jahrzehnte in einen Abwehrkampf gegen diese Ausbeutung des Landes und für die Wiederherstellung nationaler Souveränität begaben. Anti-Opium-Aktivitäten waren zugleich und in erster Linie Kämpfe um nationale Unabhängigkeit und Selbstbestimmung.

Neben der Aushöhlung der materiellen Ressourcen des politischen Systems fand eine wirtschaftliche und gesellschaftliche Umstrukturierung statt, verbunden mit der Pauperisierung großer Bevölkerungsschichten, die letztlich zum Zusammenbruch des Kaiserreiches und auch nachfolgender republikanischer Herrschaft führen sollte. Der systemisch gewordene Opiumkonsum und Opiumhandel, die fremden und einheimischen kriminellen Drogensyndikate und staatliche wie private Profiteure hatten daran maßgeblichen Anteil.

---

50 Slack wertet die Anti-Opium-Kampagnen der Guomindang sogar als „an exercise in deception" (2001: 149).

Quellen- und Literaturverzeichnis

Baumler, Alan (2000) „Opium Control versus Opium Suppression: The Origins of the 1935 Six–Year Plan to Eliminate Opium and Drugs", in Brook / Wakabayashi (Hg), *Opium Regimes, China, Britain, and Japan, 1839-1952*, S. 270-292.

Baumler, Alan (2007) The *Chinese* and *Opium under* the *Republic*: *Worse than Floods and Wild Beasts*, Albany: State University of New York Press.

Bello, David (2003) „The Venomous Course of Southwestern Opium: Qing Prohibition in Yunnan, Sichuan, and Guizhou in the Early Nineteenth Century", in *The Journal of Asian Studies* 62:4, S. 1109-1142.

Bello, David (2005) *Opium and the Limits of Empire, Drug Prohibition in the Chinese Interior, 1729-1850*, Cambridge: Harvard University Press.

Bennedict, Carol (1996) *Bubonic Plague in the 19th Century*, Stanford: Stanford University Press.

Bickers, Robert (2011) *The Scramble for China. Foreign Devils in the Qing Empire, 1832-1914*, London: Penguin Books.

Blue, Gregory (2000) „Opium for China: The British Connection", in Brook / Wakabayashi (Hg), *Opium Regimes, China, Britain and Japan, 1839-1952*, S. 31-54.

Brook, Timothy / Wakabayashi, Bob Tadashi (Hg) (2000) *Opium Regimes, China, Britain, and Japan, 1839-1952*, Berkley, Los Angeles, London: University of California Press.

Brook, Timothy / Wakabayashi, Bob Tadashi (2000) „Introduction", in Brook / Wakabayashi (Hg), *Opium Regimes, China, Britain, and Japan, 1839-1952*, S. 1-31.

Brook, Timothy (2000) „Opium and Collaboration in Central China, 1938-1940", in Brook / Wakabayashi (Hg), *Opium Regimes, China, Britain, and Japan, 1839-1952*, S. 323-343.

Bundesarchiv Berlin (BA-B) R 1401 Reichskanzleramt Nr. 119.

Chang, Hsin-Pao (1970) *Commissioner Lin and the Opium War*, New York: Norton and Company.

Chen Yung-fa (1995) „The Blooming Poppy under the Red Sun: The Yan'an Way and the Opium Trade", in Tony Saich / Hans van de Ven (Hg), *New Perspectives on the Chinese Communist Revolution*, Armonk u.a.:M. E. Sharpe, S. 263-298.

China`s External Relations - A History „Zhifu-Konvention von 1876", in <http://www.chinaforeignrelations.net/node/147>, abgerufen am 13.5.2012.

Cummings, Constanze Gordon (1888) *Wanderings in China*, Edinburg, London: W.Blackbird.

Des Forges, Alexandre (2000) „Opium/Leisure/Shanghai", in Brook / Wakabayashi (Hg), *Opium Regimes, China, Britain, and Japan, 1839-1952*, S.167-189.

Eykholt, Mark S. (2001) „Resistance to Opium as a Social Evil in Wartime China", in Brook / Wakabayashi (Hg), *Opium Regimes, China, Britain, and Japan, 1839-1952*, S.360-379.

Feldbauer, Peter (2003) *Estado da India: Die Portugiesen in Asien 1498-1620*, Reihe: Expansion – Interaktion – Akkulturation, Wien: Madelbaum Verlag.

Fairbank, John K. (1964) *Trade and Diplomacy on the China Coast. The Opening of the Treaty Ports 1842-1854*, Cambridge: Harvard University Press.

Fairbank, John / Bruner Frost, Katherine / Matheson MacLeod, Elisabeth (Hg) (1975) *The IG in Peking, Letters of Robert Hart 1868-1907*, Bd. II, Cambridge: Harvard University Press.

Flynn, Dennis O. / Giráldez, Arturo (2002) „Cycles of Silver: Global Economic Unity Through the Mid-Eighteenth Century", in *Journal of World History* 13: 2, S. 391-427.

Flynn, Dennis O. / Giráldez, Arturo (2004) „Path dependance, time lags and the birth of globalisation: a critique of O`Rourke and Williamson, in: *European Review of Economic History* 8, S. 81-108.

Flynn, Dennis O. / Giráldez, Arturo (2010) *China and the Birth of Globalization in the 16th Century*, Farnham/Burlington: Ashgate Publishing.

Gao, Xi (2010) „The Truth and Evils of Opium: The Anti-Opium Activities of British Missionary to China John Dudgeon (1837-1901)", in *Frontier History China* 5:3, S. 453-470.

Gernet, Jaques (2008) *Die chinesische Welt von den Anfängen bis zur Jetztzeit*, Frankfurt: Suhrkamp.

Hevia, James L. (2003) *English Lessons. The Pedagogy of Imperialism in Nineteenth-Century China*, Durham u.a.: Duke University Press/Hong Kong University Press.

Irigoin, Maria Alejandra (2009) „The End of a Silver Era: The Consequences of the Breakdown of the Spanish Peso Standard in China and the United States, 1780s–1850s", in *Journal of World History* 20: 2, S. 207-244.

Kobayashi, Motohiro (2000) „Drug Operations by Resident Japanese in Tianjin", in Brook / Wakabayashi (Hg), *Opium Regimes, China, Britain, and Japan, 1839-1952*, S.152-166.

Lin, Man-Houng (2004) „Late Qing Perceptions of Native Opium„ in *Harvard Journal of Asiatic Studies* 64:1 S. 117-144.

Lu, Hong / Miethe, Terance D. / Liang Bin (2009) *China's Drug Practices and Policies, Regulating Controlled Substances in a Global Context*, Burlington: Ashgate.

Madancy, Joyce A. (2000) „Poppies, Patriotism, and the Public Sphere: Nationalism and State Leadership in the Anti-Opium Crusade in Fujiuan, 1906-1916", in Brook / Wakabayashi (Hg), *Opium Regimes, China, Britain, and Japan, 1839-1952*, S.360-380.

Markovits, Claude (2009) „The Political Economy of Opium Smuggling in Early Nineteenth Century India: Leakage or Resistance?" in *Modern Asian Studies* 43, S. 89-111.

Morse, Hosea Ballu (1926) *The* Chronicles *of the* East India Company Trading *to* China, 1635-1834, Bd. 2, Oxford: Clarendon Press.

Naquin, Susan / Rawski, Evelyn N. (1988) *Chinese Society in the Eighteenth Century*, New Haven: Yale University Press.

Neumann, Karl Friedrich (1855) *Geschichte des englisch-chinesischen Krieges*, Leipzig: Teubner.

Osterhammel, Jürgen (2010) *Die Verwandlung der Welt, Eine Geschichte des 19. Jahrhunderts*, München: C.H. Beck.

Politisches Archiv des Auswärtigen Amtes, Berlin (PA AA) Peking II 2 Politische Angelegenheiten Chinas März 1875 – Dez. 1877

Politisches Archiv des Auswärtigen Amtes, Berlin (PA AA) Peking II 1120 Handel mit Opium, Morphium, Kokain Bd. 1 Sept. 1876 – Febr. 1886

Politisches Archiv des Auswärtigen Amtes, Berlin (PA AA) Peking II 1121 Handel mit Opium, Morphium, Kokain Bd. 2 Jan. 1886- August 1901

Politisches Archiv des Auswärtigen Amtes, Berlin (PA AA) R 17627 Schriftwechsel mit der Mission zu Peking sowie mit anderen Missionen und fremden Berichten über die inneren Zustände und Verhältnisse Chinas, August 1878- 31. Dez. 1878

Politisches Archiv des Auswärtigen Amtes, Berlin (PA AA) R 17972 Verhältnis Chinas zu Deutschland Bd. 1 Dez. 1885-31.7.1896

Slack, Edward R. Jr. (2001), *Opium, State, and Society, China's Narco-Economy and the Guomindang, 1924-1937*, Hawaii: University of Hawaii Press.

Steen, Andreas (2012) *Deutschland, China und die „Kulifrage". Transfer, Anwerbung, Widerstand, 1850-1914*. Typoskript 2012.

Spence, Jonathan (1990) *The Search for Modern China*, New York, London: Norton and Company.

Tan Chung (1978) *China and the Brave New World. A Study of the Origins of the Opium War (1840-42)*, Bombay u.a.: Allied Publishers Private Limited.

Trocki, Carl A. (2000) „Drugs Taxes, and Chinese Capitalists in Southeast Asia" in Brook / Wakabayashi (Hg), *Opium Regimes, China, Britain, and Japan, 1839-1952*, S. 79-112.

Trocki, Carl A. (2002) „Opium and the Beginnings of Chinese Capitalism in Southeast Asia", in *Journal of Southeast Asian Studies* 33, S. 297-314.

Trocki, Carl (1999) *Opium, Empire and the Global Political Economy: A Study of the Asian Opium Trade, 1750-1950*, London / New York: Routledge.

Vetter, Dirk (2009) „Von der Rauschgiftkolonie zum Anti-Drogen-Pionier, Chinas Anti-Opium-Kampagnen von 1838-1839 und 1906/07 im Vergleich", in *Deutsche Ostasienstudien* 8, Gossenberg.

Wakeman Frederic Jr. (1966) *Strangers at the Gate. Social Disorder in South China, 1839-1861*, Berkeley/Los Angeles: University of California Press.

Walsh, John (2007) „From Small Muslim Trading Settlement to Major Metropolis", in <http://eastasianhistory.suite101.com/article.cfm/manila#ixzz0UYdtGJT7 Manila>, abgerufen am 21.10.2009.

Wong, J.Y. (1998) *Deadly Dreams, Opium, Imperialism and the Arrow War (1856-1860) in China*, Cambridge: Cambridge University Press.

Zhou, Yongming (2000) „Nationalism, Identity, and State Building: The Antidrug Crusade in the People's Republic, 1949-1952" in Brook / Wakabayashi (Hg), *Opium Regimes, China, Britain, and Japan, 1839-1952*, S. 380-405.

Zhou, Yongming (1999) *Anti-Drug Crusades in Twentieth-Century China. Nationalism, History and State Building*, Oxford: Rowman and Littlefield.

„Kontinuität und Umbruch in Chinas Geschichte und Gegenwart", XXII. Jahrestagung der Deutschen Vereinigung für Chinastudien (DVCS), Technische Universität Berlin, 25.-27. November 2011

Die XXII. Jahrestagung der DVCS stand anlässlich des 100-jährigen Jubiläums der Xinhai-Revolution unter dem Motto „Kontinuität und Umbruch in Chinas Geschichte und Gegenwart". Die Tagung fand an der Technischen Universität Berlin statt und wurde vom dortigen „Center for Cultural Studies on Science and Technology in China" organisiert. Insgesamt interpretierten 28 Referentinnen und Referenten in neun Panels aus verschiedenen Perspektiven der klassischen und modernen Sinologie das Tagungsthema. Die Beiträge befassten sich im Wesentlichen mit der Fragestellung, welche Ereignisse als Einschnitte wahrgenommen, infolge dessen als Umbrüche dargestellt werden, und in welchem Verhältnis Unbeständiges zu Konstantem steht. Zentral war dabei, welche als Einschnitte wahrgenommenen Ereignisse sich aufgrund von Kontinuitäten, die der Blick aus der historischen Perspektive sichtbar macht, nicht als weitreichende Umbrüche charakterisieren lassen.

Eröffnet wurde die Tagung durch den Vorsitzenden der DVCS, *Prof. Dr. Helwig Schmidt-Glintzer* (Herzog August Bibliothek Wolfenbüttel), den Vorsitzenden des wissenschaftlichen Beirats des China Centers, *Prof. Dr. Wolfgang König*, und die Leiterin des China Centers, *Dr. Eva Sternfeld.*

Im Panel „Kollektiv – Revolution" wurde die Tradition von Umbrüchen in China aus begriffsgeschichtlicher und philosophischer Perspektive thematisiert. *Liu Huiru* (Universität Trier) zeichnete den Ursprung und Wandel des Revolutionsbegriffs in China nach. Die Bedeutungsänderung des Begriffs *geming* 革命 zeige, dass sozialer Wandel mit sprachlichen Neuerungen – in China durch die von der 4.-Mai-Bewegung durchgesetzte Einführung des modernen Chinesisch als Höhepunkt – einhergeht. In der modernen Bedeutung sei der Begriff *geming* 革命 erstmals Ende des 19. Jahrhunderts verwendet worden und schnell zu einem Modewort des frühen 20. Jahrhunderts geworden. *Carsten Storm* (Technische Universität Dresden) zeigte anschließend, dass die angeblich konfuzianische Tradition, auf die sich in China berufen wird, nur eine Konstruktion ist. Der Ausgangspunkt für das Verständnis der Tradition sei der Diskurs und nicht das kulturelle Erbe selbst. *Fabian Heubel* (Academia Sinica) demonstrierte, dass der zeitgenössische Neokonfuzianismus zwar Brüche mit konfuzianischen Traditionen der Kaiserzeit aufweist, aber der Bezug zu den klassischen Texten dennoch erhalten geblieben ist. Zeitgenössische Vertreter des Konfuzianismus wie Xiong Shili 熊十力 und Mou Zongsan 牟宗三 setzten sich kritisch damit auseinander, so Heubel, ob eine Neuinterpretation des Modells der inneren und äußeren Selbstkultivierung des *Daxue* 《大学》 die Vereinbarkeit des Konfuzianismus mit der Demokratisierung des Politischen ermögliche.

Im Panel „Zeit – Wandel" wurden historiographische Konzepte und ihre Anwendung in Politik und Wissenschaft diskutiert. Die Beiträge machten sichtbar, dass Ereignisse wie die Xinhai-Revolution innerhalb Chinas quasi nach Bedarf gedeutet werden und somit verschiedene parallele Verständnisse der Geschichte harmonisch nebeneinander und teilweise in Konkurrenz zueinander existieren. *Nele Noesselt* (GIGA German Institute of Global and Area Studies) ging der Bedeutung der Revolution von 1911 für die Geschichtsschreibung der Kommunistischen Partei Chinas auf den Grund. Unter anderem verwies sie auf die bemerkenswerte Nutzung des Begriffs „Revolution" durch Hu Jintao ein. Hu bezeichne neben der Xinhai-Revolution und der „Befreiung" Chinas 1949 auch die Reform- und Öffnungsperiode als Revolution. Noesselt stellte ebenso die unterschiedliche Deutung der Xinhai-Tradition durch die KPCh und die Guomindang heraus. *Nicola Spakowski* (Albert-Ludwigs-Universität Freiburg) stellte drei verschiedene Modelle von Zeitverlaufsvorstellungen im modernen China vor. Sie zeigte, dass exemplarisches Geschichtsdenken, lineares Zeitbewusstsein und zyklische Zeitverlaufsvorstellungen in China koexistieren.

Neben Nele Noesselt thematisierte auch *Astrid Lipinsky* (Universität Wien) explizit die Situation in Taiwan. Auch in ihrem Beitrag war die Deutungshoheit über die Geschichtskonstruktion ein wichtiger Aspekt. Lipinsky richtete den Blick auf die neuere und neueste Geschichte Taiwans und präsentierte die Kulturelle Renaissance-Bewegung im Panel „Kultur – Revolution" als eine „Alternative zur Kulturrevolution". Das Panel war den Wechselwirkungen zwischen politischen Ereignissen und kulturellen Entwicklungen gewidmet. *Du Weihua* (Humboldt-Universität zu Berlin) zeigte, dass die wechselnden politischen Rahmenbedingungen in der ersten Hälfte des 20. Jahrhunderts starken Einfluss auf die Reformen im Hochschulwesen hatten. *Thomas Kampen* (Universität Heidelberg) veranschaulichte hingegen, wie die revolutionären Bewegungen von 1911 und 1949 durch Personen geformt wurden, die ein Studium im Ausland absolviert hatten.

Über mehrere Panels verteilt wurde analysiert, welche Auswirkungen Dynastiewechsel auf Kontinuitäten und Umbrüche hatten. Wenn in den meisten beschriebenen Fällen Umbrüche auf verschiedenen Ebenen eine Rolle spielten, so wurde doch klar, dass insbesondere im kulturellen Bereich Traditionen weitergeführt oder nur sehr zögernd einem Wandel unterzogen wurden. *Annette Kieser* (Westfälische-Wilhelms-Universität Münster) stellte beispielsweis im Panel „Identität – Verlust" anhand von Grabfunden in Shandong den Grabkult der Han vor. Die Funde zeigten, dass bis in die späte Han-Zeit Praktiken aus der Chu-Zeit verbreitet waren. Allerdings seien auch Neuerungen wie die gemeinsame Bestattung von Ehepartnern hinzugekommen. Im selben Panel analysierte *Monique Nagel-Angermann* (Westfälische-Wilhelms-Universität Münster), wie in traditionellen Geschichtswerken die Zersplitterung des chinesischen Reiches während des fünften Jahrhunderts nach Christus einerseits als Bruch mit der Vergangenheit dargestellt wird, andererseits aber fortgeführte Elemente legitimatorischen Zwecken dienten.

Im Panel „Technik – Wissen" wurden technische und erkenntnistheoretische Dimensionen von Kontinuität und Umbruch untersucht. Der Wandel in der Ausbildung von Töpfern und Töpferinnen führe laut *Anette Mertens* (Technische Universität Berlin) zu einem Verlust des Spezialistentums, der für die chinesische Töpferei über Jahrhunderte prägend war. In ihrem gemeinsamen Vortrag thematisieren auch *Angelika Messner* (Christian-Albrechts-Universität Kiel) und *Rui Magone* (Universidade de Lisboa) die Gleichzeitigkeit von Kontinuitäten und Umbrüchen. Sie stellten die Frage, ob der Dynastiewechsel im 17. Jahrhundert auch epistemologische Brüche mit sich gebracht habe. Messner betonte die Umbrüche, die in der zeitgenössischen medizinischen Literatur sichtbar werden. Magone unterstrich die Kontinuitäten innerhalb des Beamtenprüfungssystems.

Ein großer Bestandteil des Panels „Welt – Technik" waren die gegenwärtigen gesellschaftlichen Herausforderungen. *Eva Sternfeld* beschäftigte sich mit der Frage, ob der derzeit rasant steigende Energiebedarf in China zu einem Umbruch im Sinne einer energiepolitischen Wende führen wird. Auch wenn das Land jüngst erheblich in die Förderung von erneuerbaren Energien investierte, könne man noch lange nicht von einer Energiewende sprechen. Auf absehbare Zeit bleibe Kohle Chinas primäre Energiequelle. Bezüglich der chinesischen Atomenergiepolitik verwies Sternfeld darauf, dass die Katastrophe von Fukushima zumindest kurzfristig zu einem Einschnitt beim derzeit weltgrößten Atomenergieprogramm führte, einschließlich einer Überprüfung der Sicherheitsstandards und eines vorübergehenden Moratoriums bei der Genehmigung neuer AKW-Projekte.

Im abschließenden Panel mit dem Titel „Land – Leute" spielte die Hinterfragung von altgedienten Periodisierungen eine zentrale Rolle. *Felix Wemheuer* (Universität Wien) zeigte den Bruch in der Beziehung von Staat und Bauern in der Volksrepublik China durch die Auswirkungen des „Großen Sprungs nach vorn". Wemheuer argumentierte, dass die Staats- und Parteiführung in Folge der großen Hungersnot die Urbanisierung durch die Einführung des *hukou*-Systems stoppen wollte. *Hauke Neddermann* (Freie Universität Berlin) zeigte anhand der Erfahrungen eines hanchinesischen Soldaten, der nach der Gründung der Volksrepublik nach Xinjiang siedelte, wie die Revolution Umbrüche forcieren konnte und dennoch nicht alle Beständigkeit zerstörte. *Izabella Goikhman* und *Barbara Herrmann* (beide Freie Universität Berlin) verdeutlichten, dass die Ernährungssicherheit im späten 19. und frühen 20. Jahrhundert in Südchina insbesondere dadurch weitergeführt werden konnte, dass die nicht-staatlichen Akteure die gleichen blieben und somit für Konstanz sorgten.

Die Tagung machte vor allem bewusst, dass selten klar ist, welche Auswirkungen „klassische" Umbrüche wie Dynastiewechsel auf Kontinuitäten hatten und haben. Die Konferenzbeiträge können als Anregung dienen, auch in der Wissenschaft als gegeben angesehene Ansichten und Konzepte (z.B. Periodisierungen) zu hinterfragen und dadurch im besten Fall einen genaueren Blick auf Forschungsfelder der Sinologie zu bekommen. Der sinologische Blick auf Dynastie- oder Systemwechsel sollte sich nicht auf die Veränderungen beschränken, sondern auch auf das Weitergeführte, das Konstante, die Kontinuität ausgeweitet werden. Darüber hinaus ist die Vielfalt der Tagungsbeiträge hervorzuheben. Ihren Anspruch, die deutschsprachige Chinaforschung in ihrem Facettenreichtum zu repräsentieren, hat die DVCS auf ihrer 22. Jahrestagung auch insofern erfüllt.

(Philipp Mahltig)

„Taiwan Studies in Germany – Workshop in Memory of Wang Shih-ching", Academia Sinica, Institute of Taiwan History, 2 December 2011

This small workshop brought together three German scholars who are involved in various ways in Taiwan Studies, in research and teaching. In addition to a historical overview and a presentation on the current status of Taiwan studies, there was a discussion on the future of Taiwan Studies worldwide and the relationship between German and European Taiwan studies and Taiwan Studies in Taiwan itself.

The workshop was opened by *Hsieh Kuo-hsing* (Director of the Institute of Taiwan History at Academia Sinica), *Lin Hao-tung* (The China Foundation for the Promotion of Education and Culture) and *Wang Fu-chang* (Institute of Taiwan History). Wang Fu-chang is in charge of the series of Taiwan workshops, which started some years ago, to which specialists from one country and region are invited every year. Scholars from the United States, Japan and France, amongst other countries, have already taken part.

Unlike previous workshops, all three German scholars expressed doubt as to whether a narrow focus on countries would prove useful for strengthening Taiwan Studies, being of the opinion that the key lies in issues concerning methodology and international networks. Other suggestions included linking Taiwan Studies to other area studies, increasing comparative research and overcoming national limitations.

Gunter Schubert (University of Tübingen and director of the ERCCT) started with a presentation on „Taiwan Studies in Germany and a German Approach to European Taiwan Studies: Idea, Concept and Agenda of the European Research Center in Contemporary Taiwan," a newly established post-doctorate institute, solely for research, which was partly financed by the Chiang Ching-kuo Foundation. In addition to providing an overview of the scholars, often social-science oriented, who have carried out research on Taiwan during recent decades, Schubert focused on the setting up of the ERCCT, and concluded by reflecting on the steps that need to be taken to further reduce the national "compartmentalization" of Taiwan studies in Europe.

Henning Klöter (Ruhr University Bochum), „Taiwan Research in Germany: Foray into a Neglected Field," took a historical perspective, presenting, first of all, early travelogues in the German language by the Swiss landscapist, Albrecht Herporrt (1641-1680), and then research that has been carried out by Dutch specialists. This research was partly written in German and translated into German and dealt, in particular, with Albrecht Wirth (1866-1936) and his work, *History of Formosa*, for which, Wirth (who was inclined to accept Nazi ideology) employed a traditional colonial approach. Klöter also focused on the endeavors of Helmut Martin (1940-1999), the first contemporary scholar who established a Taiwan research unit in Germany.

Jens Damm (Chang Jung Christian University and Freie Universität Berlin), „German Taiwan Studies within the Social Sciences: Berlin," described the various ways in which Taiwan-related research has been included in the research landscape of Berlin without a specific Taiwan research institute being established. Focusing on the Freie Universität, on the Institute of East Asian Studies, Sinology and Political Science in particular, Damm explained the benefits and dangers of maintaining a separate field of research in the form of Taiwan Studies.

During the roundtable discussion, all scholars rejected the ideas proposed by their Taiwanese counterparts with regard to establishing a specific organization for Taiwan Studies or establishing a central institute of Taiwan Studies in Europe. Gunter Schubert and Jens Damm made particular reference to the Europe Association of Taiwan Studies, emphasizing the positive aspects of the network character of European Studies and the advantages this offers, in contrast to the restrictive elements inherent in centralization.

(Jens Damm)

Robert Bickers: *The Scramble for China. Foreign Devils in the Qing Empire, 1832-1914,* London: Penguin Books 2011, 496 S. (ISBN 978-0-713-99749-1)

„*The Scramble for China* is an epic, dynamic account of a century of Sino-foreign interactions, confrontations and confusion. Told from both the Western and Chinese point-of-view, Robert Bickers' book examines how events such as the opium wars or the Boxer uprising have impacted upon China's relations with the world." Die Presseerklärung des Verlags hat in diesen Sätzen versucht, wesentliche Inhalte des Werkes wiederzugeben und seinen Wert zum Verständnis der gegenwärtigen Versuche Chinas, wieder eine zentrale Position in der Welt einzunehmen, betont. Es gehe dabei um das Begreifen der „dark, complex phase of its modern history", wie die „traumatic period" von 1832 bis 1914 mit den „impositions from foreign imperialists" charakterisiert wird.

So wie hier einerseits Bezug genommen wird auf die Imperialisten, die neben anderen Akteuren das Schicksal Chinas bestimmt haben, und andererseits die Phase als solche in Verschleierung imperialistischer Aggression als „dunkel und komplex" bezeichnet wird, so ambivalent – manchmal auch widerspruchsvoll – liest sich das gesamte Werk. Es ist eine kenntnisreiche, empirisch gesättigte und unterhaltsame Studie, zweifellos, und das ist viel angesichts der in der Regel recht trocken geschriebenen wissenschaftlichen Werke über diese Zeit. Warum also lässt sie mich trotz Anregungen und neuer Erkenntnisse, trotz hilfreicher Anmerkungen zum Weiterarbeiten, trotz des zeitweiligen Lesevergnügens, insgesamt doch mit einem unbefriedigenden Gefühl zurück?

Letztlich kann ich mich des Eindrucks nicht erwehren, dass mit dieser Darstellung, beabsichtigt oder unbeabsichtigt, eine große Relativierung der imperialistischen Aggression gegenüber China stattfindet, eine Revision des doch die letzten Jahrzehnte dominanten, teils modernisierungstheoretisch ergänzten und nur selten in Frage gestellten Geschichtsbildes von der Expansion westlicher Mächte und ihrer formellen und informellen Herrschaft in China, mit all den Staat und Bevölkerung tangierenden Konsequenzen kolonialer und halbkolonialer Ausplünderung, eine alle gesellschaftlichen Bereiche durchziehende Herrschaftsausübung eben. Aussagen über die Ausländer, als Mitglieder einer globalen Diaspora, die „lediglich ihre Jobs machten", die nicht aus der Perspektive des 21. Jahrhunderts gewertet werden sollten und die „geholfen haben, das moderne China zu dem zu machen, was es wurde" (S. 8) begründen diese Revision und Wende zur modernisierungstheoretischen Sicht, einer mit westlicher Modernisierung gleichgesetzten wohlgemerkt. Diese wird ergänzt durch die Perspektive des Globalen; begrifflich und inhaltlich tendiert Bickers dazu, diesem Aspekt mehr Raum zu geben, durchaus bei nicht völliger Aufgabe des „empire" und Kolonialbegriffes. Insgesamt wird das koloniale Projekt zu einem „multinational enterprise" (S. 16), ein frühes Globalisierungsprojekt, in dem viele Akteure Vieles bewirken, durchaus auch grausame Taten im „Kampf um China", doch die Gewichtungen fehlen. Und so ist eine gewisse Beliebigkeit festzustellen, die dann doch wieder System hat, auch in den Begrifflichkeiten.

Zunächst geht es um die Briten als „unwillkommene Gäste", die in ihrer „wohl-geordneten" kleinen Welt in Kanton leben und handeln. Ja, auch der Opiumhandel nahm in den 1830er Jahren zu, aber, so argumentiert Bickers, Opium war doch schon seit langem Teil der Freizeitkultur der chinesischen Elite und die Briten hatten nur noch den für sie gewinnträchtigen Markt zu schaffen. Die Unterbrechung einer Opernaufführung in einem Tempel in Shanghai 1835 durch Missionare leitet das zweite Kapitel ein. Die Unterbrechung soll als symbolischer Akt die chinesische Seite ins Spiel bringen – das abergläubi-

sche China mit einem keineswegs unbegrenzten Despotismus als „Bühne" für die Ausländer. „Lindsay's War and Peace" behandelt den Krieg, der bedingt durch Lin Zexus aggressives Vorgehen, einfach geführt werden musste. Unter Überschriften wie „Model Settlements" und „China El Dorado" wird der Auf- und Ausbau des Vertragshafens Shanghai, der, nur kurz thematisierte Zweite Opiumkrieg und nicht zuletzt die Überzeugung der ausländischen „Chinahands" von ihrer Überlegenheit gegenüber den Chinesen geschildert. „At the Heart of the Empire" befasst sich, mit Alliteration spielend, insbesondere mit Robert Hart und der großen Bedeutung des Seezolls, nun situiert in der Hauptstadt, bei der ausländischen Durchdringung des Landes und zugleich seiner Besitzergreifung, auch in der Sammlung von Kunstobjekten, nun nicht als Resultat von Plünderungen wie 1860, sondern durch Kauf. Das Kapitel „Inland Dreams" karikiert in gewisser Weise die Träume der Ausländer: Das Tianjin Massaker 1870 beendete laut Bickers die sinophilen „Platitüden" eines Burlingame oder die Hoffnungen des britischen Gesandten Alcock auf eine Revision der Ungleichen Verträge – die Ausländer, das konstatiert Bickers für diesen Zeitpunkt, wollten nicht sprechen, sie wollten gewinnen und sie wollten mit China nicht auf der gleichen Ebene verhandeln (S. 251). Das „Vertragshäfen-System" (S. 262), euphemistisch gesprochen, breitet sich nun im ganzen Land aus.
Dazu gehörte auch die Gewinnung ausländischer Einflusssphären bzw. die Abwehr dieser Versuche außerhalb des chinesischen Kernlandes: Bickers beschreibt hier die Rolle des keineswegs nur als neutrales Technologieprojekt fungierende Leuchtturmsystem, 1868 initiiert von Hart und Anfang der 1880er Jahre auf Formosa etabliert, den Aufbau eines meteorologischen Netzwerks, des Telegrafensystems, zuerst entlang der Küste, die Lobbyarbeit für den Bau von Eisenbahnen, die Zunahme ausländischer Handelsfirmen und ihrer chinesischen Partner, der Kompradoren – insgesamt eine rasante Entwicklung des Landes hin zur Modernisierung. Doch dann jäh gebrochen durch den Sieg Frankreichs in Annam, von Bickers zugleich interpretiert als Niedergang der Hoffnungen des Landes auf eine Selbststärkung ohne die Durchführung innerer Reformen – eine Position, die er teilt: Zum Überleben hatte das Land einen neuen Weg zu finden.
Um das 50jährige Jubiläum der Öffnung Shanghais als Vertragshafen, am 17. November 1893, ist das folgende Kapitel „Jubilees" konstruiert. Das innere Leben der Shanghaier europäischen Kolonie, die nach wie vor herrschende und offensiv vertretene Trennung zur chinesischen Gesellschaft – abgesehen von Dienstboten und anderen Untergebenen – wird thematisiert. Die Stadt war fester Bestandteil des europäischen Kolonialismus (S.315), formuliert Bickers in Bezug auf das Leben und Sterben in Shanghai. Das Gefühl der Unsicherheit der Europäer, die nun durch Nachholen und Gründung von Familie eine gewisse Domestizierung erfahren haben, exemplarisch verdeutlicht an einem Roman dieser Jahre, wird nun noch größer. Japanische Truppen greifen im nachfolgenden Jahr Port Arthur an. Die europäische Gegenbewegung im Zurückdrängen des neuen Konkurrenten lässt zugleich neue Bewegungen gegen die Qing-Regierung entstehen: innere Reformbewegungen mit globalen Verbindungen, aber auch erneute Bedrohungen durch die ausländischen Mächte, ebenfalls global. Russische, deutsche und japanische Truppen marschierten nun sukzessive in China ein. „Extinction", das nachfolgende Kapitel, schildert die Untergangsszenarien des Kaiserreiches, angefangen von der großen Überschwemmungskatastrophe des Huanghe-Deltas 1898 über den Boxeraufstand und den „Krieg", den alle Parteien: Boxer gegen Christen, die Qing-Truppen und die Alliierten, 1900/1901 gegeneinander führten, bis hin zum Ende der Dynastie und dem Beginn des Weltkrieges.

Dieser markiert für Bickers auch das Ende des gemeinsamen Konzertes der Mächte in China und der „multinational nature of the foreign enterprise in China“ (S. 373).
Bickers schließt mit einem lesenswerten Über- und Einblick in die chinesische und westliche Historiographie und sucht sich schließlich selbst hier zu positionieren: in der Mitte, zwischen einer Position des „foreign bafflement“ und einer in der VR China seit den 1990er Jahren verbreiteten politisierten Repräsentation der Geschichte. Das „Jahrhundert der Verträge“, so nun seine Bezeichnung der „dunklen“ Periode, war natürlich eine Geschichte des Kampfes um Konzessionen/scramble for concessions. Sie war gekennzeichnet durch „violence, honour, constraint, bafflement“ (S.396), doch, so relativiert der Verfasser, China war in dieser Phase nicht wirklich bedeutend für Großbritannien, Frankreich, Deutschland und andere Länder und es war letztlich von Vorteil, dass das Land nicht die Kolonie nur einer Macht war, sondern mehrerer, sich einander ausbalancierender Mächte.
Bickers begreift zudem seine Geschichte des Kampfes um Konzessionen als nur eine mögliche von mehreren Erzählungen über diese Periode. Als er von den großen menschlichen Kosten des geschilderten Kampfes um Konzessionen spricht, bezieht sich das auf die Ausländer. Anders als in der Presserklärung angekündigt, werden die chinesischen Perspektiven auf die Geschichte, mit Ausnahme der historiographischen Aspekte, von Bickers allerdings nicht erzählt. Die von ihm so sehr postulierte globale Vernetzung der Geschichte der Ausländer in China mit der der chinesischen Moderne bleibt damit Stückwerk. Wer sich jedoch für eine kurzweilige Erzählung der sozialen und politischen, weniger der ökonomischen Aspekte kolonialen Lebens in China, einschließlich des individuellen menschlichen Faktors, interessiert, dem sei dieses unter dem Eindruck aktueller Globalisierungstendenzen und entsprechender Paradigmen geschriebene Buch empfohlen.

(Mechthild Leutner)

Kimberly Ens Manning und Felix Wemheuer (Hg.), 2011: *Eating Bitterness. New Perspectives on China's Great Leap Forward and Famine*, Vancouver, Toronto: UBC Press, 321 S. (ISBN 978-0-7748-1726-4)

Rund sechzehn Jahre ist es her, dass Jasper Becker mit seinem kontroversen Bericht „Hungry Ghosts: China's Secret Famine“ (1996) international für Aufsehen sorgte. Mit journalistischem Blick für schicksalhafte Anekdoten und menschliche Dramen zeichnete er darin das Schreckenspanorama der „Drei bitteren Jahre“, jener gravierenden Hungersnot, die zwischen 1959 und 1961 unzählige Menschen das Leben kostete; bis heute kann nur geschätzt werden, wie viele Millionen Opfer es insgesamt gab. Beckers Buch war es, das erstmals eine breite Öffentlichkeit mit der Katastrophe im Anschluss an den verfehlten „Großen Sprung nach vorn“ konfrontierte. Inzwischen, anderthalb Jahrzehnte später, ist aus dem zuvor randständigen Thema, diskutiert nur von einer Handvoll Fachkollegen/-innen, ein zentraler Forschungsgegenstand der chinabezogenen Geschichtswissenschaften geworden – und dies außerhalb Chinas ebenso wie im Land selbst.
Nachdem das Scheitern des „Großen Sprung nach vorn“ lange mit einem Fokus auf (politische) Eliten des noch jungen sozialistischen Staates betrachtet wurde, rückt in neueren Studien vermehrt die Graswurzel- bzw. Dorfebene in den Blick, auch und gerade, weil ständig neues Quellenmaterial erschlossen wird. Gleichzeitig stellt das Feld sich fragmentiert und recht unübersichtlich dar – (mikro-) historische Studien zum Alltagsleben in den Hungergebieten stehen, häufig ganz und gar unvermittelt, neben solchen zur (offiziellen vs. nichtoffiziellen, traumatischen) Erinnerung, zum Stadt-Land-Gegensatz,

zu Geschlechterrollen, zu den institutionellen, ökonomischen und ideologischen Grundlagen der Ereignisse.

Mit „Eating Bitterness: New Perspectives on Chinas Great Leap Forward and Famine" legen Kimberley Ens Manning und Felix Wemheuer nun eine gelungene Aufsatzsammlung vor, die den Stand der internationalen Forschungsaktivitäten zusammenfasst und abbildet, indem zuvor kaum bzw. nur unzureichend verknüpfte Diskursstränge zusammengeführt werden. Ganz besonders gilt dies für chinesische und „westliche" Debatten über die Hungersnot. So vereint der Band, im Kern basiert er auf einer Konferenz an der Universität Wien im Jahr 2006, insgesamt elf teilweise recht umfängliche Beiträge von Autoren/-innen, die das Feld in den letzten Jahren allesamt geprägt und durch innovative Betrachtungsweisen befruchtet haben: Sieben von amerikanischen und europäischen Forschern/-innen, vier von chinesischen. Eine Tatsache, auf die die Herausgeber in ihrer sehr lesenswerten Einleitung mit berechtigtem Stolz hinweisen.

Die ersten sechs Texte des Sammelbandes befassen sich mit der Phase vor dem Ausbruch der Hungersnot. *Susanne Weigelin-Schwiedrzik* legt den Fokus auf Fragen der Erinnerung an den „Großen Sprung", u.a. in der parteistaatlichen, wissenschaftlichen und populärwissenschaftlichen Geschichtsschreibung sowie in literarischen Texten. *Richard King*s Aufsatz widmet sich dem Nexus aus volkstümlicher Propaganda und revolutionärer Mobilisierung der Bevölkerung in der Frühphase der Bewegung. In ihrem gendersensiblen Beitrag arbeitet *Kimberley Ens Manning* sich widersprechende Weiblichkeitskonzepte im revolutionären China heraus: Frauenbilder zentralstaatlicher Akteure unterschieden sich, so stellt sie fest, teilweise erheblich von Frauenbildern (und somit auch: Selbstbildern) z.B. weiblicher Kader in ländlichen Regionen Henans und Jiangsus. *Felix Wemheuer* stellt dar, wie die Themen „Hunger" und „Hungersnot" durch den Druck parteistaatlicher Kampagnen bereits rund anderthalb Jahre vor dem Ausbruch der Versorgungskrise mit immer weiter reichenden Tabus und Sprechverboten belegt wurden. Statt als Hinweise auf reale Probleme, als Warnungen vor einer potentiell dramatischen Schieflage, galten entsprechende Äußerungen, insbesondere wenn sie von Bauern kamen, in offiziellen Diskursen als „ideologisches Problem" – nämlich als prinzipiell rechtsabweichlerischer Ausweis eines Mangels an revolutionärem Elan. Die Verteilungsmechanismen großer Volkskommunen stehen hingegen im Fokus der Studie von *Xin Yi*. Waren sie anfangs vielerorts noch enthusiastisch begrüßt worden, führten sie, so Xin, schon bald ins ökonomische Abseits und zum Zusammenbruch der gesellschaftlichen Ordnung. Zu einem ähnlichen Ergebnis gelangt *Wang Yanni*, die sich mit den Kampagnen zur Vergesellschaftung von Arbeit und Eigentum befasst – in ihrer Darstellung wird der „Große Sprung nach vorn" zur Kampagne rücksichtsloser Industrialisierung unter den Vorzeichen totaler Militarisierung.

In der zweiten Hälfte des Buches steht die Hungersnot selbst im Zentrum der Ausführungen. So beschreibt *Gao Hua* die Versuche des chinesischen Parteistaates, Lebensmittel und Nahrungsvorräte in Anbetracht der Krise zu ergänzen bzw. durch Substitute zu ersetzen. *Chen Yixin* setzt sich mit der Frage auseinander, warum die Hungersnot in einigen Gebieten katastrophale Ausmaße annahm während andere den „Großen Sprung nach vorn" vergleichsweise unbeschadet überstanden. *Jeremy Brown* widmet sich dem entscheidenden Moment zu Beginn der 1960er Jahre, in dem die Hungersnot droht, auf Tianjin überzugreifen; das Regime entschied sich – bewusst auf Kosten der Bauernschaft – für eine Stabilisierung der Städte. *Ralph A. Thaxton Jr.* entwickelt eine neue These zum Auslaufen des „Großen Sprungs" indem er schwerpunktartig einen Blick auf Überlebensstrategien und alltäglichen Widerstand von Bauern wirft: *chiqing* (吃青), das Verspeisen unreifer Feldfrüchte, wurde, so Thaxton, phasenweise zum Massenphänomen, sodass sich der Parteistaat zum Eingreifen gezwungen sah und die Haushalte als verantwortliche Grundeinheiten rehabilitierte. Praktiken des Widerstands (und die sich wandelnde, zunehmend defensive Reaktion des sozialistischen Staates) stehen auch im Mittelpunkt der Untersuchung von *Gao Wangling*.

Kenner der Forschungsliteratur werden bei der Lektüre der Beiträge sicherlich rasch feststellen, dass manche Erkenntnis, manche These, mancher Schluss nicht völlig neu daherkommt. Tatsächlich bestehen einige der Artikel aus überarbeiteten Versionen bereits zuvor veröffentlichter Studien. In der Substanz tut dies der hohen Qualität des Buches jedoch kaum einen Abbruch. Es bleibt dabei: Der Band leistet Pionierarbeit, indem er chinesische und nicht-chinesische Forschungsprojekte gemeinsam präsentiert; das thematische Spektrum bildet die Schwerpunkte der internationalen Auseinandersetzung mit den Jahren des „Großen Sprungs nach vorn" gekonnt und vergleichsweise repräsentativ ab; methodisch und bezüglich der verwendeten Quellen spiegelt das Buch, bei aller inhaltlichen Heterogenität, in der weit überwiegenden Zahl von Kapiteln die momentan charakteristische Hinwendung zur Dorf- und Mikrogeschichte.

Insofern lässt sich der Band uneingeschränkt empfehlen. Lesern/-innen, die beginnen, sich mit dem „Großen Sprung nach vorn" zu befassen, liefert er einen fundierten, kompakten Einstieg in das Forschungsfeld. Und für all diejenigen, die sich schon länger mit den Ereignissen der späten 1950er Jahre beschäftigen, gehört das Buch zur Pflichtlektüre.

(Hauke Neddermann)

Notes on Contributors

Jens Damm is an Assistant Professor at the Graduate Institute of Taiwan Studies, Chang Jung University, Tainan, currently on leave from the Institute of East Asian Studies, Freie Universität Berlin. He is also an Associate Fellow at the European Research Center on Contemporary Taiwan (ERCCT), Tübingen. His research interests include the Chinese and Taiwanese diaspora, gender studies, and the new media.

Anett Dippner (M.A. in Sinology, Media Studies and Theatre Arts from Friedrich-Alexander-Universität Erlangen-Nürnberg) works as research associate at the Institute of East Asian Studies at Freie Universität Berlin. Her research includes Chinese art and aesthetics, focus on calligraphy, contemporary literature and gender studies.

Hans van Ess is a Professor of Sinology at the Ludwig-Maximilians-Universität Munich. He studied Sinology, Turkology and Philosophy in Hamburg. Van Ess published relevant books and articles about Confucianism, Chinese history of mind and historiography in China. He is among others editor of „Lun Wen – Studien zur Geistesgeschichte und Literatur in China".

Gu Zhengkun 辜正坤 is a Professor of Comparative Cultural Studies of the Institute of World Literature at Peking University. His research includes: English literature, poetry, translation theory and practice, history of Greek and Roman literature. Gu Zhengkun is considered as excellent Shakespeare connoisseur and translator (he is Deputy President of China's Shakespeare Association). He has published more than 40 books and 150 articles in Chinese and Western languages. He is the president of Peking University Culture and Translation Society and executive board member of the National Culture Promotion Society of China.

Li Wenchao 李文潮 is a Professor of German philology, philosophy, linguistics and political science. He studied in Xi'an, Peking, Heidelberg and Berlin. He did his PhD and habilitated at Freie Universität Berlin. After ten years of research and teaching in Germany and China he is since 2007 Director of the Leibniz-Editionsstelle der Berlin-Brandenburgischen Akademie der Wissenschaft (BBAW) in Potsdam and excellent Leibniz connoisseur, since 2006 endowed Professor at the Universität Hannover.

Lu Huilin 卢晖临 is Associate Professor of Sociology at Peking University. He received his Ph.D. at the Chinese University of Hong Kong and was a Harvard-Yenching Visiting Fellow from 2002 to 2003. His research focuses on rural development and migrant workers in China.

Mechthild Leutner is a Professor of Chinese History and Culture at Freie Universität Berlin and currently holding the chair of Chinese Studies. Her main research interests are on Chinese social and political history, German-Chinese relations and Chinese women's history.

Philipp Mahltig (studied Sinology, Sociology and Chinese Language at Freie Universität Berlin and Peking University) works as research associate at the Center for Cultural Studies on Science and Technology in China at Technische Universität Berlin.

Klaus Mühlhahn is a Professor of Chinese History and Culture at Freie Universität Berlin. He is interested in Chinese legal history in the modern period, the history of imperialism and Sino-Western exchanges in the twentieth century. His most recent monograph is *Criminal Justice in China – A History* (Cambridge MA: Harvard University Press 2009, Winner of the John King Fairbank Prize 2009 by the American Historical Association).

Hauke Neddermann is a Research Associate and PhD candidate at the Institute of East Asian Studies, Freie Universität Berlin. His research interests include history and society of modern China; especially regional history of Xinjiang and the social history of the 1950s and 1960s.

Kimiko Suda is a Research Associate and PhD candidate at the Institute of East Asian Studies, Freie Universität Berlin, and currently involved in the research project „Patterns of migrant community formation in China's megaurban Pearl River Delta (PRD) – linking informal dynamics, governability and global change", funded by the German Research Foundation. Her research focuses on contemporary China, her fields of interests include urbanization, migration and social stratification, gender politics and (trans-national) Chinese film. She is co-director of the *Asian Film Festival Berlin* (AFFB).

Tan Mingran 谭明冉, a PhD from both Beijing University and University of Toronto, is an Associate Professor in the School of Philosophy and Social Development, Shandong University, China. His research interests center on Confucianism and Neo-Confucianism, Daoism and comparative philosophy.

Kathleen Wittek is a foreign language teacher of Chinese at a Berlin Secondary School. She is currently working on contemporary Chinese literature, esp. focussing on gender issues. Her research interests further include teaching methods of Chinese as a foreign language.